Defining cult movies

MANCHESTER
UNIVERSITY PRESS

Inside Popular Film

General editors Mark Jancovich and Eric Schaefer

Inside Popular Film is a forum for writers who are working to develop new ways of analysing popular film. Each book offers a critical introduction to existing debates while also exploring new approaches. In general, the books give historically informed accounts of popular film, which present this area as altogether more complex than is commonly suggested by established film theories.

Developments over the past decade have led to a broader understanding of film, which moves beyond the traditional oppositions between high and low culture, popular and avant-garde. The analysis of film has also moved beyond a concentration on the textual forms of films, to include an analysis of both the social situations within which films are consumed by audiences, and the relationship between film and other popular forms. The series therefore addresses issues such as the complex intertextual systems that link film, literature, art and music, as well as the production and consumption of film through a variety of hybrid media, including video, cable and satellite.

The authors take interdisciplinary approaches, which bring together a variety of theoretical and critical debates that have developed in film, media and cultural studies. They neither embrace nor condemn popular film, but explore specific forms and genres within the contexts of their production and consumption.

Already published:

Thomas Austin *Hollywood, hype and audiences*
Harry M. Benshoff *Monsters in the closet: homosexuality and the horror film*
Paul Grainge (ed.) *Memory and popular film*
Julia Hallam and Margaret Marshment *Realism and popular cinema*
Joanne Hollows and Mark Jancovich (eds) *Approaches to popular film*
Nicole Matthews *Gender in Hollywood: comedy after the new right*
Rachel Moseley *Growing up with Audrey Hepburn*
Jacinda Read *The new avengers: feminism, femininity and the rape-revenge cycle*
Aylish Wood *Technoscience in contemporary film: beyond science fiction*

Defining cult movies

The cultural politics of oppositional taste

Edited by
Mark Jancovich, Antonio Lázaro Reboll, Julian Stringer and **Andy Willis**

Manchester University Press

Manchester and New York

distributed exclusively in the USA by Palgrave

Published by Manchester University Press
Oxford Road, Manchester M13 9NR, UK
and Room 400, 175 Fifth Avenue, New York, NY 10010, USA
www.manchesteruniversitypress.co.uk

Distributed exclusively in the USA by
Palgrave, 175 Fifth Avenue, New York,
NY 10010, USA

Distributed exclusively in Canada by
UBC Press, University of British Columbia, 2029 West Mall,
Vancouver, BC, Canada V6T 1Z2

British Library Cataloguing-in-Publication Data
A catalogue record for this book is available from the British Library

Library of Congress Cataloging-in-Publication Data applied for

ISBN 0 7190 6630 1 *hardback*
  0 7190 6631 X *paperback*

First published 2003

11 10 09 08 07 06 05 04 03 10 9 8 7 6 5 4 3 2 1

Typeset in Sabon with Frutiger
by Northern Phototypesetting Co. Ltd, Bolton

Printed in Great Britain
by Bell & Bain Ltd, Glasgow

Contents

Illustrations

Notes on contributors

Mark Betz is Lecturer in Film Studies at King's College, London. His articles on European cinema and archival practice have appeared in *Camera Obscura* and *The Moving Image*, and his book *Remapping European Art Cinema* is forthcoming from University of Minnesota Press. He is currently working on a study of art film distributors in New York City and on the academicization of Film Studies through book publishing.

Rebecca Feasey has taught at the University of Nottingham. She is currently working on sexuality and cultural distinction in the reception of star images, and has published on Sharon Stone and the erotic thriller in *Movie Blockbusters* (Routledge 2003) and elsewhere.

Joan Hawkins is an Associate Professor in the Department of Communication and Culture at Indiana University, Bloomington. She is the author of *Cutting Edge: Art-horror and the Horrific Avant-garde* (University of Minnesota Press, 2000).

Joanne Hollows is Senior Lecturer in Media and Cultural Studies at Nottingham Trent University. She is author of *Feminism, Femininity and Popular Culture* (Manchester University Press, 2000) and co-editor of *Approaches to Popular Film* (Manchester University Press, 1995) and *The Film Studies Reader* (Arnold, 2000). She is currently working on gender and cooking.

Leon Hunt is a Senior Lecturer in Film and TV Studies at Brunel University. He is the author of *British Low Culture: From Safari Suits to Sexploitation* (Routledge, 1998) and *Kung Fu Cult Masters: From Bruce Lee to Crouching Tiger* (Wallflower, 2003), and has written about a variety of cult genres.

Nathan Hunt has written on cult films, reception and masculinity. He is currently completing a project on fan media, particularly the magazine *SFX*, and has an article (co-written with Mark Jancovich) on cult television and the mainstream in Roberta Pearson and Sara Gwenllian-Jones, eds., *Worlds Apart: Essays on Cult Television* (University of Minnesota Press, 2002). He has also been a member of the editorial board of *Scope: An Online Journal of Film Studies*.

Peter Hutchings is a Senior Lecturer in Film at Northumbria University. He is the author of *Hammer and Beyond* (Manchester University Press, 1993), *Terence Fisher* (Manchester University Press, 2002) and *Dracula* (I. B. Tauris, 2002) as well as co-editor of *The Film Studies Reader* (Arnold, 2000). He is currently completing a book on the horror film to be published by Longman in 2003.

Mark Jancovich is Reader and Director of the Institute of Film Studies at the University of Nottingham, UK. He has written on horror, fans and cult cinema, and is the author and editor of several books including: *Approaches to Popular Film* (with Joanne Hollows, Manchester University Press, 1995); *The Film Studies Reader* (with Joanne Hollows and Peter Hutchings, Arnold/Oxford University Press, 2000); *Horror, The Film Reader* (Routledge, 2002); *Quality Popular Television* (with James Lyons, British Film Institute, 2003); and *The Place of the Audience: Cultural Geographies of Film Consumption* (with Lucy Faire and Sarah Stubbings, British Film Institute, 2003), which is the results of an AHRB-funded research project. He is also a general editor of *Scope: An Online Journal of Film Studies*; and series editor (with Eric Schaefer) of the Manchester University Press book series *Inside Popular Film*.

Antonio Lázaro Reboll is a Lector in the Department of Hispanic and Latin American Studies at the University of Nottingham, where he teaches Spanish cinema. His main research interests are art-horror in Spanish visual culture and cinema. He has published on Spanish horror cinema of the 1960s and 1970s and together with Andy Willis (University of Salford) is about to publish a volume on Spanish popular cinema (Manchester University Press).

Moya Luckett is Assistant Professor in the English Department at the University of Pittsburgh. She is completing a manuscript on movie-going in Chicago, 1905–1917, and has published widely on feminine culture. She is the co-editor of *Swinging Single: Representing Sexuality in the 1960s* (University of Minnesota Press, 1999).

Ernest Mathijs is Lecturer in Film Studies at the University of Wales in Aberystwyth. Previously, he was with the Free University of Brussels, where this research started. His current research interests include the reception of horror films and reality-TV. He has published in *Literature/Film Quarterly*, *Scope*, *Andere Sinema*, and *Cinemagie*.

Jacinda Read is Lecturer in Media and Cultural Studies at Nottingham Trent University. She is the author of *The New Avengers: Feminism, Femininity and the Rape-revenge Cycle* (Manchester University Press, 2000) and is currently working on *Charlie's Angels*.

Jeffrey Sconce is an Assistant Professor in the School of Cinema-Television at the University of Southern California and the author of *Haunted Media: Electronic Presence from Telegraphy to Television* (Duke University Press, 2000). He has published work on 'disreputable cinema' in *Film Theory Goes to the Movies* (Routledge, 1993) and in the journals *Screen*, *Science as Culture*, and *Film Quarterly*.

Julian Stringer is Lecturer in Film Studies at the University of Nottingham. He has published widely on Asian cinema and is completing a project on film festivals and transcultural exchange. He is editor of *Movie Blockbusters* (Routledge, 2003), and a general editor of *Scope: An Online Journal of Film Studies*.

Andrew Willis is a Senior Lecturer in Media and Performance at the University of Salford. He is the author of *Violent Exchanges: Genre, Nation and Cultural Traffic* (Manchester University Press, forthcoming); the co-author (with Lisa Taylor) of *Media Studies: Texts, Institutions and Audiences* (Blackwell, 1999); and co-editor (with Antonio Lázaro Reboll) of *Spanish Popular Cinema* (Manchester University Press, forthcoming). He is also a member of the editorial board of *Scope: An Online Journal of Film Studies*.

Harmony H. Wu is a doctoral candidate in the Division of Critical Studies of University of Southern California's School of Cinema-Television. She is the editor of *Axes to Grind: Re-Imagining the Horrific in Visual Media and Culture*, a special issue of *Spectator* (forthcoming, 2003), which features new essays on horror and genre theory.

1

Introduction

Mark Jancovich, Antonio Lázaro Reboll, Julian Stringer and Andy Willis

The term 'cult movies' covers a multitude of sins, and the sheer variety that composes this category is probably best summed by Jeff Sconce, who argues that it 'would include entries from such seemingly disparate subgenres as "bad film", splatterpunk, "mondo" films, sword and sandal epics, Elvis flicks, governmental hygiene films, Japanese monster movies, beach party musicals, and just about every other historical manifestation of exploitation cinema from juvenile delinquency documentaries to soft core pornography' (Sconce 1995: 372). Unfortunately, it should also be noted that even this list is not even meant to cover all aspects of the cult movie, but only those aspects that Sconce identifies as 'paracinema', a small and select subsection of a larger set.

However, despite its title, this collection will not attempt to identify what makes a specific movie into an object of cult fandom. Rather than attempt to detect the essential element that defines a film as 'cult', the collection starts out from the presumption that the 'cult movie' is an essentially eclectic category. It is not defined according to some single, unifying feature shared by all cult movies, but rather through a 'subcultural ideology' in filmmakers, films or audiences are seen as existing in opposition to the 'mainstream' (for work on 'subcultural ideology' see Thornton 1995). In other words, 'cult' is largely a matter of the ways in which films are classified in consumption, although it is certainly the case that filmmakers often shared the same 'subcultural ideology' as fans and have set out to make self-consciously 'cult' materials.

Indeed, even the 'mainstream' is not a clearly defined and fixed object, but rather an undefined and vaguely imaged Other. For example, in one classic volume on cult movies, *Incredibly Strange*

Films (1986), the mainstream is imaged as some amalgam of corporate power, lower-middle-class conformity and prudishness, academic elitism and political conspiracy. However, the mainstream remains central, despite its incoherence, because it is necessary so that cult fans can produce a sense of distinction between themselves and what Fiske has referred to as 'more "normal" popular audiences' (Fiske 1992). To put it another way, it is necessary because it is by presenting themselves as oppositional that cult audiences are able to confer value upon both themselves and the films around which they congregate.

However, even their relation to these films is not coherent. While some fans clearly revere specific films as works of true artistic and political independence, in which the distinction from the mainstream is directly associated with political and/or cultural nonconformity, other fans view the films that they celebrate either with a patronising affection or even downright contempt. In other words, many cult movies are venerated exactly because they exist to be laughed at (see Rebecca Feasey's essay in this collection). For example, in the 1970s, *Reefer Madness* became a major cult hit exactly because its outlandish anti-drugs message made it a laughing stock for young metropolitan audiences (Schaefer 1999). Similarly, the 'bad movie' is celebrated not for its artistic independence or political sophistication but for the complete failure to conform to the artistic or political 'mainstream', a failure that is often seen as revealing the conventionality of mainstream norms (see Jeff Sconce's essay in this collection).

However, if cult fans usually make claims to oppositionality, they are largely middle-class and male, and their oppositionality often works to reaffirm rather than challenge bourgeois taste and masculine dispositions. The celebration of the 'bad movie', for example, not only draws on the formal defamiliarization that Bourdieu has demonstrated is central to bourgeois aesthetics and is directly related to the material security of this class (Bourdieu 1984; Hollows and Jancovich 1995), but also involves the Othering of specific social groups. In other words, rather than a subaltern challenge to the bourgeoisie, the oppositional tastes of cult movies fans can been seen, in part, as a conflict within (rather than against) the bourgeoisie (Sconce 1995; Jancovich 2002). In these struggles, cult fandom is linked to the processes through which the cultural bourgeoisie challenges authority of the economic bourgeoisie. However, ironically, in this process the lower middle class are frequently made the scapegoat, so that this challenge works to secure the authority of the upper middle classes rather than to threaten it (Jancovich, 2002).

Furthermore, as Joanne Hollows's essay in this collection so powerfully demonstrates, this process is also related to a politics of gender. The Otherness of the lower middle classes has frequently been associated with its feminization and, as a result, it is hardly surprising that cult fandom not only works to affirm bourgeois tastes but is also related to the legitimization of masculine dispositions. The aesthetics of transgression that underpins so much cult movie fandom (as well as the personnel who create self-consciously 'cult' works) is often directly opposed to the values of domesticity that are not only associated with femininity but for which women have historically be presumed to been responsible.

As a result, while cult audiences often present themselves in direct opposition to both the academy and the market, the emergence and development of cult movie fandom is intimately related to both (see Jancovich 2002). On the one hand, as we have already seen, cult movie audiences often draw on the reading strategies of bourgeois aesthetics, particularly formal defamiliarization. Indeed, as Jancovich has argued, the development of both cult movie fandom and academic film studies have often walked hand in hand and successive waves of 'radicalization' within the discipline have been directly related to transformations in cult movie fandom. Indeed, the film studies canon is the product of successive waves of fandom. It should be no surprise, therefore, that all four of the editors of this collection were cult fans, and that it was their cultural capital and dispositions as fans that not only attracted them to academic film studies but also enabled them to function within it.

However, fandom is related also to changes in the nature of the market, and specifically with the emergence of niche markets in the postwar period. As the mass audience for films declined, many exhibitors turned to wealthy specialist audiences through the creation of art cinemas. This moment was then followed by the emergence of the repertory cinema, and the 'midnight movie' – probably the phenomenon most associated with cult movie fandom – was itself the product of market responses to changes in the nature of specific inner cities and their audiences.

Indeed, the cultural geography of cult movies is particularly significant. As Hollows demonstrates, the key spaces of congregation

were, initially, often inner-city areas that were defined as in opposition to the spaces of domestic femininity. However, it was not only
an inner-city phenomenon but one associated with specific 'cultural
capitals' (Zukin 1995), most centrally New York and even then
largely Manhattan (Gomery 1992; Jancovich 2002; and both Betz
and Hawkins in this volume).

In this way, the phenomenon is associated not only with specific
social classes but also with specific centres of cultural power and
authority. It is therefore significant that, as Andrew Willis's essay
demonstrates, many cult movies are films that have been trans-
planted from one specific cultural terrain and consumed within
another quite different one. However, not only are these products
celebrated in this new context for their supposed difference from
the 'mainstream' (although they may in fact be the mainstream of
their own culture) but this often involves an exoticization of other
cultures. In other words, cult movie fandom often relies on a celebration of the 'weird and wonderful' of world cinema, but does so
in a way that has no interest in the meaning of those films within the
contexts of their own production (see, for example, Tombs 1998).

Not only does this cultural geography account for the meanings
of specific sites of exhibition and the ways in which these might
change over time, but modes of exhibition have also altered the geo-
graphical organization of cult movie fandom. New media such as
video, cable, satellite and the internet have produced fundamental
effects on cult movie fandom. On the one hand, these technologies
have made cult movie fandom much less dependent on place, and
have allowed the distribution and diffusion of cult materials across
space. This has made possible the creation of large niche audiences
that may be spatially diffuse but can constitute a powerful market
force. On the other hand, this also threatens the sense of distinction
and exclusivity and on which cult movie fandom depends, and
threatens to blur the very distinctions that organize it. Alternatively,
new technologies not only allow fans across the world to communicate with one another and even organize themselves as a collective;
it also enables industries to construct them as just another niche
market, and so threaten their very sense of oppositionality and
hence identity. However, while these technologies aided the
processes of time-space compression, inequalities are still spatially
divided around the globe and new technologies have also, in some
cases, exacerbated these divisions.

The rise of the video, for example, threatened the exclusivity of fandom so that 'all those obscure films that I would have risked injury and death to see (literally, in some of those theatres) are now available at your local clean video store! It's a little unnerving' (Frank Henenlotter, quoted in Vale, Juno and Morton 1985: 8). But in Britain moves to regulate video also produced a whole new form of the cult movie, and one which was, for the first time, not related to theatrical exhibition: the 'video nasty'. Of course, with the video nasty, it was precisely the status of specific videos as banned items that were *not* readily available that made them precious and desirable objects that were distinguished from 'mainstream' fare.

The essays in this book all, in different ways, mediate on these various different issues and processes. Some essays are more focused on general theoretical issues and debates while many provide concrete studies of films, directors, genres and stars. Some concentrate on the contexts of their production while others concentrate on the mediation of cult movies through an analysis of their marketing, the fan media that surround them and their critical reception. In the process, many essays also entail a critical and reflexive concern with academic practice in terms of both pedagogy and research.

For example, in the first essay, Sconce explores the value of studying 'bad films', particularly as a pedagogical practice. As he demonstrates, film studies needs to question the aims and objectives of its teaching practices, an act that would not only question the nature of film studies as a discipline and its relationship to other disciplines but also force us to re-evaluate our relationship to students, most of whom come to film studies with expectations and desires that the discipline confounds and frustrates. The turn to the study of 'bad films', Sconce argues, may actually resolve some of these problems, as not only is it one way of teaching students basic issues of formal analysis; it also enables them to make the connection between this level and larger theoretical and historical concerns. In other words, it reveals the conventional nature of cinematic norms, and encourages them to ask why those norms are as they are.

In the process, the article raises central questions that not only justify the study of cult movies but also places their analysis at the centre of the discipline. Of course, there is always the danger that the ineptness of these films might simply become the object of ridicule, so that the study of them simply affirms existing norms, rather than challenging them. Furthermore, Sconce continues to see defamiliarization as central to the activities of film study, and this is a position challenged by Joanne Hollows's essay.

This second essay is primarily concerned not with the formal analysis of films, but with the processes of cultural consumption within which films are located as both texts and objects of material culture. Furthermore, she explores the ways in which these processes are related to the performance of gender and particularly the ways in which cult movie fandom not only operates around specific performances of masculinity but is also founded upon an Othering of femininity. In other words, she demonstrates that cult movie fandom is not simply opposed to an imagined Other of the 'mainstream' but that this Other is itself associated with femininity. In the process, she examines the spatial organization of cult movie fandom, and the processes of consumption and collecting with which it is often associated.

These themes are also picked up in Jacinda Read's essay, where she examines some contemporary academic work on cult movies and particularly the figure of the academic 'fan-boy'. Over the 1990s there was a legitimization and even celebration of the academic as fan as exemplified by the work of Henry Jenkins (Jenkins 1992). However, while much of this work challenged academic disdain for, and detachment from, the popular, and encouraged academics to acknowledge and explore their own investments within the popular, Read explores a more recent variant which challenges notions of academic responsibility and bears strong resemblance to the strategies of the 'lad mags' of the 1990s, a genre of British publishing that is associated with magazines such as *Loaded*, *FHM* and *Maxim* (Jackson, Stevenson and Brooks 2001). For Read, this criticism needs to be understood in terms of specific anxieties about masculinity, and particularly anxieties about its relationship to consumption. As Read points out, consumption is often associated with femininity and much of this criticism seeks to secure a sense of masculinity by distinguishing the male fan from the feminine consumer.

If these essays raise general questions about the academic study of cult movies, later essays seek to study specific aspects of the cult movie. Andrew Willis's essay, for example, examines a wave of Spanish horror films from the late 1960s and early 1970s, and demonstrates that, while they were consumed in specific ways by cult audiences outside Spain, they had quite different meanings within the context of their production. In the process, he explores the reasons why a series of directors, who were often associated with the legitimate and/or art cinema, turned to horror production at a specific moment in Spanish history. His argument is that while art movies were made solely for a select intelligentsia within Spain and an international art-house circuit beyond its borders, the turn to popular horror allowed radical Spanish filmmakers not only to deal with subversive materials in a covert form but to address a popular Spanish audience. In other words, even when it was critical of the Franco regime, the Spanish art cinema could be argued not only to have failed to address a broad Spanish audience, but even to have acted as 'window dressing' for the Franco regime: the international presence of these films made the regime appear less repressive and more liberal than was actually the case.

This is not to suggest that these films were solely made for domestic consumption. On the contrary, the reason that many were made was that horror was an easily exportable filmic product, for which there was a large international audience. As a result, Willis is suggesting not that the Spanish context enables us to access the 'real' meaning of these films, but simply that it is one important context that is often ignored and even dismissed by those sections of cult movie fandom that celebrate them as examples of the bizarre and the exotic.

It is this concern with the international and transcultural dimensions of cult movie fandom that also informs Harmony Wu's essay. In her analysis of the films of Peter Jackson, Wu also looks at the national contexts of cult movie production, but she specifically concentrates on the ways in which Jackson has 'traded in horror'. In other words, as Wu puts it, 'Peter Jackson's gross-out films . . . afforded him the capital (both economic and cinematic) to transcend the limitations of working in tiny national cinema in Hollywood's shadow and to reap success that would be otherwise available', a strategy that has paid off recently with the phenomenal success of *The Lord of the Rings*. However, while the essay concentrates on his early gross-out films, she also compares this strategy with that of *Heavenly Creatures*, a film that also traded on violence but attracted quite different cult fans. In other words, she examines not only the economic significance of cult audiences internationally but also the differences between different types of cult movie fandom.

If these essays are largely concerned with the contexts within which cult movies are produced, Ernest Mathijs looks at the critical

different types of cult fandom.

reception of cult films and particularly the reputation of David Cronenberg. In this essay, Mathijs examines the ways in which a range of publications sought to make sense of Cronenberg's film *Shivers*, and particularly the ways in which the film was discussed in terms of controversy and topicality. As Mathijs argues, this process not only constructed the meaning of the film and its director in quite specific ways but also worked to legitimate the critics themselves: 'By helping *Shivers* receive a cult reputation, these critics secured their own relevance.' Mathijs therefore looks at the mechanisms through which intertextual frames were established and developed for both the film and its director, and the processes through which it was produced as an object of 'cult' fascination.

If Mathijs looks at film criticism, Peter Hutchings's study of Dario Argento's reception compares the critical responses of fans and academics. In the process, Hutchings claims that much academic work has 'obscured the specificity of localised "cult" responses to particular objects in favour of constructing a broader picture of cultural resistance and transgression'. Consequently, he concentrates on an analysis of largely British responses and, while he certainly finds that many fans present Argento as a figure with cult status and credentials, he also stresses that most fans display a deep sense of reverence for him as a 'master', rather than practising the textual poaching, resistance or transgression often emphasized in academic accounts of fan practices (see, for example, Jenkins 1992). As a result, Hutchings argues that journalistic film criticism, the academy and fandom each 'has its own specificity, its own history, its own agendas' and that they cannot be put 'together in a cohesive whole'. This situation, however, in no way invalidates the study of cult but requires greater attention to its various concrete manifestations. As Hutchings puts it, 'the cult category is only the beginning to understanding, not an end in itself'.

As the work both on Cronenberg and Argento demonstrates, not only are many cult movies clearly identified as the work of cult auteurs within cult fandom, but these directors are often associated with specific genres. It should also be clear from Sconce's list quoted at the start of this introduction that there is a strong relation between certain genres and subgenres and cult movie fandom. Cronenberg and Argento are, for example, both strongly associated with the horror genre, which is in turn often associated with cult fandom. As Robin Wood claimed in his now classic essay on the American horror film, the genre's 'popularity itself has a peculiar characteristic that sets it apart from other genres: it is restricted to aficionados and complemented by total rejection, people tending to go to horror films either obsessively or not at all' (Wood 2002: 29–30).

Much the same is also true of other genres, and in her article on sexploitation Moya Luckett examines the films of Doris Wishman to re-evaluate the appeal of this genre from female directors and audiences. As a result she not only argues that, although it may initially seem surprising, 'sexploitation appears to have been a feminine area within low budget filmmaking', but also that 'femininity emerges as arguably *the* structuring force in cult films, and, in the process, recasts cinematic interventions into sexual difference', even if it is often 'latent and found in inopportune places'. The paper provides an overview of Wishman's career and a textual analysis of its stylistic features. Most particularly, it is claimed that Wishman not only 'repeatedly frustrate[s] masculine, goal-oriented ways of seeing' but also 'privileges the female gaze and female spectator'.

The relationship between genre and bodily spectacle is also the focus of Leon Hunt's analysis of the martial arts film. If Luckett concentrates on the relationship of a director to a genre, Hunt examines the relations between star images, star performances and genre, and he examines the ways in which authenticity is both constructed and valued within cult movie fandom. However, as he stresses, authenticity is a 'slippery term' and fans define it in different ways. Some, for example, are concerned with the purity of specific styles of fighting, which others are concerned that performances should be 'real' and not the product of cinematic trickery or special effects. Finally, even when styles become blurred and cinematic techniques become the order of the day, other fans shift their concern to issues of the body. In Jackie Chan's films, for example, their authenticity is frequently vouched for by the out-takes of mistakes in which Jackie's body is bashed and broken. In this way, Hunt examines the fan discourses through which values are assigned to films and the ways in which they are understood, but he also acknowledges that these processes need to be understood also in the context of a globalized culture. Not only is he discussing how these films are valued by western cult audiences, rather than by Hong Kong audiences; he also examines the ways in which these issues have been effected by the increasingly absorption of Hong Kong personnel and styles into the Hollywood film industry.

The physical display of the body also concerns Rebecca Feasey's essay on the cult consumption of Sharon Stone, but, if the spectacle of male physical performance is valued in martial arts fandom, the spectacle of female physical performance is denigrated in the erotic thriller. Feasey therefore examines a particular cult publication, *Bad Movies We Love*, to analyse the ways in which Sharon Stone's star image and star performances are made to mean within cult fandom. She therefore looks at the discussion of two films, *King Solomon's Mines* and *Scissors*, and demonstrates that, as an actress directly associated with sexual spectacle by the authors, she is not only treated with contempt but also cannot win. If, for cult fandom, her films are 'so bad they're good', Stone's femininity is there only to be laughed at and she is seem as responsible for her own victimization. Furthermore, when she tries to distance herself from 'nudity-friendly' roles, she is even more roundly ridiculed for her pretensions. However, as Feasey points out, Stone is not only one of the topics of *Bad Movies* but also wrote its introduction, an introduction that presents her in a very different way. Rather than someone who is blissfully ignorant of her own awfulness, Stone presents herself as fully in on the joke and able to mock herself and her career. However, as Feasey demonstrates, she is still required to ridicule and distance herself from her own femininity and hence to become 'culturally one of the boys' (Thornton 1995). In this way, Feasey demonstrates the problematic position of female stars, and femininity more generally, within cult movie fandom.

Nathan Hunt's essay also focuses upon a specific cult publication, but in this case it is a magazine, *SFX*. The essay examines the function of trivia within this magazine, and Hunt argues that it cannot be simply dismissed as either an obsession with that which has no value or meaning, nor as a radical act of textual reinterpretation. Instead he demonstrates the ways in which trivia operate to regulate fan communities and particularly the ways in which they used to define ownership of specific cultural texts. In other words, while most texts will also be consumed by those outside a particular fan community, trivia are used by fans to assert a special and privileged relationship to texts which is used to establish a sense of ownership over them. This inevitably enables fans to police the boundaries of fandom; to distinguish a 'real' fan from a cultural interloper or 'tourist'. Finally, trivia are used to produce, maintain and negotiate hierarchies within fandom, a realm which often has little to do with the communal utopia that Jenkins discusses but is often distinguished by homosocial competition (Jenkins 1992; Hollows in this volume).

Finally, the last two essays address the relationship between the cult movie and the art cinema. The cult movie is often seen as a popular and even subaltern scene but it is precisely its sense of itself as a kind of oppositional and underground culture that it shares with the European art cinema. Not only do both the art cinema and cult movie fandom emerge out of similar developments in both exhibition and the academy (Jancovich 2002), but they have therefore frequently interacted and even overlapped with one another.

Mark Betz's essay therefore concentrates on the reception of the European art cinema in the postwar period, but he does so to demonstrate not only the relationships between the art film and the cult movie but also the extent to which the marketing of the European art cinema shared very similar qualities with the marketing of the exploitation cinema. He even goes so far as to suggest that the former may have displaced the latter. As he points out, not only does Schaefer identify 1959 as the end of the period of classical exploitation, but it was also 'the first cresting of the French New Wave and New Italian Cinema, a crucial marker in art cinema historiography for the beginning of its high modernist phase'. As a result, Betz not only asks us to rethink the relationship between the art cinema and the cult movie, but he also seeks to recuperate the art cinema through the 'use of the kinds of extratextual materials that are so much of current film and media historiography'. In other words, he wants not only to escape the inverse snobbery through which the art cinema is now routinely ignored and even dismissed but to do so without returning to an uncritical celebration of its aesthetic superiority. In other words, he is concerned to study its meanings in terms of its precise social and economic location, and to examine its marketing and exhibition as central elements in the generation of those meanings. In other words, he refuses the notion that the art cinema could exist 'in a state of splendid isolation from economic and material life' (Hollows 1995: 30)

These issues are somewhat updated by Joan Hawkins in her study of what she terms the 'downtown avant-garde'. This group are defined through their 'common urban lifestyle, a shared commitment to formal and narrative experimentation, a view of the human body as a site of social and political struggle, an interest in radical identity politics, and a mistrust of institutionalized mechanisms of wealth and power'. Like earlier avant-gardes, they share a sense of themselves as an artistic underground, but unlike these earlier avant-gardes they 'borrow heavily from "low" culture – erotic thrillers, horror, sci-fi, and porn'. In other words, they are one of the key points at which the cult movie and the art movie intersect, overlap and cross-fertilize one another, and it is this point of intersection, overlap and cross-fertilization that Hawkins outlines and analyses.

However, there is an awareness in both Betz, and Hawkins's essays that the movements discussed are not only largely geographically specific but also historically contingent. Not only have they been radically affected by changes in political, economic and cultural developments but they have also been subject to the aftershocks of 11 September 2001, a date that has dramatically changed the social and cultural landscape of Manhattan, to say nothing of the world beyond it.

In the process, it is hoped that the essays in this volume will raise a series of issues about the cult movie and its cultural politics, and if the book refuses to provide a definition of the cult movie this is for two reasons. First, as we have argued, it is the process of making definitions and distinctions that is central to the cultural politics of the cult movies and, second, we have attempted to construct a book that does not assert a party line, but in which there is a productive dialogue and exchange of definitions and ideas. We are therefore very grateful to all our contributors for their time, energy and generosity, and for their commitment to the current book. We admire the quality of their work and are privileged to have been able to draw this work together.

References

Bourdieu, Pierre (1984) *Distinction: A Social Critique of the Judgement of Taste*. London: Routledge.

Fiske, John (1992) The Cultural Economy of Fandom, in Lisa A. Lewis (ed.), *The Adoring Audience: Fan Culture and Popular Media*. London: Routledge.

Gomery, Douglas (1992) *Shared Pleasures: The History of Movie Exhibition in the United States*. Madison: University of Wisconsin Press.

Hollows, Joanne (1995) Mass Culture Theory and Political Economy, in Joanne Hollows and Mark Jancovich (eds.), *Approaches to Popular Film*. Manchester: Manchester University Press.

Hollows, Joanne, and Jancovich, Mark (1995) *Approaches to Popular Film*. Manchester: Manchester University Press.

Jackson, Peter, Stevenson, Nick and Brooks, Kate (2001) *Making Sense of Men's Magazines*. Oxford: Polity.

Jancovich, Mark (2002) Cult Fictions: Cult Movies, Subcultural Capital and the Production of Cultural Distinctions, *Cultural Studies*, 16 (2), pp. 306–322.

Jenkins, Henry (1992) *Textual Poachers: Television Fans and Participatory Culture*. New York: Routledge.

Lewis, Lisa A. (ed.) (1992) *The Adoring Audience: Fan Culture and Popular Media*. London: Routledge.

Schaefer, E. (1999) *'Bold! Daring! Shocking! True': A History of Exploitation Films, 1919–1959*. Durham: Duke University Press.

Sconce, Jeffrey (1995) 'Trashing' the Academy: Taste, Excess and an Emerging Politics of Cinematic Style, *Screen*, 36 (4), pp. 371–93

Thornton, Sarah (1995) *Club Cultures: Music, Media and Subcultural Capital*. Oxford: Blackwell.

Tombs, Pete (1998) *Mondo Macabro: Weird and Wonderful Cinema Around the World*. London: Titan Books.

Vale, V. and Juno, Andrea (eds.) (1986) *Re/search 10: Incredibly Strange Films*. San Francisco: Re/search.

Wood, Robin (2002) The American Nightmare: Horror in the 70s, in Mark Jancovich (ed.), *Horror, The Film Reader*. London: Routledge, pp. 25–32.

Zukin, Sharon (1995) *The Cultures of Cities*. Oxford: Blackwell.

2

Esper, the renunciator:
teaching 'bad' movies to good students

Jeffrey Sconce

Every academic discipline encounters the occasional 'turf war', moments when the competition for institutional resources and prestige becomes especially heated. Film studies is no exception. Though still one of the youngest recognized disciplines on the university campus, film studies has been no stranger to such conflict; indeed, its relative 'youth' and struggle for legitimization has often made it one of the most contested sites within the academy (and one of the most continually imperiled). Such struggle takes place on four fronts. First, cinema scholars must even today justify their very existence to an 'old guard' of humanists often still trying to come to terms with the 'dime novel' and the 'penny dreadful', much less the unholy spectre of movies and television. Second, film scholars must defend themselves from the current boundless institutional enthusiasm for the study of 'new media' – a discipline everyone is certain will be of vital importance in the not-too-distant future, yet which must content itself in the meantime by predicting the death of cinema, the death of television, the death of books and so on. Closely related to this phantom field is the emerging academic omnivore known as visual culture studies, a discipline humbly dedicated to the theoretical dissection of every historical object to have ever been illuminated in the spectrum of visible light. Finally, even those within film studies itself, as a narrower field, like those internal to any discipline, must argue among themselves over appropriate objects and methodologies. Often such debates take the form of mutually devolving caricatures. Thus David Bordwell's and Kristin Thompson's advocacy of neo-formalism becomes the nebulous (and slightly menacing) 'Wisconsin project', evoking images of students hunched over Steenbecks on a holy mission to provide an accurate shot count for each and every postwar Republic western.[1] Those keeping the Francophilic vigil of so-called 'apparatus theory' fare little better, dismissed by their foes as engaged in a predictable search for the omnipresent 'gaze', writing up endless accounts of the spectator's subjective construction by the supreme, totalizing omnipotence of the cinematic apparatus.[2] Then there is the cultural studies approach, lambasted by its enemies as an eternally optimistic and increasingly routine search for resistance, subversion or emancipation in the face of mass cultural dominance, sloppy research conducted by 'critics' who have given up questioning the ideological dimensions of their own pleasures so that they may more convincingly argue that a *Dukes of Hazzard* website is actually a hotbed of engaged political activism.[3] Finally, there is Foucault, the critic who appears (at the moment anyway) to have won the intellectual sweepstakes of the twentieth century and become the theorist of absolutely everything, a trend that would no doubt horrify 'Foucault' himself had his 'author-function' lived to see all manner of culturally unrelated phenomena collapsed into his quite historically specific conceptual frameworks.[4]

In the midst of these battles are those of us in the teaching trenches of academia, faced with a yearly army of undergraduates looking to us to learn something about 'film'. Often these students lack the interest (or philosophical background) to understand Althusser's break with Marx, or why 'relative autonomy' might be important in understanding *Top Gun*. Those vain enough to place Lacan, Deleuze or Baudrillard on an undergraduate syllabus, meanwhile, are almost guaranteed a series of truly hilarious rote responses defining the 'mirror-phase', 'rhizome', and 'simulation' on the final exam, answers that, once the laughter dies down, demonstrate depressingly that students in fact have learned very little during the previous semester. Then again, one might try to empower the students by assuring them that their repeated viewings of Adam Sandler films, far from being infantile, are in fact a way of thumbing their noses at the power-bloc, but this is a conclusion even they will begin to suspect after a time. If film instructors are unhappy with this situation, our students are probably even less satisfied. Children of Enlightenment naivety that they are, students have actually enrolled in film classes hoping to learn something about film itself, as an 'art', as a practice, as an *object*. This leaves us with a recurring and discomforting question in our field: what exactly are we to teach undergraduates in film classes? What makes film classes different from those in art history, sociology, or English literature, to name but a few of the other institutional homes, poachers, and rivals of film studies?

At this point, some will no doubt suspect a covert formalist agenda at work: force students to learn the history of editing and mise-en-scène – audiences, ideology and 'techniques of the observer' be damned! While sympathetic to the neo-formalist call for greater attention to the filmic object itself, my goal here is not to call for film studies to retreat into a fantasy of disciplinary autonomy or to imagine that formal issues can be understood independently of ancillary historical inquiries into perception and reception. Nor am I arguing that formalism itself presents an objective science somehow removed from the historical forces that produced and developed it over the past century. This chapter will argue, however, that a close examination of the formal, technological and economic histories of film should remain a crucial foundation in film studies. Rather than bombard students with reductive accounts of the greatest hits in French cultural theory, all the while assuming that the ability to engage film form is a self-evident skill in most students, how might we teach undergraduates the basic mechanics of film construction (yes, editing, mise-en-scène, etc.) while simultaneously sensitizing them to the political dynamics of representation itself? For those engaged in graduate and postgraduate cultural analysis, meanwhile, I would argue some facility with the history and mechanisms that have produced film form are a necessary prerequisite for integrating the cinema into larger debates over vision, history, and power, regardless of one's ultimate theoretical ambitions.

Obviously, debate over such issues of 'form' and 'content' (and 'form as content') predate the institutional emergence of film studies. The Bakhtin circle's engagement (and partial reconciliation) with Russian formalism in the 1920s and 1930s presents one important example, as do the famous debates between Lukács and Goldmann over the political potential of bourgeois realism (see Bakhtin and Medvedev 1985; Goldmann 1975; Lukács 1963). By no means am I suggesting that any definitive resolutions to such quandaries are to be found in the following pages. I would like to argue, however, that film studies might once again prioritize film within its curriculum, even as it, like so many other disciplines within the humanities, merges and morphs with the larger academy project of mapping vision, culture and power. This strikes me as particularly crucial in terms of undergraduate education, where faculty intoxicated with the latest trends in the field often forget that undergraduate learning is more of a process of steady accumulation than of immediate revelation. A film instructor's goal may be to lead students to the Foucauldian epiphany that finally exiles humanity itself from the stage of human history, but such insight would seem unlikely without brief detours through Cartesian philosophy, the Enlightenment, and Marxism (as well as a provisional explanation to impatient students as to how the cinema might fit into this scheme in the first place). Similarly, before we blow students' minds by teaching them that vision itself may be a historically variable phenomenon, we might first provide them with the skills (however suspect) that will allow them to engage the cinema as a changing historical object of perception. To those who abhor formalist approaches, we might suggest that films are more than plots and shots to be opportunistically harvested in service of abstract cultural claims. If style and form *are* content (as most of us would no doubt agree) then they require the cultivation of both the historical knowledge and critical skills necessary for understanding these techniques. To those who attack the imprecision of symptomatic criticism – as Bordwell himself does quite eloquently in *Making Meaning* (1989) – we might argue that even if the film academy has become 'interpretation, inc.', a factory for generating endless readings of occluded cinematic meaning, audiences (like critics) nevertheless still 'make meanings' whenever images are projected on a screen. The study of 'meaning' may prove a futile task, as fluid, provisional and unknowable as the science of stacking greased marbles. And yet limiting film studies to a historical inventory of formal devices, while certainly a useful foundation, is akin to studying the flavour of a nation's cuisine by measuring its flatware.

The disciplinary 'impasse' presented above is, of course, somewhat of a caricature (as the chain of similes might suggest). Even the most delirious post-structuralist concedes that films possess some principle of organization, while Bordwell, even as he argues 'why not to read a film', advocates a map of film studies that includes not only the object itself but also the forces leading to its production and those impacting its reception. In practical terms, however, such distinctions and allowances are often lost in the bid to amplify arguments and/or defend entrenched institutional positions. Whatever our interest in art, culture and representation, however, the question remains as to how best to engage beginning students in the logic, history and debates of cinematic signification. To help address this problem, I make the following (modest) proposal: we can greatly increase our pedagogical efficacy as film instructors by giving more attention to the largely forgotten work of director Dwain Esper, and in particular his 1934 sexploitation classic, *Maniac*.

Sub-zero degree cinema

In the ongoing critical mission to discover and consecrate 'auteurs', Dwain Esper has little hope. Working on the fringe of the fringe in Hollywood's shadow exploitation industry of the 1930s, he directed only a few films, of which only one or two are readily accessible. According to the more conservative criteria of auteurism, Esper possesses not even the requisite technical competence to reach for Andrew Sarris's first rung on the ladder to the pantheon. And, in an age where even Ed Wood, Jr has entered Bazin's 'aesthetic cult of the personality', Esper's work remains relatively unknown to most audiences (even within the thriving cinematic subculture dedicated to 'bad' movies). The most detailed account of his life and work can be found in Eric Schaefer's excellent history of the exploitation film, *Bold! Daring! Shocking! True!* (1999), which examines the production and promotional context in which Esper laboured. Esper was one of many entrepreneurs working in the shadow of legitimate Hollywood product, producing and directing a series of films devoted to topics forbidden under the Production Code. These directors had limited access to capital, equipment and distribution, often accompanying their salacious features from town to town in scandalous 'roadshow' exhibitions. As Schaefer documents of this industry, low budgets and lack of access to other production resources frequently led to restrictions on rehearsal time, set-ups, retakes and other elements directly impacting the exploitation filmmaker's ability to 'polish' a film. Working on budgets of less than $8000, Esper clearly faced an almost insurmountable challenge in terms of assembling the talent and resources necessary to mount a 'competent' production; or, as Schaefer states more charitably, 'Lower budgets meant that those who labored in exploitation films usually had not had the opportunity to hone their skills to a degree comparable to those working in mainstream pictures' (Schaefer 1999: 92).

Those hoping to find a 'vision' or 'signature' in Esper's work are sure to be disappointed. Of those who do know Esper's work, few would argue that he had any agenda beyond producing a sensationalistic film as cheaply as possible. Without projecting too much on Esper's now distant subjectivity, we can probably assume that he aspired to little more than reasonably matching the reigning codes of performance, mise-en-scène and editing at work in classical Hollywood cinema, all the while inserting the moments of 'forbidden' spectacle expected by his audience. This volatile mix of Hollywood classicism, sensationalism, poverty and ineptitude makes Esper's films unfold like fever dreams, profoundly distorted narratives that somehow remain strangely familiar by virtue of their distant relationship to Hollywood practice. Consider, for example, the plot mechanics in the first half of *Maniac*. Maxwell, a schizophrenic vaudevillian renowned for his uncanny ability to impersonate almost any living being, is on the lamb from the law. He goes into hiding with a mad scientist and quickly finds himself an accomplice in the doctor's plans to raise the dead. Having stolen one corpse and assisted the doctor in its resurrection, the frightened vaudevillian fights with the scientist about returning to the morgue for another specimen. In the fray, the doctor is killed. Soon a patient arrives at the door. The vaudevillian quickly breaks out his make-up kit and acting skills to impersonate the deceased doctor. A woman has brought her extremely disturbed and agitated brother in for his weekly injection. New to the doctor business, the schizophrenic vaudevillian accidentally injects the already raving lunatic with a hypo of adrenaline, inspiring actor Ted Edwards to deliver one of the most histrionic depictions of mania ever captured on celluloid. Edwards treats viewers to the prolonged display of lunacy promised by the film's title before escaping, absconding with, and molesting the recently resurrected corpse of the young woman (who happens to be wandering about in a trance in the doctor's home). Neither is ever seen on screen again.

As Schaefer observes, 'the story of *Maniac* may sound odd, but a synopsis of the film cannot begin to convey the disjointed, confusing experience of an actual viewing.' (1999: 92) Interesting, one might argue, but hardly a replacement for *Citizen Kane* on the undergraduate film syllabus. My argument here is not that *Citizen Kane* should be replaced by *Maniac*; rather, I believe introducing students to a film like *Maniac* will better position them to understand, analyse and appreciation *all* forms of cinema. One advantage of beginning with a film like *Maniac* is that it carries none of the critical baggage of a *Citizen Kane* nor the weighty reputation of Welles, or Hitchcock, or any other director whose popular persona precedes the consumption of their work. It is difficult to introduce students to film analysis via *Vertigo*, *Psycho* or *North by Northwest* owing to the enormous 'cult' of Hitchcock cultivated over the past forty years by critics, theorists and the director himself. Examining the history and mechanics of any of these films is inevitably clouded by the now ubiquitous mythology of Hitchcock as the perverse genius secreted within the text, somehow in control of every micro-detail of cinematic signification. Esper, on the other hand, is a cinematic cipher, less the master 'enunciator' – as Bellour (1977) dubs Hitchcock – than a 'renunciator', a director surrounded by minimal talent and funding barely concerned with (much less in control of) style and narration. Not so much a puppeteer, a textual metapresence or a neurotic subject position read off the symptomology of his films, Esper remains more the unwitting enabler of a signifying catastrophe.

Of course, to dub Esper as 'the renunciator' is to contribute to the director's own process of mythologization; indeed, the romanticization of low-budget auteurs as frustrated and demented geniuses (*à la* Ed Wood) or courageous problem-solvers (*à la* Corman) has been a central project of the bad cinema cult over the past twenty years or so. No doubt all those involved in teaching film and media would want to eventually address such issues – how it is that extratextual circuits of exchange and fantasy inform our engagement of individual films – but this is a topic for more advanced study. Suffice it to say, for the introductory freshman film course, the name 'Dwain Esper' means nothing, and *Maniac* elicits no expectations. Unencumbered with the baggage of auteur status, Esper is a perfect ambassador for negotiating the perceived impasse between the 'historical poetics' of neo-formalism and the 'poetics of history' informing so much contemporary cultural analysis.

Fault lines

Having screened *Maniac* in a number of introductory film courses, I can attest to the film's ability to stimulate discussion of both the techniques and politics of film form. An excellent starting point for analysis is the adrenaline-induced, borderline-necrophilic sex rampage described above. When confronted with this incredible display of lunacy, most viewers cannot help but comment upon the sheer 'excess' of Edwards's performance (figures 1–3). The question, then, is how to take students beyond the obvious 'scenery chewing' of this sequence and channel their encounter with 'excess' into a useful lesson on representation itself. In a previous article I have argued that such excess can present moments when representational logic breaks down to foreground usually invisible codes organizing the narrative, a process even more pronounced in 'exploitation' films that seek (but fail) to replicate dominant codes of Hollywood realism (Sconce 1995). This would seem a prime example. It is almost impossible to view this explosion of lunacy without thinking of it as a highly stylized performance *of* lunacy, and a hammy one at that. To put it another way, the campy excess and theatricality of this scene, like so many others in exploitation cinema, compel even the most complacent viewer into adopting a reading position marked by that rare combination of incredulous amazement and critical detachment. To invoke Susan Sontag's famous notion of camp as a sensibility that sees all cultural phenomena in 'quotation marks', here the lunatic becomes the 'lunatic' (or given the truly superlative effort in Edwards's acting, perhaps even the *'lunatic!'*).

At a most basic level, such performative excess draws attention to the very codes of performance itself, and with further prodding, the greater realization that all codes of acting and realism are historically specific and culturally determined. This is a fact that beginning film students often intuitively recognize but have yet to contemplate fully. Although most audiences would no doubt recognize that performance styles change over time, it is a much more significant insight to realize that 'realism' itself changes across history. Such insight (when it does occur) often focuses almost exclusively on obsolescent mise-en-scène ('fake' sets, outmoded costumes, unconvincing special effects etc.). The foregrounding of outmoded (or just plain bad) performances, however, forces students to confront obsolescent strategies for *portraying* realism. Such excesses in exploitation cinema, I would argue, provide an excellent foundation for engaging the historically variable construction of cinematic realism, not only as a visual field of obsolete objects but as a nexus of obsolete codes and systems once believed to be 'realistic'. Once cued to the performative excesses in a film like *Maniac* it is a short step

1 Maniac

2 Maniac

3 Maniac

toward reconsidering the currently invisible codes governing 'naturalistic' acting in our own cultural moment, be it the ever-simmering agitation of a Robert De Niro or the deadpan vacuity of a Keanu Reeves. Indeed; it might be particularly instructive to have students compare Edwards's maniacal outburst with the method-fidgeting of Anthony Perkins in *Psycho* or the calculated aplomb of Anthony Hopkins in *Hannibal* – a representational archeology that could lead one either to other variable components in cinematic realism or directly into the preface of *Madness and Civilization*. In either case, histrionics ideally leads to history.

The kidnapping of the resurrected corpse and the subsequent disappearance of both the maniac and his victim foregrounds another important lesson to be drawn from *Maniac*. Esper's film is a model of 'faulty' narrative motivation and logic. In discussing this specific scene, Schaefer notes, 'the girl that Buckley [Edwards] carries off appears out of nowhere. No cues are given to indicate her presence and status as a possible victim before she is whisked away' (Schaefer 1999: 92). Only having recently risen from the slab, the young girl appears on the scene for the sole purpose of serving as a convenient victim for the maniac's rampage (figures 4–6). Her abduction leads to more histrionic lunacy by actor Edwards and a few brief glimpses of nudity. Once both characters have contributed their parts to the film (the nut and the nude), their services are no longer required in this 'narrative' and so they vanish, despite the clear distraction and danger they must present to the surrounding diegetic community. Their primary purpose, as Schaefer argues, is to provide 'spectacle', that foundation of exploitation cinema that links it to the early 'cinema of attractions' discussed by Tom Gunning (1986).

As with Edwards's acting, the narrative implausibilities and dangling fates of characters within *Maniac* present a case study in the artificial nature of all narrative design. Again, when the codes of Hollywood realism are working successfully, even the most critical viewer can find it difficult to resist the illusion of immersion into a seemingly real and plausible world. As exploitation films are usually only minimally concerned with story, employing narrative as a mere pretext for delivering lurid moments of spectacle, their narrative mechanics are frequently awkward and perfunctory. As Schaefer notes, 'the centrality of spectacle in exploitation films tended to disrupt or over-ride the traditional cause-and-effect chain in the narrative, while it also permitted filmmakers to be slack with classical

4 *Maniac*

5 *Maniac*

6 *Maniac*

devices like continuity editing. As a result, forbidden sights stood out in relief from the shambling wreck of the diegesis' (Schaefer 1999: 80). The 'shambling wreck' of Maniac, as in many other exploitation titles, provides a useful tool for interrogating the routines of all Hollywood narrative practice. For those hoping to teach students basic issues in narration, the strange structure of *Maniac* foregrounds a number of interesting issues concerning the general relation of story and plot in all cinema. What does a narrative choose to show? What does it choose to conceal? How does the narration manipulate duration and temporal order, on-screen and off-screen space? By virtue of their ambiguous and often troubled relation to Hollywood realism, exploitation films such as *Maniac, Glen or Glenda, Bloodfeast* and *Let Me Die a Woman* (to name only a few prominent examples) can often hurl a narratological grenade into such time-honored critical apparati as Genette's *Narrative Discourse*, Metz's Grand Syntagmatique, or Gremais's semiotic square.

The argument here is that 'faulty' narratives may be more valuable teaching tools than 'complex' ones, especially in introducing students to the basics of narrative construction. *Last Year at Marienbad* may be a more sophisticated construction of narrative space and time, but Maniac is undoubtedly a more instructive and useful 'counter-example' to the normalizing processes of Hollywood realism. Indeed, *Last Year at Marienbad* may ultimately be more interesting to students once they have seen and discussed a film like *Maniac*. Such utility exists not only at the level of providing students with a formal vocabulary in narrative analysis, but also in introducing them to larger representational issues concerning the usually naturalized relationship between story and plot. Once students see the pathetically motivated zombie-girl appear from nowhere only to be swept up and carried away by the maniacal Edwards, one can begin to explore the ideological implications of this scene's rather gratuitous and transparent inclusion in the film. What are the 'pleasures' of such spectacle, and what are the implications of the flimsy pretexts the film uses to motivate such a moment? This narratively dissonant episode, by virtue of its inexplicable eruption in the text, calls attention to the entire history of usually more naturalized and invisible gender exploitation in the cinema, an example that would no doubt be of use to feminist inquiry ranging from the 'image criticism' of Molly Haskell to the post-structuralist gender theory of

Judith Butler. At the same time, those interested in more conventional questions of realism and narratology might use the episode to interrogate the entire concept of narrative unity. Why do we find it so distracting that the characters vanish for the remainder of the story? Why does classical Hollywood cinema typically avoid 'loose ends', and how might this relate to a larger ideological critique of 'realism' itself? Once students understand in formal terms how narrative is a process of selection and assemblage, they can begin to question the logic of this construction, linking formal devices to cultural work.

Questions of narration lead us directly into the issue of continuity editing and the construction of time and space, practices long regarded by critics as both the 'basic language' of scene construction and the ideological foundation of Hollywood cinema. As fate would have it, Maniac provides another excellent sequence for considering these issues. Looking for a narrative conceit to organize his tale of maniacal excess, Esper turned to Poe's famous short story 'The Black Cat'. Thus, even as Maxwell must negotiate wandering corpses and adrenaline-crazed lunatics, he must also endure the hideous gleaming eye of the murdered doctor's cat. Midway through the film, the now insane Maxwell chases the cat through the house, a sequence Esper attempts to orchestrate through a series of 'match-cuts' linking the various rooms of the house. Facing time and budget restraints, however, these cuts are less than convincing. Many of the shots begin with the unfortunate feline rather unceremoniously tossed into the set from an offscreen assistant, all in an attempt to create a sense of the cat's desperate flight through the house (figure 7). Once Maxwell captures the cat, he begins throttling it (figure 8). In the close-up, we notice that the once black cat has assumed noticeably lighter tabby markings. The purpose behind the continuity error soon becomes clear. Esper has replaced his lead black cat with a very special one-eyed stunt cat (figure 9). With glee, Maxwell squeezes the offending eyeball from the tabby cat's socket and then, in a moment of stunning excess, even by today's rather jaded standards, eats the eyeball, proclaiming, 'Why, it is not unlike an oyster or a grape.' A cut-away returns the lead black cat on screen to jump through a pane of candy-glass and bring the sequence to dramatic closure. For those who know Poe, such a shot is essential for illustrating that the cat has survived this attack and will exact his yowling revenge later in the story.

7 *Maniac*

8 *Maniac*

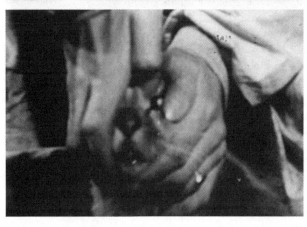

9 *Maniac*

If *Maniac*'s narrative holes and overall illogic draw attention to larger issues of narration, sequences such as this attract scrutiny to the more localized practices of continuity coverage and the construction of time and space within a scene. As in the previous examples, 'faulty' construction can lead to critical insight. This sequence provides an excellent example of the formal devices characteristically employed to maintain clarity, screen direction and spatio-temporal continuity. If beginning students are oblivious to the fact that films are most often not shot in real time and space (still a major revelation for many), such sequences provide a clear example of how editing brings disparate scraps of film together in an illusion of coherence. Not to belabour the point, but it should be obvious by now that such sequences allow those inclined toward any number of other critical approaches to exploit these faults and fissures in the text. Building on *Maniac*'s unwitting demystification of the formal strategies used to maintain spatio-temporal 'coherence', instructors can quickly engage students in debates over the social, psychical and historical mechanisms that produce the need for and shape of such 'coherence'. And again, I would argue that exploitation titles such as Maniac are often the more valuable objects for introducing students to such debates. For example, one might say that the same function could be fulfilled by that venerable citizen of the introduction to film syllabus, Godard's *Breathless*. For many novice students in film, however, Godard's famous 'jump-cuts' often read as missing splices in a bad print of the film; that is, it is difficult to discern whether they represent artistic intervention or celluloid deterioration. Esper's audaciously incongruent 'match-cuts', on the other hand, almost inevitably lead to a more thorough understanding of film mechanics and can better provoke debate over the relationship of time, space and editing.

There is another 'fault line' worthy of exploitation in *Maniac*, one that returns us to larger issues of film form. Midway through the film, the following (and highly antiquated) intertitle appears:

Maxwell had forgotten his wife, and she he, until. . . .

Esper cuts to a scene of several young women in a hotel room, banded together in poverty and sharing expenses for the evening. Contributing to the film's overall need for forbidden spectacle, the women lounge in the bathtub, dance in their underwear and, in a particularly gratuitous shot, jiggle their buttocks with a vibrabelt (figure 10). In yet another improbable narrative development,

10 Maniac

Maxwell's ex-wife discovers that her ex-husband has unknowingly come into a substantial amount of money. She resolves to find him and find a way to share in the fortune. If the mad scientist, the raid on the morgue and the raising of the dead make the first half of the film evoke *Frankenstein*, this jarring shift in genre takes us to a code-violating version of *Gold Diggers of 1933*. While genre mixing was not unheard of in the studio system, Esper's *Maniac* indiscriminately raids a variety of sources (Poe, Universal horror, Warner Bros back-stage drama) to provide a semblance of narrative organization on which to drape the more important moments of spectacle. There is little effort here to provide a novel variation or synthesis of genre, only an opportunistic plundering of familiar generic devices. As in the previous examples, however, this rather crude juxtaposition of highly discordant genres provides for mutual defamiliarization. Emeshed in the codes of 1930s genre films, this shift may have not seemed too unnatural to an audience of the period (who did not pay admission for a story in the first place). With historical distance, however, the codes and conventions of this intertextual collage become more apparent.

Much of the work in genre theory has devoted itself to avoiding tautological definitions of a group of films (i.e. westerns are westerns because they are set in the Old West, which means they are westerns – see Tudor 1995). Understanding genres as fluid rather than fixed entities has thus been a central project in genre analysis. One of the most useful devices for introducing students to these dynamics has been Rick Altman's work on the distinction between syntactic and semantic definitions of a genre. To review, semantic definitions typically centre on issues of mise-en-scène (westerns = horses, frontier towns, cowboys etc.) while syntactic definitions are more concerned with a 'deep structure' or grammar (western = nature versus civilization; individual versus society). In revisiting this work, Altman has added the category of the 'pragmatic' to involve historically changing sets of audience expectations (Altman 1999). Taken together, these three spheres describe a process of industry, audiences and films in perpetual dialogue, a 'conversation' that allows genres to arise, mutate, transmigrate, hybridize and eventually disappear. A function of larger cultural cycles rather than specific formal features, this dialogue is at work in even the most banal and seemingly 'typical' embodiment of a genre.

With its strange hybridity, *Maniac* mixes semantics and syntax to the point of ungrammatical irrationality. Is this a monster movie, a documentary, a backstage comedy? As with the other 'fault lines' discussed above, the inelegant suturing of genres in *Maniac* makes possible debate over all forms of product conventions in the cinema. Extrapolating into the contemporary moment, students might be asked to consider why some recent genres and genre blends have worked (*Titanic* as romance and disaster film) while others seem doomed to failure (the box-office flop of *Wild, Wild West* suggests that the 'sci-fi western' is not a growth hybrid). Again, the pedagogical strength of *Maniac* resides in its clumsy execution. When introducing students to the techniques and politics of cinematic form, watching one film 'fail' is a useful method to prepare them for the analysis of more apparently 'seamless' productions (which, of course, can also be subjected to equally rigorous critical dissection).

Bleeding out

Each of the areas discussed above – excess in performance, narrative illogic, faulty continuity editing and genre dissonance – ultimately brings us (and our students) back to the relationship between aesthetics, politics and history. *Maniac*'s defamiliarized relationship to its own historical model of Hollywood classicism, and, in turn, classical Hollywood's defamiliarized relationship to our own contemporary models of narrative film, make *Maniac* doubly removed and doubly estranged from the experience of most beginning film students. It is a narrative film that seemingly forces its contemporary audience to regard it not as a compelling story but as the photographic record of a historical period. It is not so much a narrative as an 'attempt' to tell a narrative, and as such is invaluable as a teaching tool, forcing students to confront almost immediately cinematic practices of form, signification, and representation. Of course, there are hundreds of *'Maniacs'* that can serve a similar function; beach blanket films, Elvis pictures, 1950s monster-movies – any film where history and technique remove students from the 'effects' of representation and plunge them headlong into the quagmire of signification itself.

In this respect, film scholars might take a page from practices of their most vocal popular competition – the now international audience of 'cult' film fans dedicated to the taxonomy and critical elucidation of a diverse body of so-called 'fringe' cinema (of which *Maniac*, beach blanket films, Elvis pictures and 1950s monster-movies are perfect examples). The very concept of 'cult cinema', of course, is vague, problematic and perhaps even misleading, suggesting as it does that 'cult value' is inherent in the films themselves, as if the 'cult film' is its own recognizable genre. But 'cult', as Benjamin would no doubt remind us, has as much to do with ritual as object. The 'cult film' phenomenon has less to do with a body of work than with the emergence of a particular reading protocol, one wholly promiscuous in its choice of object and unified only by the relative homogeneity of the social formation from which it arises. This audience tends to consist of white, middle-class men who, for complex social, historical and even psychoanalytic reasons well beyond the scope of this chapter, have dedicated a significant portion of their life not just to watching movies but to knowing about certain movies in incredible detail. What is often dismissed in this audience as pointless obsession, however, is a close analogue to the work of legitimate film scholars, and often the purported project of our work with students. Comparisons work both ways of course. If 'cult' audiences mimic film scholars, film scholarship is not unlike a cult. We all pledge rather strict and long-lasting allegiance to a certain theoretical paradigm (or worse, to a set of unquestioned beliefs), returning again and again to the favourite films, directors, issues, rhetoric, theories and theorists on which we have fixated.

This returns us, finally, to issues of pedagogy. In between our individual and often esoteric searches for *petit objet a* or the 'transcen-

dental signifier', we have scheduled our students for screenings of
The Searchers, *Jeanne Dielman* or *Rescued by Rover*. Why these
films, we might ask? Why films at all? Obviously, those who teach in
film departments teach the films with which they are most comfort-
able or which they feel will best illustrate a particular point in the
syllabus. In this respect, the above case for *Maniac* is merely a pedagogical observation based on my own teaching experience. It is certainly not a manifesto! But, in closing, I would reaffirm that all
involved in film (and media) studies can only benefit from occasional
reflection on the 'goal' of their teaching at all levels of instruction.
Beyond improving pedagogy, such reflection is valuable in basic
terms of professional self-preservation. Shortly after winning the
Oscar for Best Director in 2001, for example, Steven Soderberg
scandalized the professional and academic film industries by claim-
ing that any reasonably intelligent person could be taught to direct
a film in less than an hour. Anyone can figure out how continuity
editing works, reasoned Soderberg, simply by watching DVDs and
studying the mechanics of screen direction and scene construction.
Those involved in the professional study of film may have similar
feelings and fears about their own chosen careers. Judging by its
increased presence on syllabuses in English literature, history, sociology, French, Spanish, anthropology, art history and so on, the
cinema is undeniably popular with students, professors and administrators. And, if any bright person can be taught to direct in an hour
or less, should not a very intelligent person be able to teach film history, theory and criticism within, say, a week . . . a month . . . a year?
What, then, should film scholars teach students in film courses? The
question is of more than theoretical interest, having very real ramifications in terms of the allocation of university resources and the
future of film studies as a discipline. This question, moreover, will
no doubt become increasingly pressing for younger scholars enter-
ing the field of film studies, academics who will find themselves even
more torn by the need to publish 'cutting-edge' research within the
interdisciplinary momentum of the field as a whole, yet all the while
having to justify to university administrators why their positions
cannot be subsumed, annexed or replaced by other homes in the arts
and humanities. A generation of Dwain Esper specialists, of course,
is not the answer to this conundrum (any more than generations of
Lacanians, Foucauldians and Derrideans have been in the past). But,
as I hope the above pages have demonstrated, film scholars who

hope to specialize within the perhaps inevitable 'bleeding out' of media studies into the humanities would be well served to actually know something about film itself – as a practice, as an art, as an object. While the very concepts of 'disciplines', 'boundaries' and 'objects' have become increasingly loathsome to the intellectual vanguard of the humanities, they remain rather useful benchmarks for both students and administrators, two populations with which film scholars would be wise to keep in open dialogue.

Notes

1 Such 'attacks' appeared in the wake of Bordwell, Thompson and Staiger's now canonical work *The Classical Hollywood Cinema: Film Style and Mode of Production to 1960* (1985). They continued through the early 1990s, and have recently been addressed in Bordwell and Carroll (1996).
2 For an engaging deflation of such theory see Bordwell 1989.
3 A most pointed attack on the cultural studies paradigm can be found in Morris 1990.
4 Desperate to avoid charges of ahistoricism, psychoanalytic criticism has found Foucault a useful (if unwilling) ally in attempts to spread the word of Lacan backwards across film history.

References

Altman, Rick (1999) *Film/Genre*. London: British Film Institute.

Bahktin, M. M., and Medvedev, P. M. (1985) *The Formal Method in Literary Scholarship: A Critical Introduction to Sociological Poetics*. Cambridge, Mass.: Harvard University Press.

Bellour, Raymond (1977) Hitchcock, the Enunciator, *Camera Obscura*, 2 (Autumn), pp. 66–91.

Bordwell, David (1989) *Making Meaning: Inference and Rhetoric in the Interpretation of Cinema*. Cambridge, Mass.: Harvard University Press.

Bordwell, David, and Carroll, Noel (eds.) (1996) *Post-Theory: Reconstructing Film Studies*. Madison: University of Wisconsin Press.

Bordwell, David, Thompson, Kristin, and Staiger, Janet (1985) *The Classical Hollywood Cinema: Film Style and Mode of Production to 1960*. New York: Columbia University Press.

Goldmann, Lucien (1975) *Towards a Sociology of the Novel*. London: Tavistock.

Gunning, Tom (1986) The Cinema of Attractions: Early Film, its Spectator and the Avant-Garde, *Wide Angle* 8 (3–4) (Autumn), pp. 63–70.

Lukács, George (1963) *The Meaning of Contemporary Realism*. London: Merlin.

Morris, Meaghan (1990) Banality in Cultural Studies, in Patricia Mellencamp (ed.), *Logics of Television: Essays in Cultural Criticism*. Bloomington: Indiana University Press.

Schaefer, Eric (1999) *'Bold! Daring! Shocking! True!': A History of Exploitation Films, 1919–1959*. Durham: Duke University Press.

Sconce, Jeffrey (1995) 'Trashing' the Academy: Taste, Excess, and an Emerging Politics of Cinematic Style, *Screen* 36 (4) (Winter), pp. 371–393.

Sontag, Susan (2001 [1964]) Notes on Camp, in *Against Interpretation*. New York: Picador.

Tudor, Andrew (1995 [1973]) Genre, in Barry Keith Grant (ed.), *Film Genre Reader II*. Austin: University of Texas Press.

3

The masculinity of cult

Joanne Hollows

The expanding literature within film studies which has attempted to specify the characteristics of cult has often done so through an opposition between the characteristics of cult and its audiences and those of 'mainstream cinema' and its audiences. Indeed, any sense of coherence that cult has is usually produced by what it is not: as Jancovich (2002) has argued, cult texts are 'defined according to a subcultural ideology in which it is their supposed difference from the "mainstream" which is significant, rather than any unifying feature'. This chapter builds on these insights to argue that these distinctions between the subcultural world of cult and 'mainstream cinema' are gendered. It also suggests that these distinctions are reproduced not only by cult fans but also by academic criticism on cult (an argument developed elsewhere in this volume by Jacinda Read).

Both academic criticism and fan discourses frequently employ the notion that cult is a subculture. Some critics have drawn explicit connections between subcultural theory and cult movies fandom: for example, Joan Hawkins argues that mail-order video companies 'comprise and address what Dick Hebdige might recognize as a true video subculture, a subculture identified less by a specific style than by a certain strategy of reading' associated with the avant-garde (2000: 14). Many other critics attribute implicitly to cult those features frequently associated with youth subcultures: for example, cult is often described as transgressive and resistant (Telotte 1991; Juno and Vale 1986, among others). However, in the process, cult criticism also reproduces some of the problematic assumptions of subcultural theory: not only is the very way in which subculture has been conceptualized gendered, but so also are many of the practices that give an identity to subcultures. Although in the following sec-

tions I examine in more detail how fan practices in cult are constructed as masculine, and can also work structurally to exclude
women, this section goes on to examine how the very concept of
subculture has been naturalized as masculine.

McRobbie and Garber have noted how the very concept of subculture 'has acquired . . . masculine overtones' (1991: 3), a tendency
strengthened by the frequent identification between the subcultural
theorist and the subcultural activities (s)he studies (McRobbie
1981). These ideas are developed by Sarah Thornton (1995) in her
ethnographic work on club cultures which examines how subcultural identities and ideologies are produced through an opposition
with, and rejection of, 'the mainstream'. Thornton analyses the discourses employed by clubbers and subcultural critics to demonstrate
how we 'create groups with words' (Pierre Bourdieu cited in Thornton 1995: 101). Subcultures are valued positively by both groups
because they are actively produced by young people themselves;
defined by their distance from commerce; are more 'authentic'; are
a means for young people to express their difference; and are, therefore, deviant, resistant or transgressive. These, as Jancovich (2002)
has pointed out, are exactly the same as the ways in which both fans
and critics frequently imagine cult. However, Thornton argues, subcultural identities are also produced by the ways in which they are
distinguished – in both senses of the word – from the majority of
young people. The 'mainstream' is imagined as reproducing passively the dominant culture; as consuming a ready-made commercially produced culture; as inauthentic; as homogeneous; as straight
and conformist. However, Thornton argues, a further opposition
can be mapped on to this opposition between subcultures and the
mainstream: the characteristics associated with subcultures are those
commonly associated with masculinity and the characteristics
derided in portraits of the mainstream are those associated with
femininity. Indeed, she argues, the 'inconsistent fantasies of the
mainstream' which are used by clubbers – and, I would argue, by cult
– frequently equate the mainstream with mass culture which has
often been identified with the feminine as a means of devaluing it
(see Huyssen 1986).

Jancovich has demonstrated how Thornton's ideas can be applied
to the ways in which cult imagines 'mainstream cinema' and its audiences. Indeed, he argues, there is a need to examine 'one of the most
problematic concepts within film studies – "the mainstream com-

mercial cinema" – and the ways in which its inconsistent and contradictory uses arise from its function as the Other, the construction
of which allows for the production of distinctions and a sense of cultural superiority' (Jancovich 2002). However, because of his interest in the ways in which struggles over taste are 'classed', Jancovich
pays little attention to the ways in which they are also gendered: that
is, in much criticism, mainstream cinema is imagined as feminized
mass culture and cult as a heroic and masculinized subculture. For
example, in Juno's and Vale's work, *Dynasty* and *Terms of Endear-
ment* are offered as examples of the antithesis of cult and associated
with a feminized audience, as demonstrated in the following
exchange between the authors and the cult auteur Larry Cohen:

AJ: What kind of films influence you?
LC: Oh I've seen almost everything.
VV: You've even seen *Dynasty*?
LC: Once or twice. If you go over to somebody's house, it's inevitable
– like my mother *has* to watch it . . . but I can't sit through it . . .
(Juno and Vale 1986: 126)

In a different but related vein, in the introduction to the more
recent *Unruly Pleasures*, Harper and Mendik distinguish between
the cult and mainstream audience using metaphors of male and
female orgasm: while the 'hardcore' cult audience experiences an
'intense physical and emotional involvement' and a 'violent excitement', the audience for mainstream film is associated with 'random,
directionless, entertainment-seeking' (2000: 9). In the process, the
mainstream 'Other' of the cult fan is characterized using a familiar
image of the distracted female television viewer, well-documented in
feminist media studies (see, for example, Brunsdon 2000). In discussions such as these cult is naturalized as masculine and the mainstream as feminine, and this, I would suggest, has implications for
the ways in which the politics of cult have been formulated. If cult
is continually seen to be characterized by the ways in which it resists,
challenges and transgresses the mainstream, and if the mainstream is
persistently gendered as feminine, cult would seem to reproduce
existing power structures rather than simply challenge them.

This chapter focuses on the ways in which the masculinity of cult
is naturalized in many of the key consumption practices that constitute cult fandom. This gendering of cult as masculine does not mean
only that it is based on a refusal of competencies and dispositions

that are culturally coded as feminine; it may also work structurally to exclude women from participation in cult movie fandom.

However, before proceeding, it is worth clarifying this argument in relation to possible objections. First, it could be claimed that the narrow ways in which cult is employed in what follows might work against a more expansive understanding of cult movie fandom. However, this would be to ignore the ways in which the production of more expansive definitions of cult is dependent , in part, on questioning both the residual and dominant ways in which cult has been, and is, mobilized across a range of academic and popular discourses. While there is considerable disagreement about what is a cult movie, it would none the less be unlikely to see *Titanic* or (my own favourite) *Pretty Woman* listed among *Something Weird*'s top fifty movies among the likes of *The Sinful Dwarf* and *Big Bust Loops Vol. 15*. Likewise, they are unlikely to figure among Cinebizarre's catalogue of 'Art films, Cult films, Avant-garde films, Giallobizarre, Hong Kong cinema, International Erotica, Midnight Movies, Exploitation & Sexploitation, gory Horror, sexy vampires, classic science fiction, European sex comedies, shock films and drive-in trash'. *Titanic* might have a 'cult' following but its associations with a feminine and 'mass' audience on one hand, and 'middlebrow' discourses of 'quality' on the other (see Nash and Lahti 1999), mean that it is unlikely to be easily accepted into academic or popular cult canons unless the supposedly 'dominant' and 'conservative' meanings of the women's film can be subverted by the strategies of cult fans.

Second, while many of the arguments may be more generally applicable, this chapter tends to focus on what might be called 'low-end' cult based around 'obscure and trashy titles' (Klinger 2001: 136). As suggested above, it is this meaning of cult that is most commonly employed by cult film media, distributors and retailers, and which has also preoccupied academic writing. However, it is crucial to note at this point that the argument about cult is far less applicable to camp. The distinction between these categories is obviously extremely blurred as there is extensive overlap between the two in terms of the fans themselves, the types of movies in camp and cult canons, and in sites of exchange and distribution. None the less, Greg Taylor has argued that the roots of cult often privileged 'connoisseurship' and were based on 'identification and isolation of marginal artworks' in defiance of 'mass' taste and the wider logic of consumer culture (1999: 15). Camp, on the other hand, is concerned less with the selection of objects and more with 'interpretation', demonstrating that 'potentially *any* mass culture object can be re-created aesthetically' (16). For Staiger, the midnight movies of the early to mid-1960s in the USA not only contributed to the formation of a camp aesthetic but also acted as a site for the 'expression of community and a site for community building' that, in some ways, acted as a foundation for the gay liberation movement (2000: 126). In what follows, the emphasis is on the cult side of the cult/camp divide with a corresponding emphasis on heterosexual, rather than gay, masculinity.[1]

Third, this chapter does *not* intend to suggest that cult movies constitute a 'men's genre' nor that the films elected to cultdom are inherently masculine. Instead, my aim is to examine the fan practices that produce cult and the ways in which they privilege masculine competencies and dispositions. As Andrew Ross argues, 'Cultural power does not inhere in the content of categories of tastes. On the contrary, it is exercized through the capacity to draw the line between and round categories of taste' (1989: 61). Thus, despite the frequent appearance of horror, science fiction and softcore porn within the cult pantheon (arguably 'men's genres'), other more feminized films such as *Valley of the Dolls* can be redeemed by processes of reclassification. In this way, any attempts to redefine cult must examine the power relations that sustain current definitions.

Finally, to suggest that cult has been naturalized as masculine is *not* to argue for an essentialist position which claims that there is something inherently male about cult and its fans. This is not to say that the cult fan is never explicitly constructed as male: Something Weird's copy for *Touch of Sweden* suggests that 'Sexploitation fans will be fanning their penises over this all-star lineup!' However, in what follows, I want to argue that cult has been culturally constructed as masculine and examine how this not only is based on a rejection of the feminine but may also work to exclude 'real' women from some of the practices associated with cult fandom. However, cult fandom is open to women who opt to be 'culturally "one of the boys"' (Thornton 1995: 104) and seek to distance themselves from the negative associations of femininity. My own adventures to 'alternative' cinemas to see 'cult movies' as a teenager in the early 1980s were very much motivated by a desire to distance myself from the mainstream 'girly' tastes of my friends. Indeed, female fans of films such as *Titanic* are still frequently 'aware of the stamp of devaluation their fandom carries in this society' (Nash and Lahti 1999: 83). Although girls may opt to be 'one of the boys', this does little to challenge the power relations which sustain a position in which there are few opportunities to capitalize on femininity within cult movie fandom.

It is perhaps for this reason that even feminist academics working within the field of cult cinema have tended to generate analyses that reproduce, rather than question, the masculinity of cult.[2] This tendency is particularly apparent in the work of Pam Cook (1976) and Carol Clover (1992) which, in attempting to appropriate elements of exploitation cinema (the films of Stephanie Rothman and rape-revenge films respectively) for feminism, colludes with the rejection and repression of the feminine found elsewhere in cult movies fandom and criticism. This tendency manifests itself, in particular, through the way in which both analyses are predicated on the assumption that in order to claim these films for feminism they must be distinguished from a mainstream which is perceived to be feminized and depoliticized. Cook, for example, argues that although the naturalized, conservative forms of mainstream Hollywood cinema 'may be less offensive to women . . . In fact, exploitation films are potentially less offensive than mainstream Hollywood cinema because of their resistance to the "natural", and the way they offer the possibility of taking a critical distance on the metalanguage of mainstream cinema' (1976: 124–125). Clover's feminist analysis of the rape-revenge film depends on drawing a similar, and perhaps more explicit, distinction with the genre itself. In other words, as Read has argued elsewhere:

> while the low-brow rape-revenge film is elevated to the status of a politicized avant-garde (consumed by male audiences), the mainstream version is implicitly analysed within a framework that condemns mass culture as a feminized and, therefore, depoliticized culture (consumed by 'normal', that is, mixed audiences). For example, the kind of adjectives Clover uses to denigrate and exclude mainstream examples of the rape-revenge film betrays a belief that they are too feminine to be feminist. In other words, they are variously described as 'civilized' (p. 147), 'pretty' (p. 150), 'safe' (p. 235), 'glossy' (p. 232), 'nice' (p. 20), and 'feel-good' (p. 147). (Read 2000: 9)

Consequently, for both male and female fans and academics alike, the rejection of the feminine functions not only to secure the masculinity of cult but to assure its (allegedly) oppositional politics.

Why would a nice girl be in a place like this?

As I have demonstrated, the processes of classification and catego-
rization through which cult gains a sense of its masculinized identity
are produced in opposition to an imagined feminized 'mainstream'.
However, many of the practices of cult fandom work also to naturalize cult as masculine through the ways in which they structurally
exclude women. Again, feminist critiques of subcultural theory provide a useful starting point. For example, critics such as McRobbie
(1981) have noted how subcultural theorists locate youth subcultures in the masculine space of 'the street'. For McRobbie, the division between public and private spheres therefore structures access
to subcultural membership and activities.

Cinemagoing might seem initially to run counter to this example
– cinema has frequently been identified as a public space in which
women 'feel at home'. However, the sites in which cult is consumed
are far removed from (and may indeed operate as a refusal of) the
picture palaces which courted the female audience (see, for example: Peiss 1986; Stacey 1994). For example, Henenlotter celebrates
the 'sleazo movie theatres' in which 'the more peeling paint, the
more smell of urine, the more exciting it seemed to be' (in Juno and
Vale 1986: 8). These cinemas are hardly feminized consumption
spaces, and the sleaze, dirtiness and transgressiveness of cult movies
theatres is emphasized by the fact that, in the 1960s and 1970s, cult
movies were often screened in porn cinemas or in picture-houses
that existed in close proximity to them.

The sleaze of the cinema itself is also a product of their location
in parts of the city's underbelly or 'twilight zones'. This works to
confirm the figure of the cult fan as a (frequently heterosexual)
'manly adventurer' who sets out into the urban wilderness (Straw
1997: 13), a position less open to women. Although the city is no
longer represented as a dangerous and inappropriate place for
women as it was in the nineteenth century (Nava 1996; Ryan 1994),
the city of the 1960s in which cult flourished was increasingly seen
as a threatening place: not only was there a re-emergence of images
of the city as a 'place of decay' (Hall 1996: 11) but also 'city leisure
areas acquired a litany of ills' (Hannigan 1998: 43). While the location of cult in these disreputable city spaces may work to confirm a
heroic masculinity in its female fans, for women they can signify
fear. Indeed, contemporary studies of women's use of city space

indicate that 'a fear for personal safety was an influential factor in women's avoidance of certain places in the city, particularly at night, in ways which were not apparent among men' (Taylor *et al.* 1996: 228). As the 'particularly at night' in this quotation suggests, the tradition of the midnight movie, which was central to the creation of cult, works further to exclude women. Yet as critics such as Barry Keith Grant have suggested, the 'midnight screening' was central to the construction of cult as transgressive, as anti-respectability and as 'against the logic of "prime-time" exhibition' (2000: 19). The construction of cult as masculine, therefore, needs to be understood in relation to these cinematic sites of social centrality. This points to the ways in which particular sites come to 'symbolize an alternative set of values and beliefs around which a group can develop an identity and sense of belonging' and play a role 'in the reproduction of marginal or outsider identities' (Hetherington 2000: 25–26). It is these masculinized spaces which, in part, allow for the identity renewal and symbolic escape from everyday life (and the domestic) which have historically been important in producing cult (Hetherington 1996; Hollows and Milestone 1998). The sleazo cinemas became 'socially important not only for their empirical facilities but for their qualities as what William Whyte once called "schmoozing" spaces which support personal and group identifications' (Shields 1992: 16).

However, the rituals and sites of social centrality in cult movie fandom have changed, with public collective consumption in 'enchanted' sites increasingly being replaced by individual consumption of movies in the 'unsacralized space' of the home (Hawkins 2000: 41). While cult movies have found a home on television, its status as a domestic medium is obviously problematic for the way in which cult has been constructed. Not only does television viewing take place in what traditionally has been seen as the feminized sphere of the home, but television has also been strongly associated with the 'family viewing' against which youthful audiences have defined themselves. Indeed, the movement of cult films on to television in the 1970s via 'midnight movies' slots can be seen as an attempt to distance these films from 'normal' schedules providing 'family viewing'. Furthermore, television's status as a 'mass' medium which is accessible to all threatens the 'integrity' of cult by offering to reveal its insider knowledges to all. Finally, television appears antithetical to cult because it is persistently presented as an agent of feminization, its audience identified with the passive, distracted and complicit female viewer (Petro 1986) against which cult fans define themselves.

On one hand, as Klinger (2001) argues, the growth of 'home film cultures' organized around new technologies has refigured what was once an antagonistic relationship between the cinephile and domestic viewing to produce new conditions of film consumption in domestic space. As Tashiro notes, his film collection not only provides a 'set of objects in space which provide a potential that I can control', but also 'possession' of a film is intensified in the domestic context (Tashiro 1996: 17). Whether there is equal opportunity to experience this sense of 'control' and 'ownership' remains open to debate given that work in media studies suggests that the gendering of domestic labour (at least within 'traditional' nuclear family contexts) continues to structure relationships to communications technologies within the home (see, for example, Morley 1996).

However, on the other hand, the consumption of cult films on video also allows the cult fan to keep the domestic at a distance. Initially, video was treated with hostility by cultists because of its associations with the feminine: as Henenlotter put it, 'the only films that were available were *The Sound of Music* and *Hello Dolly*' (in Juno and Vale 1986: 8). However, the development of video as a format has offered opportunities for it to be repositioned within cult. This puts emphasis on the means of distribution and retailing, rather than the viewing context, as a means of refiguring the cult fan as 'manly adventurer'. Mail-order distributors often highlight the illicit or illegal nature of buying videos with claims such as 'ORDER AT YOUR OWN RISK' (Hawkins 2000: 45). Indeed, the aesthetics of these tapes can also work to secure cult's illicit nature: low production values that privilege a 'raw' image become 'both a signifier of the tape's outlaw status and a guarantor of its authenticity' (ibid.: 47). Cult shops are frequently located on the seedy fringes of the city centre where they often co-exist with the porn trade. This is sometimes reproduced in an online retail environment where home pages offer links to softcore and hardcore porn sites.[3] The relationship between cult video retailers and the porn industry not only places the girl who wishes to be 'one of the boys' in an awkward position (not least because the porn is frequently addressed to a heterosexual male audience), but also the proximity to hardcore porn works to secure the thrill that comes from cult's illicit and 'outlaw' status.

These factors work to sustain the masculinity of cult through the emphasis on a gendered prowess. However, they are also homologous with those aspects of cult which seek to measure 'hardness' by demonstrating how far or low you can go. This is frequently used as a retail ploy with claims such as 'too horrific for most audiences' used to promote video sales.[4] Hoxter claims that the pleasures of watching horror involves a 'game of "dare"' for fans 'no matter their gender' (Hoxter 2000: 178). However, he none the less goes on to liken this 'dare' to what has become a ritual test of specifically masculine hardness in a UK context, 'the adolescent "Vindaloo test"' (178) in which lads compete to eat the hottest curry. In this way, the viewing of cult, even in the domestic context, can still be naturalized as a manly activity.

Cult, collecting and commodity exchange

This section examines in more depth the ways in which consumption practices and strategies work to construct cult as a 'subculture'. In the process, I examine how relationships between cult fans are created and sustained through a range of media and through modes of commodity exchange. In doing so, I again draw on Sarah Thornton's work which demonstrates that, while subcultures define themselves as anti-media and anti-commerce, various media and forms of commodity exchange are often central in giving subcultures a sense of coherence. This is used as the basis for a more extended discussion of the ways in which the cult consumer is envisaged more specifically as a collector, which enables a distance to be produced from the feminine associations of consumption.

As Jancovich (2002) has argued, despite their frequent hostility to the media:

> cult movie audiences are themselves brought together, and a sense of 'imagined community' is produced and maintained, *through* the media. However, the value of membership within these subcultures is based on a sense of exclusivity and hence the media also threatens these subcultures by blurring the very sense of distinction which underpins the sense of community.

Therefore, while varieties of niche media – magazines, fanzines and websites – circulate the subcultural knowledges which are central to membership of the 'imagined community' of cult, they also threaten to make these knowledges available to all. For these reasons, cult media are a source of ambivalence for the cult fan.

However, certain strategies can also be employed to ward off 'outsiders' and maintain a sense of exclusiveness. Some of these strategies can be related to the importance of 'hardness' in cult discussed above. For example, Sanjek has noted the 'self-conscious misogyny, racism and sexism' of horror fanzines, arguing that 'this intentionally juvenile hard-boiled tone goes hand in hand with the fanzines' belief that only the most hardened sensibilities can bear the assault of offensive imagery' (1990: 154). Indeed, Brigid Cherry's work confirms how this can work to exclude female readers whose low rates of consumption of niche media aimed at horror fans is partly attributed to a distaste for 'gore' on one hand, and the sexism and semi-pornographic imagery found in these magazines on the other (1999: 181–182). However, Cherry's research also points to other reasons for low consumption of these niche media among women. Some fans objected to the 'obsession with trivia' in the magazines (ibid.: 182), an obsession which, as Nathan Hunt's chapter in the present volume makes clear, is crucial in constructing a sense of shared expertise and subcultural capital within cult fandom. Furthermore, Klinger (2001) sees trivia as having an important currency within film fandom more generally. Cherry's work suggests that most female fans find these dispositions towards films either incomprehensible or irrelevant (see Morley 1986). Cherry's research also supports the idea that the sites of cult consumption work to exclude women from its 'imagined community': the women in her study tended to buy only magazines available in high-street newsagents' and did not tend to frequent specialist stores. While this work is largely concerned with horror, similar strategies are also more generally identifiable in cult fandom. Indeed, they are also familiar tropes in academic criticism about cult, as Jacinda Read discusses elsewhere in the present volume. As a review of *Unruly Pleasures* published in *Sight and Sound* put it, 'the nipple count and the references to Lacan are roughly equal . . . the book could at times be mistaken for an academic version of the *Sunday Sport*' (Williams 2000: 38).

If the strategies of exclusivity in the niche media that create and sustain cult construct its 'imagined community' as something of a 'boyzone', then so do the ways in which its commerce and commodity exchange is organized. The importance of commodity exchange in constructing cult has tended to be disavowed because cult shares with the subcultures discussed by Thornton 'the idea that authentic culture is somehow outside of media and commerce' (1995: 116). This can be seen in the frequent use of budget as a means of classifying cult against the mainstream. For example, Juno's and Vale's defence of the low-budget as the vision of an auteur and genuinely 'of the people' is made in opposition to 'commercial' film making: 'When a corporation decides to invest $20 million in a film, a chain of command regulates each step, and no one person is allowed free rein. Meetings with lawyers, accountants, and corporate boards are what films in Hollywood are all about' (1986: n.p.). This is implicitly mirrored in some of the sales tactics of distributors: for example, screenedge.com defines itself as 'radical', 'cutting edge' and 'nothing like Hollywood'. Because the very category of cult is based on a rejection of the products of consumer capitalism, it becomes problematic to think of the cult fan as a consumer, an identity associated with the passive feminized consumer of 'mainstream' cinema. Indeed, this also reproduces a tendency in conceptualizations of subcultures more generally. As Angela McRobbie has argued, 'shopping has tended to be subsumed under the category of domestic labour with the attendant connotations of drudgery and exhaustion. Otherwise it has been absorbed into consumerism where women and girls are seen as having a particular role to play' (1994: 136). Cult fans who browse their xeroxed catalogues of illicit videos do not think of themselves as catalogue shoppers because the fact that participation in cult depends on shopping for goods is at odds with the allegedly transgressive, and laddish, nature of some forms of cult fandom.

For these reasons, cult fans must distance themselves from the feminine shopper and adopt dispositions towards consumption which are more assertively masculine. One of the key mechanisms through which this is achieved is through the construction of the cult fan as collector rather than mere consumer. The idea that the collector's activities somehow exceed that of the ordinary consumer is frequently produced in theories of collecting (see, for example: Belk 1995; Danet and Katriel 1994). Historically, the collector has been imagined as masculine: 'Women were consumers of objects; men were collectors. Women bought to decorate and for the sheer joy of buying, but men had a vision for their collections, and viewed their collections as an ensemble with a philosophy behind it' (Saisselin cited in Belk and Wallendorf, 1994: 241). In cult collecting, as in record collecting, this philosophy can be informed by 'anti-consumerist ethics which tie the collector's investment in the obscure to the bohemian's refusal of the blatantly commercial' (Straw 1997: 10).

It is important to note at this point that I am not suggesting that the collector is an 'essentially' masculine figure. Klinger argues that, 'despite a strong male presence in the collecting world', film collectables are marketed to a heterogeneous range of consumers (2001: 136). While research on collecting in general indicates that that both men and women collect, it also suggests that different modes of collecting can be seen as a means of constructing or performing gendered identities (Belk and Wallendorf 1994). Women's collections have frequently been found to be more personal, more intimate and more related to people whereas 'male practices of accumulation take shape in an ongoing relationship between the personal space of the collection and the public discursive systems of ordering or value . . . [that] tie each male's collection to an ongoing, collective enterprise of cultural archaeology' (Straw 1997: 6). The importance of various media discussed above to the construction of cult is crucial in constructing these public systems of ordering and value through which collections can be given meaning and value. Yet it is also the practices of collecting, fandom and the exchange of materials which help to produce the masculinity of cult: the material culture of cult provides 'the raw materials around which the rituals of homosocial interaction take place. Just as ongoing conversation between men shapes the composition and extension of each man's collection, so each man finds, in the similarity of his points of reference to those of his peers, confirmation of a shared universe of critical judgement' (Straw 1997: 5). This is demonstrated in Charles Tashiro's acknowledgement that not only does an acknowledged rarity make an object more desirable but also that part of the pleasure in acquiring additions to the collection (which in turn shapes the 'value' of a particular video) may be in 'acquiring titles before friends' (1996: 15). The emphasis on 'authenticity' and 'rarity' in cult collecting 'helps to stimulate the competitive gamesmanship and "sport" characteristic of this enterprise' (Klinger 2001: 139). The practices and processes of exchange create and sustain cult while also creating and sustaining its masculinity.

The construction of the cultist as 'manly adventurer' also offers a way of distinguishing cult consumption from an everyday feminized practice. As Charles Tashiro has suggested, part of the thrill of video collecting in general comes from the sense of 'bravado' generated by acquiring a rarity that 'provides a mark of distinction that the widely released director's cut of *Blade Runner* doesn't' (1996: 15). Cult collecting also draws on much older images of the collector as anthropologist and updates them: today's expeditions are 'into the natural wilderness of discarded styles' (Straw 1997: 13). Although this manly adventurer's skill is largely measured by his ability to find cult in unlikely places, some specialist cult outlets also take care to define themselves against more 'mainstream' shopping spaces: the interiors of cult shops are frequently painted in dark colours, dimly lit, with products frequently in the dusty plastic bags used in sex shops, and catalogues celebrate their low production values in a rejection of the 'glossy' qualities of regular catalogues.[5] Web retailers may also use gory or sexual graphics (combined with a fondness for black) to signify their difference from retailers such as Amazon and Blackstar. However, while these consumption spaces are based on a refusal of 'mainstream consumer culture', they are none the less part of consumer culture: indeed, their characteristics offer a means of 'branding' their outlets as 'authentic' consumption sites for a niche audience who wouldn't be seen dead in W. H. Smiths.

As Jancovich (2002) argues, the world of cult is based on practices which are not simply premised on a rejection of the mainstream but also on a rejection of 'improper' cult fans. I have tried to suggest that not only is 'proper' fandom based on a form of homosocial bonding but also that the hipness associated with the figure of the manly adventurer works to gender cult as masculine. As Straw argues, 'It is within the social constructions of hipness that values which we might call masculinist and strategies whose effect is to reproduce social stratification interweave in interesting ways' (1997: 9). If this hipness acts as a form of subcultural capital within cult, 'what ultimately defines cultural capital as capital is its "convertibility" into economic capital' (Thornton 1995: 12). While for most the rewards of hipness are a sense of distinction, for some this subcultural capital will be converted into economic capital through the pursuit of subcultural 'careers' in magazines, retailing and distribution. In this way, some fans will operate as 'intellectuals' within the scene in much the same way as DJs operate within club cultures (Straw 1991). The rewards of cult fandom are thus open to those who have the most mastery of its masculine dispositions. Other fans may opt to convert their subcultural capital into 'proper' or legitimate cultural capital which, I would argue, is why subcultural ideologies are frequently reproduced in academic accounts of cult. The ways in which the masculinity of cult is reproduced – or, indeed, fetishized – within academic writing is explored elsewhere in the present volume by Jacinda Read.

In this chapter, I have aimed to open up debates about how cult movie fandom is a gendered practice. The reasons for doing so are not motivated by a desire to rid cult of its 'big bust loops' on the off-chance that some easily shocked girl and/or feminist might find them offensive. Nor is it, as one critic suggested, 'to paint half the walls pink in every cult movie store' (although, once visualized, this suggestion has an amusing appeal!). Instead, the aim of this piece is to demonstrate the ways in which cult, although it is usually associated with a challenge to cultural hierarchies and with resistance, transgression and radicalism, serves also to reproduce cultural distinctions and cultural hierarchies along the lines of gender. Therefore, this is less a call for 'equal opportunities' in cult fandom and more a reminder that in every act of transgression there is always something, or someone, that is transgressed. The 'radicalism' of cult is only sustained by processes of 'othering' and it is always important to remain aware of who, and what, is being 'othered'.

Notes

1   However, it should be noted that camp also reproduces cultural distinction, particularly on the basis of class, as Andrew Ross (1989) makes clear. Furthermore, camp has also been seen as 'gender specific and hence problematic for lesbians' (Wilton 2000: 348).

2   As I have argued elsewhere (Hollows 2000), this can be seen as part of a wider tendency in some feminist criticism for the critic to align herself with the masculine because the identity' feminist' is frequently based on a rejection of the feminine.

3   For example, a visit to retailer bizarrovideo.com throws up links to the sextracker website offering '1000s of Hardcore XXX Movies!!' to download (http://enter.sextracker.com/Hetero). Indeed, online retailers may also seek to distinguish themselves from each other by the extent of their 'adult' content. For example, cinebizarre.com promises that 'you won't be confronted with any pornographic videos' whereas bizarrovideo.com promises clips of 'live girls' and warns that you should not enter the site if you 'find images of adults engaged in sexual acts to

be offensive and objectionable'. Contextual material suggests that the primary reasons behind these distinctions lies in uncertainty about how cult retailers should position themselves in relation to the legal implications of their content, particularly in relation to minors.

4   From the copy for *Cannibal Holocaust* at Film Wizards Cult Movie Arcade   (www.filmwizards.com/Merchant2/merchant.mv?Screen=PROD &Store_Code=1&Product_Code=C03&Category_Code=C).

5   Nonetheless, it is also acknowledged that there has been a 'high-streetization' of cult. I the UK, the science fiction retail chain Forbidden Planet has opened some more high-end shops which are at odds with the 'dingy' qualities that still exist in some of their stores. This might be understood in terms of wider transformations in the ways in which masculine consumption practices are constructed so that to be 'masculine' and a 'high-street shopper' are no longer mutually exclusive. These themes have been developed in Nathan Hunt's ongoing research into *SFX* magazine.

References

Belk, Russell W. (1995) *Collecting in a Consumer Society*. London: Routledge.

Belk, Russell W., and Wallendorf, Melanie (1994) Of Mice and Men: Gender Identity and Collecting, in Susan Pearce (ed.), *Interpreting Objects and Collections*. London: Routledge, pp. 240–253.

Brunsdon, Charlotte (2000) *The Feminist, the Housewife and the Soap Opera*. Oxford: Oxford University Press.

Cherry, Brigid (1999) *The Female Horror Film Audience: Viewing Pleasures and Fan Practices*. Unpublished Ph.D. thesis, University of Stirling.

Clover, Carol (1992) *Men, Women and Chainsaws: Gender in the Modern Horror Film*. London: British Film Institute.

Cook, Pam (1976) 'Exploitation' Films and Feminism, *Screen*, 17 (2) (Summer), pp. 122–127.

Danet, Brenda, and Katriel, Tamar (1994) No Two Alike: Play and Aesthetics in Collecting, in Susan Pearce (ed.), *Interpreting Objects and Collections*. London: Routledge, pp. 220–239.

Grant, Barry Keith (2000) Second Thoughts on Double Features, in Graeme Harper and Xavier Mendik (eds.), *Unruly Pleasures: The Cult Film and Its Critics*. Guildford: FAB Press, pp. 13–27.

Hall, Peter (1996) *Cities of Tomorrow*. Second Edition. Oxford: Blackwell.

Hannigan, John (1998) *Fantasy City: Pleasure and Profit in the Postmodern Metropolis*. London: Routledge.

Harper, Graeme, and Xavier Mendik (2000) Several Theorists Ask 'How Was It For You Honey?' Or Why the Academy Needs Cult Cinema and

Its Fans, in Graeme Harper and Xavier Mendik (eds.), *Unruly Pleasures: The Cult Film and Its Critics*. Guildford: FAB Press, pp. 7-11.

Hawkins, Joan (2000) *Cutting Edge: Art-Horror and the Horrific Avant-garde*. Minneapolis: University of Minnesota Press.

Hetherington, Kevin (1996) Identity Formation, Space and Social Centrality, *Theory, Culture and Society*, 13 (4), pp. 33–52.

Hetherington, Kevin (2000) *New Age Travellers: Vanloads of Uproarious Humanity*. London: Cassell.

Hollows, Joanne (2000) *Feminism, Femininity and Popular Culture*. Manchester: Manchester University Press.

Hollows, Joanne, and Milestone, Katie (1998) Welcome to Dreamsville: A History and Geography of Northern Soul, in A. Leyshon, D. Matless and G. Revill (eds.), *The Place of Music*. New York: Guilford, pp. 83–103.

Hoxter, Julian (2000) Taking Possessions: Cult Learning and *The Exorcist*, in Graeme Harper and Xavier Mendik (eds.), *Unruly Pleasures: The Cult Film and Its Critics*. Guildford: FAB Press, pp. 171–185.

Huyssen, Andreas (1986) Mass Culture as Woman: Modernism's Other, in Tania Modleski (ed.), *Studies in Entertainment: Critical Approaches to Mass Culture*. Bloomington and Indianapolis: Indiana University Press, pp. 188–207.

Jancovich, Mark (2002) Cult Fictions: Cult Movies, Subcultural Capital and the Production of Cultural Distinction, *Cultural Studies*, 16 (2), pp. 306–322.

Klinger, Barbara (2001) The Contemporary Cinephile: Film Collecting in the Post-video Era, in Richard Maltby and Melvyn Stokes (eds.), *Hollywood Spectatorship*. London: British Film Institute, pp. 132–151.

McRobbie, Angela (1981) Settling Accounts With Subcultures, in T. Bennett, G. Martin, C. Mercer and J. Woollacott (eds.), *Culture, Ideology and Social Process*. London: Batsford, pp. 111–124.

McRobbie, Angela (1994) *Postmodernism and Popular Culture*. London: Routledge.

McRobbie, Angela, and Garber, Marjorie (1991) Girls and Subcultures, in Angela McRobbie, *Feminism and Youth Culture: From Jackie to Just Seventeen*. Basingstoke: Macmillan, pp. 1–15.

Morley, David (1986) *Family Television: Cultural Power and Domestic Leisure*. London: Comedia.

Nash, Melanie, and Lahti, Martti (1999) 'Almost Ashamed to Say I Am One of Those Girls': *Titanic*, Leonardo DiCaprio, and the Paradoxes of Girls' Fandom, in Kevin S. Sandler and Gaylyn Studlar (eds.), *Titanic: Anatomy of a Blockbuster*. New Brunswick, NJ: Rutgers University Press, pp. 64–88.

Nava, Mica (1996) Modernity's Disavowal: Women, the City and the Department Store, in M. Nava and A. O'Shea (eds.), *Modern Times:*

Reflections on a Century of English Modernity. London: Routledge, 56–91.

Peiss, Kathy (1986) *Cheap Amusements: Working Women and Leisure in Turn-of-the-Century New York*. Philadelphia: Temple University Press.

Petro, Patrice (1986) Mass Culture and the Feminine: The 'Place' of Television in Film Studies, *Cinema Journal*, 25 (3), pp. 5–21.

Read, Jacinda (2000) *The New Avengers: Feminism, Femininity and the Rape-Revenge Cycle*. Manchester: Manchester University Press.

Ross, Andrew (1989) *No Respect: Intellectuals and Popular Culture*. London: Routledge.

Ryan, Jenny (1994) Women, Modernity and the City, *Theory, Culture and Society* 11 (4), pp. 35–64.

Sanjek, David (1990) 'Fans' Notes: The Horror Film Fanzine, *Literature/Film Quarterly*, 18 (3), pp. 150–160.

Shields, Rob (1992) Spaces for the Subject of Consumption, in R. Shields (ed.), *Lifestyle Shopping: The Subject of Consumption*. London: Routledge, pp. 1–20.

Stacey, Jackie (1994) *Star Gazing: Hollywood Cinema and Female Spectatorship*. London: Routledge.

Staiger, Janet (2000) *Perverse Spectators: The Practices of Film Reception*. New York: New York University Press.

Straw, Will (1991) Systems of Articulation, Logics of Change: Communities and Scenes in Popular Music, *Cultural Studies*, 5 (3), pp. 368–388.

Straw, Will (1997) Sizing Up Record Collections: Gender and Connoisseurship in Rock Music Culture, in Sheila Whiteley (ed.), *Sexing the Groove: Popular Music and Gender*. London: Routledge, pp. 3–16.

Tashiro, Charles (1996) The Contradictions of Video Collecting, *Film Quarterly*, 50 (2) (Winter), pp. 11–18.

Taylor, Greg (1999) *Artists in the Audience: Cults, Camp and American Film Criticism*. Princeton: Princeton University Press.

Taylor, Ian, Evans, Karen, and Fraser, Penny (1996) *A Tale of Two Cities: Global Change, Local Feeling and Everyday Life in the North of England: A Study in Manchester and Sheffield*. London: Routledge.

Telotte, J. P. (1991) Beyond All Reason: The Nature of the Cult, in J. P. Telotte (ed.) *The Cult Film Experience: Beyond All Reason*. Austin: University of Texas Press, pp. 5–17.

Thornton, Sarah (1995) *Club Cultures: Music, Media and Subcultural Capital*. Cambridge: Polity Press.

Vale, V. and Juno, Andrea. (1986) *Re/search 10: Incredibly Strange Films*. San Francisco: Re/search Publications.

Williams, Linda (2000) *Unruly Pleasures*: Review, *Sight and Sound*, 10 (11) (November), p. 38.

Wilton, Tamsin (2000) On Not Being Lady Macbeth: Some (Troubled)

Thoughts on Lesbian Spectatorship, in Joanne Hollows, Peter Hutchings and Mark Jancovich (eds.), *The Film Studies Reader*. London: Arnold, pp. 347–355.

4

The cult of masculinity:
from fan-boys to academic bad-boys

Jacinda Read

In her contribution to this volume, Joanne Hollows observes that attempts to specify the characteristics of cult within academic literature often depend on constructing an opposition between the subcultural characteristics of cult and its audiences and those of 'mainstream cinema' and its audiences. She goes on to argue, however, that 'in the process, cult criticism also reproduces some of the problematic assumptions of subcultural theory including the ways in which both the conceptualisation of, and the practices of subcultures, are implicitly and explicitly gendered'. Drawing on the work of McRobbie and Garber (1991) and Thornton (1995), she demonstrates how the very concept of subculture has been naturalized as masculine. While Hollows's main focus is on the way in which many of the practices of cult fandom, like the practices of subcultures, work to naturalize 'the masculinity of cult', following Thornton, she also points towards the convertibility of the subcultural capital acquired through cult fandom. Thus while for some 'subcultural capital will be converted into economic capital through the pursuit of "careers" in magazines, retailing and distribution . . . other fans may opt to convert their subcultural capital into "proper" or legitimate cultural capital'. It is perhaps for this reason that the work of academics such as Telotte (1991), Harper and Mendik (2000), Cook (1976) and Clover (1992), discussed by Hollows, tends to reproduce, rather than question, subcultural ideologies, and thus the masculinity of cult.

As the title of this piece suggests, it is this transformation from fan to academic that I want to trace here. In so doing, however, I want to explore the ways in which the masculinity of cult described by Hollows has intersected in quite specific ways, in the recent work of two British academics, with an historically and nationally specific 'cult of masculinity' which emerged in Britain in the latter part of the 1990s and which was embodied in the figure of the 'new lad'. Hollows's discussion has already pointed towards some of the ways in which the masculinity of cult might intersect with this contemporary British cult of masculinity. For example, as Hollows observes, Hoxter (2000) likens the 'game of "dare"' involved in cult consumption with 'what has become a ritual test of specifically masculine hardness in a UK context, the adolescent "Vindaloo test" in which lads compete to eat the hottest curry'. Similarly, Williams, in her review of a recent collection of cult movies criticism, *Unruly Pleasures* (Mendik and Harper 2000), likens the book to 'an academic version of the *Sunday Sport*' (Williams 2000), a British newspaper widely identified with a 'laddish' sensibility. Although the intersections between the cultish sensibility of *Unruly Pleasures* and the laddish sensibility of the *Sunday Sport* are clearly visible throughout in what Williams describes as the 'nipple-count', in this piece I want to explore in detail one particular instance of this intersection, Ian Hunter's defence of *Showgirls*. The piece is interesting for my purposes because, along with the work of Chibnall (1997 and 1998) and Sconce (1995), it is one of the few which, in exploring the relationship between the fan and the academic, explicitly addresses what is at stake in academic appropriations of cult movies. In comparing Sconce's argument, written in the context of the USA, and Hunter and Chibnall's arguments, written within the context of the UK, however, I will also endeavour to point up and account for the situated, contingent, historically and culturally specific nature of these appropriations.

This piece, then, builds on Hollows's contribution through a consideration of the way in which the identification of the critic with the cult fan in this work reproduces subcultural ideologies in an attempt to guarantee not only the masculinity of cult but, in Hunter and Chibnall's case, the cult of masculinity. The move from looking at how cult is constructed in fan discourse to looking at how it is constructed in academic discourse, however, involves the introduction of a more complex set of oppositions complicated not only by the overlapping relationship between the fan and the academic but by the academic institutionalisation of feminism in the 1980s and particularly of what Charlotte Brunsdon describes as 'feminist canons of femininity'. According to Brunsdon, this field of study ... has been mainly established through avowedly political criticism which has often had the implicit critique of conventional femininities installed as centrally as the more explicit critique of patriarchy. Much early feminist media criticism involved a passionate repudiation of the pleasures of consumption which, by extension, morally rebuked those who consumed. (1991: 364)

The male academic critic of cult movies thus risks attack from feminism on two fronts: as a man and as a consumer. This can be seen as resulting in a 'double-bind' for the academic critic of cult movies. In other words, in opposing the feminist critique of patriarchy, and particularly the way in which (feminist) film theory has tended to 'problematise and pathologise male heterosexual pleasure in the text' (Chibnall 1997: 88), the academic critic of cult movies has been forced to identify with and defend the (feminine) pleasures of consumption. Clearly, there is much to be gained from such an identification, not least that it enables a shift from the position of the oppressor to that of the oppressed from which an oppositional politics can be articulated. Some academic discussions of cult are thus characterized by a desire to identify the cult critic or fan with an oppressed, 'feminine' position examples include Sconce's (1995: 379) and Chibnall's (1997: 85) descriptions of the graduate student and critic of cult movies respectively as 'disempowered'; Telotte's suggestion that 'In going to a cult film, we embrace the other in us' (1991: 14); Hunter's (2000) and Osgerby's (2000: 121) use of the term 'fan-boy'. Never the less, these discussions are nevertheless frequently plagued by anxieties about the potentially emasculating effects of this identification. The ambivalent and contradictory nature of this position perhaps finds its clearest expression in Hunter's (2000) description of himself as a 'fan-boy', a description which combines the 'girly' connotations of fandom with the youthful, knowing sensibility of the 'new lad'. In what follows, then, I take Hunter up on his somewhat self-conscious invitation to read his interpretation of *Showgirls* as symptomatic of his position in the academic field and Hunter himself as 'a case study in cultural negotiation. Exhibit One: the postmodern white male academic' (197). In so doing, I suggest that such discussions and the (albeit self-conscious) positions they construct can be read as symptomatic of a wider crisis in masculinity brought about by anxieties concerning the location of the academic as consumer or fan and by the impact of feminism on the politics of the academy in Britain. These discussions, I argue, reveal a set of responses which, by asserting the masculinity of cult, function also to reassert the cult of masculinity.

My starting point for such an analysis is Simon Frith's (1992) discussion of academic writing on pop music. Frith compares his own somewhat 'dull' sociological approach to pop music (characterized through a view of pop music as an *ordered* kind of social and symbolic structure') to the 'flashy' cultural studies approach of pop music critics such as Iain Chambers (characterized through a view of pop music as a *disruptive* . . . myth of resistance through rituals') (178–179). As Hollows argues in this volume, cult movies fans draw on similar kinds of subcultural ideologies or myths in order to characterize their fanship as a form of resistance to mainstream culture, a culture implicitly gendered as feminine. What such a cultural studies of pop music reveals, according to Frith, however, is that 'popular music is a solution, a ritualized resistance, not to the problems of being young and poor and proletarian but to the problems of being an intellectual' (179). In other words, intellectuals make pop music 'a site for the play of their fantasies and anxieties' (179). For Frith, then, cultural studies of popular music are academic not working-class fantasies and, more significantly, for my purposes, 'what's at stake in such writings are what it means to be male, to be white, to be middle class' (180). Coming as it does out of the nationally specific critical discourse of British cultural studies, Frith's argument would seem to offer a useful way of thinking about what is at stake in the appropriation of cult movies by some British academics. Indeed, a comparison with Sconce's discussion of what is at stake in North American appropriations of cult will reveal how different cultural, political and critical contexts have shaped the development of cult movies criticism in the UK and the USA.

Before going on to flesh out and illustrate this argument in more detail, we first need to be a little more specific about exactly how the fantasies and anxieties Frith describes are manifested in academic writing. Frith approaches this issue through a revealing comparative reading of Raymond Williams's *Resources of Hope* and Dick Hebdige's *Hiding in the Light*. If, for Frith, *Resources of Hope* reveals Williams's rootedness as a man, as a thinker and as a political activist, *Hiding in the Light* reveals Hebdige's anxieties about his *lack* of roots. According to Frith, this is reflected both in their respective writing styles – Williams's has a 'measuredness, an authority' while Hebdige's is 'jittery, unwilling to take itself seriously, punctuated by puns' (Frith 1992: 179) – and in their choice of examples; while Williams draws on both high culture and working class cultural practices, Hebdige draws almost exclusively on popular culture. In short, if Williams is placed in a tradition, a geography, a family and a politics, Hebdige is placed simply '*as a consumer*, a place defined, in Iain Chambers's words, by a sense of homelessness' (180).

What are at stake here, therefore, are anxieties of consumption, defined by Frith as 'the problem of having no place from which to speak' (1992: 180). Clearly, anxieties about being a consumer or fan of popular culture are inevitably also anxieties about feminization which are symptomatic of a wider crisis in masculinity 'as the figure of "the fan" conventionally and empirically female, is translated into the "feminized" man . . . the ideal male consumer' (181). However, if the shift from a masculine culture of production (Williams) to a feminine culture of consumption (Hebdige) has left the male academic with 'no place from which to speak', then the decline of left politics in Britain and the institutionalization of feminism, I would suggest, has also had similar effects. As Frith observes, 'if Williams has no doubt about the need to speak, Hebdige wonders why anyone should listen' (179). In other words, as feminism has moved into the mainstream it has allegedly simultaneously colonized the margins leaving few spaces from which a masculine oppositional politics can be articulated. According to Frith, for cultural studies commentators the solution to these anxieties and crises is music. Not only does it provide a place from which to speak, but in its discursive exclusion of women and gays, subcultural writing provides a fantasy of the '"non-sexualized" community of boys' (Frith 1992: 181) which not only militates against the feminizing effects of consumption and fandom but provides a model for active, resistive and empowering popular cultural consumption. While, in Thornton's schema (1995: 115), this model of consumption is unequivocally masculine, it is, as I have argued, ultimately based on an identification with a feminine position of oppression and, subsequently, with a feminist model of oppositional consumption. The way in which these feminine and feminist positions are negotiated and disavowed and a masculine model of resistive consumption reasserted will be explored in subsequent paragraphs. For now I want to use the similarities and differences between Frith's description of the sense of homelessness experienced by contemporary British cultural studies commentators and Jeffrey Sconce's characterization of the North American graduate student of paracinema ('bad' cinema) as an 'intellectual in limbo' (1995: 377) as a means of exploring and accounting for some of the differences in British and American appropriations of paracinema.

For the graduate student of paracinema this sense of limbo, of having no place from which to speak, is produced from the way they find themselves 'caught between the institutional discourses (and agendas) of the film elite as represented by the academy, and the "fan" activities of the paracinematic community with which they feel a previous affinity' (Sconce 1995: 378). Paracinema, then, like music, offers a solution to this sense of homelessness or limbo: 'It should not be surprising, then, that paracinematic fans, as exiles from the legitimizing functions of the academy, and many graduate students, as the most disempowered faction within the academy itself, both look to trash culture as a site of "refuge and revenge"' (379). What is surprising, however, given his characterization of the paracinematic community as primarily 'male, white, middle-class, and "educated"' (375) four pages earlier, is Sconce's insistence on their status as disempowered exiles. Indeed, writing within the context of the UK, Chibnall has identified similar 'feelings of disempowerment and marginality among straight white males' (1997: 85). In what follows, however, I want to argue that the reasons for this sense of disempowerment and the subsequent adoption of paracinema as a site of 'refuge and revenge' are not identical for North American graduate students and British academics.

At the risk of simplifying what is clearly a complex set of differences, I think Sconce's emphasis on and characterization of graduate students of paracinema should alert us to the nationally specific periodization at work here, as should his reference to the way in which their desire to push 'the limits of the traditional cinematic canon and the constraints of conventional academic enterprise' was influenced 'by the importation of cultural studies to the USA during the 1980s' (1995: 377). In other words, what I want to argue is that the longer history of cultural studies in Britain (see Hall 1992) – and particularly the approach to graduate study in the 1970s at the Centre for Contemporary Cultural Studies which produced many of the early (sub)cultural studies of pop music and youth culture – means that Sconce's explanation of the graduate student's appropriation of trash cinema in terms of the generational or class politics of the canon in the academy is not applicable in Britain. Instead, as Frith's exploration of academic writing on pop music suggests, for some British critics, paracinema, like pop music, represents a solution not to the problem of being exiled from the legitimising functions of the academy on the basis of class or age, but to the problem of being a white, male, middle-class intellectual.

Turning to the work of Steve Chibnall and Ian Hunter, then, we can begin to analyse how we might understand Sconce's characterization of paracinema as a site of 'refuge and revenge' within the context of the UK. Following Will Straw, I want to suggest that, within this context, paracinema functions in a similar way to music for the male protagonist of Nick Hornby's novel *High Fidelity*. What both the novel and the work of Chibnall and Hunter reveal are 'an ageing male's strategies for survival in a cultural realm in which his place is no longer certain' (Straw 1997: 11), a realm in which a 'consumption-based ethic of oppositionality' (Weisbard cited in Straw: 12) is 'the only readily accessible political stance' available (12). I want to take as my starting point for this discussion Steve Chibnall's claim that 'Paracinema has provided opportunities for (predominantly) young straight white male academics to reclaim marginalised areas of cinema's history and to resist the dominant paradigms of film theory which have tended to problematise and pathologise male heterosexual pleasure in the text' (1997: 87–88). Chibnall's argument here clearly relies on the reproduction of a number of subcultural ideologies and oppositions (dominance/resistance, mainstream/margins, conformity/deviance) in order to manoeuvre the straight white male academic into the position of a deviant, resistant 'disempowered' minority, and feminism (what else can 'the dominant paradigms of film theory which have tended to problematise and pathologise male heterosexual pleasure in the text' be a reference to?) into the position of the conformist, dominant mainstream.

Thus, while the graduate student described by Sconce and the academic critic described by Chibnall are both concerned to 'resist the dominant paradigms of film theory', the way in which these paradigms are conceived by these writers is quite different. In other words, as I have indicated above, for Chibnall 'the dominant paradigms of film theory' are primarily associated with explicitly political (feminist) discourses, whereas for Sconce they are associated with aesthetic ones. This is not to say, of course, that Sconce's counter-aesthetic position is not also a political argument. Indeed, he argues that paracinema's aesthetic of excess 'represents an explicitly political challenge to reigning aesthete discourses in the academy' (1995: 380). In so doing, however, he also points out a number of continuities between aesthete and paracinematic discourses on cinema which are suggestive of a desire to situate paracinema, the challenge it represents and the students who study it *within* aesthetic film culture. Hunter's and Chibnall's project, on the other hand, is to argue for their *marginal* position within the academic community on the basis of paracinema's subcultural status *vis-à-vis* the reigning political (feminist) discourses in the academy. In this way, Hunter's and Chibnall's adoption of paracinema as a site of 'refuge and revenge' can be seen as a response to the sexual, rather than the cultural, politics of the academy.

For these critics, then, paracinema represents an opportunity to reassert a masculine (sub)culture and politics in the face of the perceived institutionalization of feminism and its subsequent colonization and feminization of the margins. In other words, under the influence of feminism, previously 'illegitimate', and thus marginal, cultural forms such as magazines, comics, popular fiction and, in particular, soap operas have become 'legitimate', and thus 'mainstream', objects of analysis. Thus, like mainstream cultures of femininity, feminism and the women's genres it has helped to canonize are presented as decidedly uncool and unhip in cult movie criticism. As Gripsrud observes: 'Presenting oneself as a soap-fan in scholarly circles could be considered daring or provocative some ten years ago. Nowadays it is more of a prerequisite for legitimate entry into the academic discourse on soaps in some Anglo-American fora' (cited in Sconce 1995: 377). As Brunsdon points out, however, alongside this 'loosening and leavening of the canons of many disciplines within the humanities' has come 'a general revaluation of cultures of consumption' (1991: 370). In particular, against earlier characterizations of the female consumer as the 'passive victim of media manipulation' (371), feminism has been largely responsible for initiating the 'consumption-based ethic of oppositionality' described above. Thus, in a post-feminist milieu, in which the opposition between feminism and femininity is becoming decidedly less distinct (Brunsdon 1997; Hollows 2000; McRobbie 1994; and Read 2000), the cult movie critic's adoption of a 'consumption-based ethic of oppositionality' must inevitably be based on an *identification* with both a feminine position (oppression and consumption)

and a feminist position. Yet, for the reasons I outlined in the introduction, this is clearly a problematic identification. On closer inspec-
tion, then, what we find in some British academic appropriations of
cult movies is not so much a 'counter-aesthetic' (Sconce 1995: 372)
as a counter-politics, or 'politics of incorrectness', which simultaneously acknowledges and disavows both feminine competences and
feminist politics. In other words, and somewhat worryingly, what
we begin to see in the work of academics such as Chibnall and
Hunter is the (ironic?) celebration of the kind of laddish political
incorrectness made famous in the 1990s by publications such as
Loaded and described here by Suzanne Franks:

> As feminism went mainstream, its subtle presence pervaded every ad
> campaign, every TV programme and the consciousness of every
> woman in the West – so men felt threatened . . . So they went on the
> offensive and liberated themselves. They joyfully revelled in the right
> to scratch and belch and love football more than anything else in the
> world, to get pissed and leer at women with big breasts. The message
> was 'Stop patronizing me; *I understand the equal rights thing.* Now
> let's have a laugh for Christ's sake.' (2000: 167, my emphasis)

The message of psychotronic criticism, as described by Chibnall, was
uncannily similar:

> Politically, the new psychotronic criticism ran counter to dominant
> streams of political correctness in the academy. *Although aware of fem-
> inism and the politics of difference*, the new criticism shows no desire
> to 'do the right thing', but rather to ironically elevate texts that often
> exhibit a naive disregard for sexism, misogyny, racism and other pre-
> enlightenment sins. (1997: 85, my emphasis)

Of course, the ironic reading of politically incorrect texts is not
unique to British work on paracinema. As Sconce observes, 'many
paracinematic texts would run foul of academic film culture's political orthodoxy. But, of course, this is precisely why such films are so
vociferously championed by certain segments of the paracinematic
audience, which then attempts to "redeem" the often suspect pleasures of these films through appeals to ironic detachment' (1995:
383–384). What is unique, however, is the way in which British publications such as *Loaded* have successfully made political incorrectness and ironic reading strategies a part of the subcultural sensibility
of young men. Political incorrectness is thus seen as, and associated
with, the 'cool', 'hip' masculinity of the 'new lad'. The failure of

Men Behaving Badly, one of the key televisual representations of lad-dism, to translate successfully into the US context is indicative of the national specificity of this formation of masculinity (see Whelehan 2000: 71–72). Within the context of the UK, therefore, the ironic reading of politically incorrect texts we find in the work of critics such as Hunter and Chibnall intersects in specific ways with an his-torically and nationally specific cult of masculinity. Within such a context, the kind of claims for ironic reading strategies made explic-itly in the Chibnall quotation above and implicitly in *Loaded* and its siblings (*Maxim, FHM*) make such political incorrectness very diffi-cult to engage with seriously, since to do so is to risk accusations of not 'getting the joke', and therefore of being uncool and unhip. In this way, irony functions not only to deflect accusations of sexism and prevent serious engagement with the issues, but to exclude anyone who is unable or unwilling to read texts in this way. Thus, as Franks argues: 'For many women the most disturbing aspect of all this was the boy's own gang mentality that laddism encouraged. If you were not prepared to enthuse about Page 3 girls, living off lager and chips, and toenail clippings on the sofa you were dubbed uncool, uptight and a bad sport' (2000: 168). It is perhaps not sur-prising, therefore, that in 1990s Britain, the model for hip, cool fem-ininity was the figure of the 'ladette' – a figure who, as the name suggests, was clearly 'culturally "one of the boys"' (Thornton, 1995: 104).

Ian Hunter's (2000) defence of *Showgirls* reveals a similarly lad-dish sensibility. However, it lacks the conviction and authority of Chibnall's writing. Instead, Hunter's writing, like Dick Hebdige's, is 'jittery, unwilling to take itself seriously, punctuated by puns' – the title of the piece, for example, is 'Beaver Las Vegas! A Fan-Boy's Defence of *Showgirls*. Like Hebdige's work, then, Hunter's article reveals a similar set of ambivalences and anxieties about his status as a 'fan-boy'. Indeed, one wonders whether Hunter's fondness for *Showgirls* has anything to do with the fact that the film's central premise is also the one which runs through the article, that is, 'that under consumerism, there are no authentic identities but merely a series of performances. Throughout the film names are exchanged' (Hunter 2000: 192). Similarly, throughout this article there is a series of 'slippages' whereby the feminized fan-boy is transformed through the mobilization of subcultural ideologies – not least those of the new lad – into an academic bad-boy.

The title itself functions as one of the ways in which Hunter distances himself from the feminine associations of fandom. 'Beaver Las Vegas' would not look out of place on the front cover of *Loaded* and, indeed, both this scatological pun and the use of the suffix 'boy' work to secure his youthful, 'naughty' and laddish credentials while simultaneously letting him off the hook of adult responsibility. This refusal of adult responsibility is also evident elsewhere in British writing on cult movies, not least in scriptwriter David McGillivray's claim that Peter Walker's films are 'a harmless outlet for overgrown schoolboys who were really doing little more than trying to see how much they could get away with before they were sent to bed' (cited in Chibnall 1998: 21). Hunter's description of himself as a 'fanboy', however, is clearly open to contradictory interpretations. Bill Osgerby, for example, whilst recognizing the clichéd nature of the characterization of 'audiences for 'cult' texts [as] entirely composed of spotty, anorak-wearing fan-boys who do not get out much and have trouble getting girl-friends', nevertheless acknowledges that '"cult" texts cast a fascination that can border on the fanatical and obsessive' (2000: 121). In this respect, the fan-boy clearly shares some of the (albeit stereotypical) characteristics of the 'immature, homosocial world' of the (record) collector and the failed masculinity of the nerd in particular (Straw 1997: 11). Hunter is clearly aware of these potentially nerdish associations, however. Thus, despite his description of his obsessive private accumulation of all things *Showgirls* and of the way in which 'lurking in public I talk about the film, bore my friends with opinions about it' (2000: 196), he successfully distances himself from the failed masculinity of the nerd this description conjures up. Implicitly, this is achieved, if I may be allowed a little scatological joke of my own, by Hunter's insistence that 'the clippings file on my desk *bulges inches thick*' (196, my emphasis). Explicitly, however, for Hunter, fandom as a '"sad" and inappropriate enthusiasm' is associated with fans of *Star Trek* and, as he is quick to point out, 'by *Star Trek* standards I'm not a proper fan at all' (195). In making such distinctions, Hunter thus simply reinforces rather than questions the cult masculinities constructed in fan discourses and described here by Sconce: 'a subscription form for *Film Threat* features a drawing of the 'typical' *Film Threat* reader, portrayed as a dynamic, rockabilly-quiffed hipster surrounded by admiring women. This is juxtaposed with a drawing of the 'typical' Psychotronic reader, depicted as passive, overweight and asexual, with a bad complexion' (1995: 375).

Hunter is also keen to distance himself from the reading strategies of 'ordinary punters' (2000: 196). Clearly this rests on a distinction between the alternative reading strategies of the minority and the mainstream reading strategies of the majority. Reading on, however, reveals that this distinction is also gendered. In other words, for Hunter, 'the point of identification in *Showgirls* was not with any of the characters but rather with the director himself' (197). As Henry Jenkins's work on fans of *Twin Peaks* has revealed, while female fans were interested in how the plot illuminated 'character psychology and motivations' (1992: 109), male fans were interested in how 'knowledge about Lynch as an author' (110) made possible specula-tion on plot development. Thus, while Hunter explicitly distin-guishes his reading practices from those of 'ordinary punters', he implicitly distinguishes them from those of female fans. What Hunter identifies himself with instead is Verhoeven, 'the unapologetic "bad-boy" of flash-trash cinema, the intellectual Dutchman who frolics among the clichés of Hollywood blockbusters' (2000: 197).

The transformation from feminized fan-boy to academic bad-boy is thus complete. It is no surprise, then, to find Hunter reproducing the Chibnall quotation cited above (Chibnall, 1997: 85) to secure this move into the position of a deviant, resistant minority. Indeed, as I suggested prior to my discussion of this quotation, what appears to be at stake here is a counter-politics, or 'politics of incorrectness', rather than a counter-aesthetics. Thus, while Hunter repeatedly claims that neither the film nor his reading of it is politically trans-gressive or subversive, what *is* politically transgressive or subversive for Hunter is *liking* the film. This is not because, as he suggests, it was widely perceived as bad but because, I would suggest, it was *not* politically transgressive or subversive. As Hunter himself points out, above all, critics deplored the film not for its aesthetic shortcomings but for 'Verhoeven's hypocrisy in exploiting the very sleaze and voyeurism that his film purported to expose' (2000: 189). Thus, against Hunter's claim that 'by trying to reclaim *Showgirls* for myself ... I risk seeming to want to "straighten out" the camp interpreta-tion and dismiss gay fans as delinquent misreaders' (195), I would suggest that by describing his fondness for *Showgirls* as both 'per-verse' (197) and 'pathological' (198) Hunter characterizes *himself* as the 'delinquent misreader'.

Indeed, the article is pervaded by anxieties about what he sees as his own misreading – 'how could I be so wrong?' (190), 'my unreliability in matters of aesthetic value' (196), 'goaded by the error of my interpretation' (201) – and, as I have already suggested, by anxieties about his status as a fan-boy. By the end of the article, however, we find Hunter deciding he 'might as well relax into being a fan-boy and a one-man cult audience' on the basis that 'society, history and habitus have rigidly shaped my tastes and sensibility' (198). Not only does this fail to question or problematize the social construction of taste, the power relations implicit in this construction or the effects of those power relations, it overlooks the way in which the entire article has been based on a series of distinctions which function to assert and naturalize not only the masculinity of cult but the cult of masculinity. In other words, as we have seen, Hunter clearly hasn't relaxed into being a fan-boy since the article is premised on a rejection of the feminine associations of the fan and the failed masculinity of the nerd in favour of a characterization of himself not as a fan-boy but as an academic bad-boy.

Thus I would have to disagree with Hunter's claim that 'this chapter . . . muddles any distinction between fan and academic, enthusiastic partisan and severe enforcer of political rectitude' (2000: 187). Clearly, both Hunter's and Chibnall's association with non- or semi-academic publishing ventures (both *Unruly Pleasures* and *Making Mischief* were published by FAB Press) might be seen to position them *between* the fan community and the academic community. Indeed, it is the explicit aim of *Unruly Pleasures* 'to build bridges between the cult film fan and the cult film theorist' (Harper and Mendik 2000: 7). However, I would suggest that Hunter's and Chibnall's association with 'alternative' publishing outlets such as FAB functions to construct distinctions *within* academic culture rather than blur the boundary between fan and academic. In other words, the subcultural nature of these publishing ventures functions as another of the ways in which the straight white male academic is manoeuvred into the position of deviant, politically incorrect minority and feminism into the position of conformist, mainstream 'enforcer of political rectitude', thus securing the latter's position within an *academic* subculture of bad-boys. The academic bad-boy, in this respect, is 'bad' precisely because, whilst enjoying the legitimacy his position in the academy bestows, he refuses to play by the 'rules' of mainstream academic culture (elite academic publishing, 'political rectitude'). Indeed, Hunter's characterization of himself as a one-man cult audience functions to identify him as an aficionado rather than a fan, while his identification of himself with 'a growing number of academic connoisseurs of trash cinema' (197) not only helps to distance him from the failed masculinity of the nerd, but is the process through which his individual, private, domestic consumption practices are moved into the collective, public, productive space of the academy of 'bad-boys'. As Imelda Whelehan writes of the boyish gang mentality of the new lad: 'This sense of "community" is perhaps one response to the idea of the male identity crisis, in that it offers a powerful sense of belonging to a group which has its insiders and outsiders' (2000: 64).

Chibnall makes no bones about this laddish psychotronic sensibility being a response to a masculinity under threat: 'Drawing on developing feelings of disempowerment and marginality among straight white males, the psychotronic sensibility was a reassertion of the right to look, to make anything the object of the knowing, sardonic, ironising and frankly excited gaze' (1997: 85). Clearly, such a stance can be partially read as a response to the growing objectification, eroticization and commodification of the male body in the 1980s and to the way men are increasingly being addressed as consumers. What concerns me, however, is the way in which such a response to the feminization of men as both objects of the gaze and as consumers politicizes laddish political incorrectness through 'the deployment of vacuous sociological terms (resistance, empowerment)' (Frith 1992: 180) and thereby legitimizes its anti-feminist and feminine tendencies through the reproduction, rather than analysis, of oppositional subcultural ideologies.

Thus, for Chibnall, what unites most psychotronic aficionados is 'the rejection of censorship for adult viewers' and the desire to 'expose what was previously hidden (sleaze)', an exposure which 'itself becomes an act of empowerment enhanced by reactions of shock and disbelief in others' (1997: 85). Sconce's description of these processes more clearly reveals the subcultural ideologies at work here: 'Paracinema . . . presents a direct challenge to the values of aesthete film culture and a general affront to the "refined" sensibility of the parent taste culture. It is a calculated strategy of shock and confrontation against fellow cultural elites, not unlike Duchamp's notorious unveiling of a urinal in an art gallery' (1995: 376). Punk's appropriation of the swastika has been seen as a similarly calculated strategy of shock and confrontation and, indeed, in his book on Peter Walker, Chibnall sees the 'game of shock-and-gasp' (1998: 21) involved in Walker's films as the precursor to punk. Moreover, throughout the introduction (tellingly titled 'Shocks to the System') attempts are made to link Walker's movies with the shocking subcultural sensibility of punk: Walker himself, for example, is likened to The Sex Pistols' manager, Malcolm McClaren (13), while the absence of heroic figures in his films is seen to anticipate punk rhetoric of 'no more heroes' (15). Despite their similarities, the differences between Sconce's and Chibnall's analogies here are, I think, indicative of the different projects behind some US and UK appropriations of paracinema. In other words, despite, and maybe because of, the challenge it represents to aesthete film culture, Sconce wants to position paracinema, like Duchamp's urinal, within aesthetic (film) culture in order to invigorate it. Chibnall's association of paracinema with punk, on the other hand, is suggestive of a desire to generate a set of marginal subcultural credentials and thus to evacuate mainstream academic culture. In this way, the cult movie aficionado becomes the punk of the movie world, a part of a cool, hip, rebellious, youthful masculine culture. The clearest reproduction of such subcultural ideologies comes, then, in Chibnall's claim that the psychotronic sensibility has resulted in 'the generation of new fields of fandom served by a plethora of amateur and professional fanzines with assiduous researchers unearthing esoteric knowledge about forgotten films, fresh sources of alternative cultural capital for autodidacts' (1997: 86). Many of the oppositions mapped out by Sarah Thornton are clearly in evidence here: specialist genres ('forgotten films') versus pop, insider information ('esoteric knowledge') versus easily accessible information, 'alternative' versus mainstream and, ultimately, masculine culture versus feminine culture (1995: 115). The world of psychotronic criticism as it is described by Chibnall, then, like the world of rock criticism described by Straw, seems 'characterised by shared knowledges which exclude the would-be entrant, this functions not only to preserve the homosocial character of such worlds, but to block females from the social and economic advancement which they may offer' (Straw 1997: 10). And yet, in the 'assiduous researcher', there lurks a potentially nerdish failed masculinity, suggesting that the masculinity of cult can never entirely guarantee the cult of masculinity.

References

Brunsdon, Charlotte (1991) Pedagogies of the Feminine: Feminist Teaching and Women's Genres, *Screen*, 32 (4) (Winter), pp. 364–381.

Brunsdon, Charlotte (1997) *Screen Tastes: Soap Opera to Satellite Dishes*. London: Routledge.

Chibnall, Steve (1997) Double Exposures: Observations on *The Flesh and Blood Show*, in Deborah Cartmell, I. Q. Hunter, Heidi Kaye and Imelda Whelehan (eds.), *Trash Aesthetics: Popular Culture and Its Audience*. London: Pluto Press, pp. 84–102.

Chibnall, Steve (1998) *Making Mischief: The Cult Films of Pete Walker*. Guildford: FAB Press.

Clover, Carol (1992) *Men, Women and Chainsaws: Gender in the Modern Horror Film*. London: British Film Institute.

Cook, Pam (1976) 'Exploitation' Films and Feminism, *Screen* (Summer), pp. 122–7.

Franks, Suzanne (2000) *Having None of It: Men and the Future of Work*. London: Granta Books.

Frith, Simon (1992) The Cultural Study of Pop Music, in Lawrence Grossberg, Cary Nelson and Paula A. Treichler (eds.), *Cultural Studies*. London: Routledge, pp. 174–186.

Hall, Stuart (1992) Cultural Studies and its Theoretical Legacies, in Lawrence Grossberg, Cary Nelson and Paula A. Treichler (eds.), *Cultural Studies*. London: Routledge, pp. 277–294.

Harper, Graeme, and Mendik, Xavier (2000) Several Theorists Ask 'How Was It For You Honey?' Or Why the Academy Needs Cult Cinema and Its Fans, in Xavier Mendik and Graeme Harper (eds.), *Unruly Pleasures: The Cult Film and Its Critics*. Guildford: FAB Press, pp. 7–11.

Hollows, Joanne (2000) *Feminism, Femininity and Popular Culture*. Manchester: Manchester University Press.

Hoxter, Julian (2000) Taking Possession: Cult Learning and *The Exorcist*, in Xavier Mendik and Graeme Harper (eds.), *Unruly Pleasures: The Cult Film and Its Critics*. Guildford: FAB Press, pp. 171–185.

Hunter, I. Q. (2000) Beaver Las Vegas! A Fan-Boy's Defence of *Showgirls*, in Xavier Mendik and Graeme Harper (eds.), *Unruly Pleasures: The Cult Movie and Its Critics*. Guildford: FAB Press, pp. 189–201.

Jenkins, Henry (1992) *Textual Poachers: Television Fans and Participatory Culture*. New York: Routledge.

McRobbie, Angela (1994) *Postmodernism and Popular Culture*. London: Routledge.

McRobbie, Angela, and Garber, Marjorie (1991), Girls and Subcultures, in Angela McRobbie, *Feminism and Youth Culture: From Jackie to Just Seventeen*. Basingstoke: Macmillan.

Mendik, Xavier and Harper, Graeme (2000) *Unruly Pleasures: The Cult*

Film and Its Fans. Guildford. FAB Press.

Osgerby, Bill (2000) 'Stand-By For Action!': Gerry Anderson, Supermarionation and the 'White Heat' of Sixties Modernity, in Xavier Mendik and Graeme Harper (eds.), *Unruly Pleasures: The Cult Film and Its Critics*. Guildford: FAB Press, pp. 121–135.

Read, Jacinda (2000) *The New Avengers: Feminism, Femininity and the Rape-revenge Cycle*. Manchester: Manchester University Press.

Sconce, Jeffrey (1995) 'Trashing' the Academy: Taste, Excess, and an Emerging Politics of Cinematic Style, *Screen*, 36 (4) (Winter), pp. 371–393.

Straw, Will (1997) Sizing Up Record Collections: Gender and Connoisseurship in Rock Music Culture, in Sheila Whiteley (ed.), *Sexing the Groove: Popular Music and Gender*. London: Routledge, pp. 3–16.

Telotte, J. P. (1991) Beyond all Reason: The Nature of the Cult, in J. P. Telotte (ed.), *The Cult Film Experience: Beyond all Reason*. Austin: University of Texas Press, pp. 5–17.

Thornton, Sarah (1995) *Club Cultures: Music, Media and Subcultural Capital*. Cambridge: Polity Press.

Whelehan, Imelda (2000) *Overloaded: Popular Culture and the Future of Feminism*. London: The Women's Press.

Williams, Linda (2000) Review of *Unruly Pleasures*, *Sight and Sound*, 10 (11) (November), p. 38.

5

Spanish horror and the flight from 'art' cinema, 1967–73

Andrew Willis

One of the areas most readily given the label 'cult cinema' is European horror, in particular those films produced in the 1960s and 1970s (Hawkins 1999; Hawkins 2000; Hunt 1992, Tohill and Tombs 1995). In many ways these products fit certain notions of 'cult' perfectly: they are often low-budget, sleazy, exploitation fare; they have devoted fan groups; they often circulate through specialist video outlets (legally, semi-legally and illegally); and they are often difficult to find. Within the stock of such outlets one will always find a smattering of Spanish horror films from the late 1960s and early 1970s. Their cult status is secured by references to them in fanzines devoted to horror and sleaze such as *Flesh and Blood, Is it Uncut?, Shock Cinema* (Hawkins 1999; Duncombe 1997; Sanjek 1990).

Indeed, it was in my pursuit of just such films that I stumbled across the titles that made me consider the issues that form the focus of this chapter. Amongst the Spanish horror titles available from cult sources are a number of films that bear the names of directors who have reputations that extend way beyond the field of European cult cinema, or exploitation films generally. Crucially, these directors had established critical reputations *before* they made low-budget horror films, and, significantly, made films that sustained or enhanced those reputations, *after* (Hopewell 1986; Stone 2001). This marks them out as different from those 'cult' works that are early low-budget efforts made by directors who would later seek to establish more mainstream reputations. I'm thinking here, for example, of the directors associated with Roger Corman: Jonathan Demme, Joe Dante, Martin Scorsese etc. (for more on Corman and his company New World see Hillier and Lipstadt 1981, and Hillier 1992). This aspiration to mainstream success also shows a very different career trajectory from those 'cult' directors who have existed exclusively within the sphere of low-budget filmmaking such as, in the Spanish context, Jesús Franco and José Larraz (for more detail on Jesús Franco see Hawkins 2000; Tohill and Tombs 1995).

In order to consider these films further they need to be placed firmly into their broader historical and social context: Spain and Spanish cinema in the late 1960s and early 1970s. Here, rather than seeing them simply as examples of an unspecific, exotic and loosely defined 'European cult cinema', I want to consider them as particular reactions against the approaches of what has become widely known as the 'New Spanish Cinema' of the 1960s. As this 'New Spanish Cinema' is often discussed in terms of its artistic merit, a clear separation of 'art' cinema and 'popular' cinema provides a useful starting point. It certainly begins to indicate a different set of responses and strategies adopted by those filmmakers working in the field of horror.

Despite the important work they have done, few of the works that look at the New Spanish Cinema touch upon the more popular films made by established Spanish directors with serious critical reputations, let alone consider why these directors chose to work in genres associated with low-budget, exploitation, filmmaking (see for example Hopewell 1986; Kinder 1993). However, equally problematically, few of the predominantly fan-based works mentioned earlier that address the low-budget European horror film place these works into their context of production. Rather, they seem to simply explore or merely celebrate their generic qualities. What I want to do here is suggest reasons why certain directors, associated with some of the most challenging films produced within Spanish cinema of the 1950s and 1960s, elected in the early 1970s to work in the field of horror, a genre that was undoubtedly one of the most popular of the day.

Spanish cinema in the 1960s

Following a period of arch-conservatism, after the nationalist victory in the Civil War, Spanish cinema in the 1960s is marked by a clear liberalization of the government's attitude towards films that might be seen as critical of the regime. John Hopewell argues that 'from 1962 part of the Spanish regime attempted to rejuvenate the national film industry from above. The resultant "New Spanish Cinema" was part of a cautious attempt at political liberalisation' (1986: 63). One of the key moves in this liberalization was the re-appointment of José María García Escudero as Under Secretary of Cinema. He is often presented as someone who encouraged artistic ambition within the Spanish film industry. He modified the board of film censors, pushed through changes at the national film school, the Escuela Oficial de Cine, and increased the funding for films that were deemed to be of 'special interest' (Hopewell 1986; Besas 1985: 72–74).

Both Hopewell (1986) and Marsha Kinder (1993) see these moves as an attempt to create a more internationally visible Spanish cinema. This process included supporting directors and films that were lauded at international festivals even if they were received with caution or criticism by the authorities in Spain. Carlos Saura's *Los golfos* (*The Hooligans*) (made in 1959 but not released in Spain until 1962) is representative of this as it displeased the official censor but was shown at the Cannes international film festival as the official Spanish entry (Kinder 1993: 87). Hopewell sees this as a move to 'Europeanize' Spanish cinema, making it seem contemporary, modern and relevant (1986: 65), whilst Kinder argues that such films can be seen as 'taking an important step toward developing an innovative cinema with international appeal' (1993: 89). This was certainly part of García Escudero's stated aim to create a Spanish cinema of ideas, which is reflected in his much-quoted statement that, 'If you can't beat Hollywood on its own ground (a commercial cinema), you can, and Europe has actually done this, on Europe's home ground: intelligence' (Hopewell 1986: 65). Part of this process was the establishment of specialist 'art' cinemas where these 'intellectual' films could be shown. In 1967 a series of 'Salas de Arte y Ensayo' were opened to exhibit these 'special interest' films alongside subtitled foreign works. For the most part these were in major cities and tourist spots frequented by foreigners, neither of which were usually frequented by ordinary, working-class film-goers (D'Lugo, 1997).

These moves towards an intellectual, international 'art' cinema resulted in two very significant problems: first, supposedly radical and ideologically challenging films and filmmakers became, arguably, international representatives of the regime. In other words, the creation of 'art' cinema meant that such films and their directors became easily assimilated by the regime. As Kinder observes, 'Saura could be transformed into a cultural commodity that would help sell the liberalized reinscription of *Franquismo* in international markets' (1993: 93). Second, these films, through the official distribution and exhibition policies, were restricted to specialist cinemas. In this case, films that wanted to be socially engaged were consigned to what Hopewell describes as the 'cultural ghettos of 'art' cinemas' (1986: 65).

So, whilst the championing of 'art' cinema offered a model of the creative, committed, oppositional auteur, that supposed figure of resistance was easily assimilated by the interests of the regime as an example of their increasingly liberal attitudes. For some filmmakers, not willing to be assimilated by this process, another direction had to be found, one that lay outside the realm of officially sanctioned 'art' cinema. John Hopewell begins to suggest what this alternative might be with his observations about the so-called 'Barcelona School' of filmmakers. He argues that directors such as Vicente Aranda and Gonzalo Suárez chose to 'distract attention from covert political implication by the use of stock film genres' (1986: 68). However, he fails to explore the implications of this in any great detail. Indeed, most of the critics who articulate the inherent contradictions of 'New Spanish Cinema' still focus their critical attention on the works of 'compromised' auteurs such as Carlos Saura.

However, 1967 was not only the year in which the 'Salas de Arte y Ensayo' were established; it is also acknowledged as the breakthrough year for Spanish horror film production. More specifically, this was the year that *La marca del hombre lobo* (*Mark of the Werewolf*) was released and found an eager audience for its gothic-trimmed horror. With this embracing of popular genres by audiences in Spain, it is possible to argue that those politically oppositional filmmakers who wanted to seek an area of filmmaking that was less clearly controlled by the government potentially found it – in particular within one of the most popular genres of the day, the horror film.

Spanish horror in the late 1960s

Internationally, the 1960s had been a period of sustained production and popularity for the horror film. Films produced in Britain, Italy and the USA had found audiences throughout the decade (see

Hutchings 1993 and Hunt 1992), and as already noted Spain joined the ranks of horror producers with the success of *La marca del hombre lobo* released in 1967. A West German co-production, shot in 3D and 70mm and starring Paul Naschy, *La marca del hombre lobo* was successful enough internationally – including the US version *Frankenstein's Bloody Terror* – to kick-start horror genre production in Spain. This success was consolidated in 1969 with the release of the enormously popular *La residencia* (also known as *The Finishing School*), directed by Narcisco Ibáñez Serrador. Joan Hawkins has noted the potential of these genre pictures to address contemporary issues, arguing that 'even when horror films were not especially graphic, they served to make strong political points' (Hawkins 2000: 94).

It is therefore no surprise to find the names of directors and writers who had previously been closely associated with oppositional filmmaking on the credits of some of the most politically engaged horror films of the period. As they attempted to find a space to work that existed outside the 'art' cinema assimilated by the regime, they arrived in the arena of popular genre filmmaking. In this context they were able to continue to explore contemporary social and political issues in their films. The need for such directors to embed, almost camouflage, themselves in popular genres was made more apparent in 1969 when the government, reacting to what they perceived as increased social unrest, tightened censorship and began to move away from the more liberal tendencies of the mid-1960s. A new minister for Information and Tourism, Alfredo Sánchez Bella, was appointed, and in 1972 he called for the censorship board to 'accentuate its vigour in classifying films' (Hopewell 1986 :80). This increased repression after the period of supposed liberalization can also help explain why certain directors chose to continue to submerge themselves in popular genres. Again, as Hawkins argues, 'the existence of these films is extraordinary, given the social and political climate of the time. Even the tame, domestic versions . . . hint at illicit sexuality, lesbianism and other activities officially designated as perversions by General Franco's government' (2000: 93). Whilst Hawkins goes on to consider the case of Jesús (or Jess) Franco, a director already associated with low-budget exploitation filmmaking by the late 1960s, I want to focus on directors who had more clearly established 'art' film reputations in earlier periods and therefore, it might be argued, more consciously reject that 'art' cinema in favour of the freedoms offered by genre production – in particular, the already mentioned Vicente Aranda and Claudio Guerín Hill, as well as some from an earlier generation such as Juan Antonio Bardem.

Juan Antonio Bardem was one of the major figures in the anti-fascist film movement within Spain. A graduate of the national film school and a member of the illegal Communist Party, he had helped establish the film magazine *Objetivo* in 1952. In 1955 he made his famous address at the University of Salamanca that asserted that, 'Spanish cinema is politically ineffective, socially false, intellectually abject, aesthetically nonexistent and commercially crippled' (Besas 1985: 40). His cinematic reputation was established with socially engaged films such as *Muerte de un ciclista* (*Death of a Cyclist*) (1955) and *Calle Mayor* (*Main Street*) (1956). In 1972 Bardem directed the psychological horror film *La corrupción de Chris Miller* (*The Corruption of Chris Miller*), which deals with issues of power and sexuality through its story of two isolated women who are visited by a mysterious young man. Simply to dismiss this work is naive. As Bardem shows, for committed filmmakers in this period the generic codes and conventions of the horror film could be utilized in order to explore social and political issues. The fact that certain directors consciously turned to popular forms is further suggested by the fact that Bardem returned to more directly political subject matter once the regime had fallen, such as his 1978 film *The Warning*, shot in Bulgaria, which tells the story of the communist leader, Dimitrov.

Eloy de la Iglesia was another Spanish filmmaker who was a Communist Party member and chose to work in popular genres (Hopewell 1986; Smith 1992; Tropiano 1997). Like the others, his horror films carried clear engagements with the social injustices of Franco's Spain, in his case showing horrific acts as the result of the repression and alienation of the working class. De la Iglesia's work is marked by a strong sense of social realism. Although many of the Spanish horror films produced in the 1960s and 1970s involved supernatural elements, he maintained a strong fidelity to the reality of the repressive atmosphere that engulfed Spain during the Franco years. His most widely known film of this period, *La semana del asesino* (1971), certainly sidesteps supernatural causes for the horror in the film in favour of believable, socially rooted causes for 'real' horrific acts. This film was marketed internationally, and built a cult reputation as *Cannibal Man* even though it contains no direct cannibalism. The horror genre, or perhaps more specifically the psychological horror film, offered de la Iglesia space to explore an array of contemporary issues such as masculinity, sexuality and class. Later in his career, after the end of the Franco regime, he turned his attention to more directly political melodramas that focused on youth, sexuality and corruption, once again, showing his awareness of how popular forms offer the potential to talk to ordinary people in a language they understand.

Like Bardem, Vicente Aranda also had a strong filmmaking reputation before he turned to the horror genre (Besas 1985; D'Lugo 1997; Hopewell 1986). His experimental 1966 film *Fata Morgana* had been well received and was seen as a key work in the short lived 'Barcelona School' of the period. After establishing his art house credentials he too turned to the horror genre in the late 1960s and early 1970s, making *La novia ensangrentada* in 1972. Clearly, Aranda was personally committed to the project as it was the first film made by his own production company, Morgana. The film achieved a wider cult status as *The Blood Spattered Bride*. The film, a vampire story, offers a scathing critique of Spanish machismo, linking it to the established male social order of Franco's Spain. This is achieved through the careful association of the central male character, played by Simon Andreau, with the ideas, values and beliefs of Francoist patriarchy. Indeed, it seems that inviting the audience to be critical of these values is one of the major aims of the film. The setting of the story of two newly weds in the world of the horror film allows Aranda to reject the constraints of social realism in favour of an approach that invites the audience to question the reality of what they see. In turn, alternative views of the world, in particular relating to gender and sexuality, become something that it is possible to suggest and represent. Indeed, Aranda's work in this period is marked by a willingness to embrace excess as a way of moving away from the codes and conventions of social realism and representing an alternative world.

Soon after the arrival of the newly weds at the husband's family home in the countryside he goes hunting with an old family retainer who refers to him only as master. As they walk through the countryside, the pair discover a female fox caught in a trap, and the master shoots the helpless creature. Following this encounter we see the man walking in the countryside with his wife. He begins to embrace her romantically but then suddenly aggressively forces her to perform oral sex on him. Shortly after this he again attacks her, this time in an aviary. The bride, like the birds, is trapped by the social conventions that privilege men; because of this even when attacked she does not know how to help herself. As John Hopewell has observed, machismo played an important part in the creation of images of masculinity that were prevalent in the Franco era. He argues that

> Machismo mixes a sense of male honour with shows of physical valour; in practice, it has become a hotchpotch of right-mindedness and wrong-headedness, unsophisticated male chauvinism, a petty and petulant insistence on getting one's own way, a tendency when challenged to round on your enemy, puff out your chest like a pouter pigeon, and dare your antagonist to throw the first punch. Franco encouraged *machismo*: sexual chauvinism went hand in hand with political and national chauvinism. (1986: 31)

This idea seems to inform *The Blood Spattered Bride* directly. It is a film that links 'sexual chauvinism', as shown in the sequences mentioned, with wider social and political ideas. It is critical of the sexual machismo prevalent at the time but uses this as a way of also subtly criticizing other social and political ideas and beliefs. The film therefore can be read as a critique of the wider ideological beliefs of the dominant social order in Spain at the time. Aranda may well have found it difficult to offer such critiques of Spanish society outside popular genres, in this case the horror film. Following this Aranda went on to achieve a level of notoriety with his post-Franco film *Cambio de sexo* (*Change of Sex*) in 1976, once again showing his desire to explore social and political issues, something his career has continued to do since.

Claudio Guerín Hill was also a filmmaker who had begun to establish 'art' film credentials. Educated at the national film school in the 1960s, he had contributed to the three-part *Los desafíos* (*The Challenges*) in 1969 alongside José Luis Egea and Víctor Erice, and directed *La casa de las palomas* (*The House of Doves*) (1971) before choosing to work in the horror genre. An ambitious work, *La campaña del infierno* (*The Bell of Hell*) is a clear critique of the established political order. This is achieved through the clear opposition between the young lead and the corrupt middle-aged characters who inhabit the Galician village where the film is set. The film's opening sequences show John, the film's young lead, leaving a mental institution and heading back to his village. He is asked to report back to the institution in six days but rips up his appointment card as he passes through the hospital gates suggesting at the outset that he has rejected the order of the authorities. We soon learn that John had been placed in the institution at the behest of his aunt in order for her to spend his inheritance. The film's perspective on authority is suggested through the way it represents John's actions, in particular, his constant playing of practical jokes and his challenging attitude to the sexual mores of the older generation. Indeed, it is possible to see John's placement in a mental institution as more symbolic of the efforts of the older generation to suppress the more radical, new ideas of the younger generation. John's actions can be read as a rejection, even rebellion, against the values of a generation that was victorious in the Civil War and enthusiastically supported the Franco regime in the years that followed.

Guerín Hill creates a clear opposition between John, who is continually associated with the trappings of 1960s rebellious youth (long hair, a motorbike, smart answers, sex), and the older figures of authority (his aunt, the priest, the town elders). He also practises that archetypal 1960s alternative, artistic medium, photography. This generational opposition, which is clearly signified in the early part of the film when John returns to the village, also operates to suggest that perhaps he had been committed to the asylum for more than financial reasons. Indeed, upon his return to the village John systematically attacks characters that represent the existing social order, while John's only friendly encounter is with an old man who lives on the margins of society deep in the woods. This is made more significant by the fact that he is old enough to have been part of the resistance to the Franco regime, and therefore is not implicated in the corruption endemic in the system and its oppressive practices. Indeed, by the end of the film the old man seemingly helps in the destruction of the film's most Francoesque character, Peter.

In the early stages of *The Bell of Hell* the mental institution is clearly represented as part of the authoritarian system. The doctor is being paid to keep John institutionalized, and it is his greed, not medical ethics, that dictates his actions. The link between mental institutions and the interests of the state has, of course, been forcefully made by Michel Foucault in his *Madness and Civilization* (1971). Considering the way in which Guerín Hill represents the mental institution within *The Bell of Hell*, it is likely that he may have been familiar with this work, first published in French in the early 1960s. Foucault, broadly, argued that 'madness' was that which lay outside the realm of 'reason', and that this 'reason' was identified by those who were most powerful within society and therefore in a position to exert their power. In the preface to *Madness and Civilization* he writes: 'we have yet to write a history of that other form of madness, by which men, in an act of sovereign reason, confine their neighbours, and communicate and recognize each other through the merciless language of non-madness' (1971: xi). In this sense, then, the clinic is that institution in which those who do not embrace the socially constructed, accepted patterns of behaviour are placed. Within *The Bell of Hell* this is explicitly shown as those who refuse to accept the values and beliefs of the ruling Franco regime, based as it was on ideals of family, nation and the Catholic church. The character of John represents a rejection of those values and is someone who refuses the behavioural norms of Spanish society at the time. John continually plays practical jokes that push the boundaries of 'good taste' – for example, in his suggestion, in a note to Peter's wife, that he has raped her whilst she was unconscious – which play with the accepted sexual mores of that fiercely Catholic society.

It is central to the radical edge of *The Bell of Hell* that John continually acts outside the accepted moral codes of Spanish society at the time. Here it is possible to see the influence of R. D. Laing and the anti-psychiatry movement. If John is a character who represents much of the 1960s counterculture, his 'madness' can be read as a rejection of the morals and values of the state. As Kenneth Cmiel states, Laing argued that 'it was the "normal" people who were the real crazies. In such an insane world, precisely those who knew enough to ignore the rules – the schizophrenics – were the sane ones' (Cmeil 1994: 271). This aspect of John's character also plays with the generic codes and conventions of the horror film. As the film progresses, the audience is presented with a character who is a monstrous outsider, yet is also the most sympathetic character owing to the fact that society, as represented in the film, is not something one would want to be part of. However, the character of John, with his particularly troublesome attitude to sex and notions of consent, may also be seen as challenging any simply liberal rejection of the values of the established order.

One of the other central elements in the film that contribute to the critical edge of *The Bell of Hell* is the casting of Alfredo Mayo in the role of Peter, a local building contractor who is the focus of John's revenge. The generational oppositions, which I have already argued structure the film, take on an even wider resonance when one considers the casting. Mayo, according to John Hopewell a '40s heart-throb', was closely associated with pro-Franco roles, in particular through his playing the central role in *Raza* (*Race*, 1941), a film which was supposedly based on the dictator's experiences. Although he later became involved in more critical works, Mayo is clearly used in *The Bell of Hell* as a persona associated with the regime either through his earlier work or the roles he took in the 1960s. This has the effect of overlaying meaning on to sequences that on the surface might be seen to simply work generically. For example, a hunting sequence occurs about twenty minutes into the film. It is there to reveal information about the village leaders and their morals but owing to Mayo's presence takes on wider significance. His costume echoes photographs of Franco on his many hunting trips and his appearance in Carlos Saura's art house film *La caza* (*The Hunt*). Indeed, hunting is a traditionally masculine pursuit, and its use as a symbol of the older order is based upon linking such leisure activities to the ideological position of the right in Spain. One of the ways that Guerín Hill does this is through the casting of Mayo and the assumption that audiences will make links between the actor's persona and the regime. John Hopewell discusses the reasons for the use of the hunt as an image of critique in Spanish cinema from *La caza* to Borau's *Furtivos* (*Poachers*, 1975). He states that 'hunting also has specifically political connotations as the favourite sport-cum-slaughter of Franco and many of his ministers. And the high society hunt, a several day shoot for bankers, businessmen, aristocrats and politicians, provided an important scenario for establishment power struggles' (1986: 27). I would argue that Guerín Hill clearly uses these connotations in *The Bell of Hell*. Although in *La caza* the hunters pursue animals before turning on each other, in Guerín Hill's film the hunters turn on an innocent young girl. This makes their exploitation and corruption even more explicit. It is significant that the hunting party is made up of characters whom we later see sitting in the front row of the church acting piously and as respectable members of the community. Within the structure of this psychological horror film there is a clear critique of the establishment. It is highly likely that a film less immersed in these generic codes and conventions would have suffered from the same limited release that befell *La caza* in the mid-1960s. Whereas Guerín Hill is unable to articulate his criticism of the social order in an overly explicit way owing to the state censors, he is able to use the audiences' knowledge, particularly in relation to the social significance of hunting and the history of the featured performers, to create links between narrative, character and the ideology of the Franco regime. I would argue that the codes and conventions of the horror film provide him with a perfect vehicle for exploring the contradictory value system of Spanish society in the early 1970s and those who administered it.

Although clearly not all the horror directors of this period had the same political agenda as those I have mentioned, some of the works produced can clearly be seen as enormously subversive. This subversion comes not only from the content of their works but also from their use of popular genres as a way of escaping the assimilating tendencies of a regime as it attempted to present a more liberal face to the outside world. They also choose to work in forms that were popular with working-class audiences and therefore were not restricted to the government-sanctioned 'art house' cinemas. Few of the films that I have touched upon in this chapter have received any sustained critical interest, perhaps due to the fact that many of the directors mentioned have produced more 'art house' works in their careers. However, as Spanish horror becomes of more interest to critics in the wake of the box-office successes of *Los otros* (*The Others*, Alejandro Amenábar, 2001) and *El espinazo del diablo* (*The Devil's Backbone*, Guillermo del Toro, 2001), it is to be hoped that the products of the late 1960s and early 1970s will receive more serious attention. What the works I focus on in this chapter suggest is that the historical context of production is something that should not be ignored, especially when considering cult cinemas. Indeed, as in the cases I have outlined, this context of production can contribute enormously to an understanding of 'cult' films.

References

Besas, Peter (1985) *Behind the Spanish Lens*. Denver: The Arden Press.
Cmiel, Kenneth (1994) The Politics of Civility, in David Farber (ed.), *The Sixties: From Memory to History*. Chapel Hill: The University of North

Carolina Press.

D'Lugo, Marvin (1997) *Guide to Spanish Cinema*. Westport: Greenwood Press.

Duncombe, Stephen (1997) *Notes From the Underground: Zines and the Politics of Alternative Culture*. London: Verso.

Evans, Peter William (ed.) (1999) *Spanish Cinema: The Auteurist Tradition*. Cambridge: Cambridge University Press.

Graham, Helen, and Jo Labanyi (eds.) (1995) *Spanish Cultural Studies: An Introduction*. Oxford: Oxford University Press.

Hawkins, Joan (1999) 'Sleazemania, Euro-trash and High Art: The Place of European Art Films in American Low Culture', *Film Quarterly* (53) (Winter).

Hawkins, Joan (2000) *Cutting Edge: Art-horror and the Horrific Avant-garde*. Minneapolis: Minnesota University Press.

Hillier, Jim (1992) *The New Hollywood*. London: Studio Vista.

Hillier, Jim, and Lipstadt, A. (eds.) (1981) *Roger Corman's New World Pictures*. London: British Film Institute.

Hopewell, John (1986) *Out of the Past: Spanish Cinema after Franco*. London: British Film Institute.

Hunt, Leon (1992) A (Sadistic) Night at the Opera: Notes on the Italian Horror Film, *Velvet Light Trap*, 30.

Hutchings, Peter (1993) *Hammer and Beyond: The British Horror Film*. Manchester: Manchester University Press.

Jordan, Barry, and Morgan-Tamosunas, Rikki (1998) *Contemporary Spanish Cinema*. Manchester: Manchester University Press.

Kinder, Marsha (1993) *Blood Cinema: The Reconstruction of National Identity in Spain*. Berkeley: University of California Press.

Kinder, Marsha (ed.) (1997) *Refiguring Spain: Cinema/Media/Representation*. Durham: Duke University Press.

Sanjek, David (1990) Fans' Notes: The Horror Film Fanzine, *Literature/Film Quarterly*, 18 (3).

Smith, Paul Julian (1992) *Laws of Desire: Questions of Homosexuality in Spanish Writing and Film*. Oxford: Oxford University Press.

Stone, Rob (2001) *Spanish Cinema*. Harlow: Longman.

Tohill, Cathal, and Tombs, Pete (1995) *Immoral Tales: Sex and Horror Cinema in Europe 1956–1984*. London: Titan Books.

Tropiano, Stephen (1997) Out of the Cinematic Closet: Homosexuality in the Films of Eloy de la Iglesia, in Marsha Kinder (ed.), *Refiguring Spain: Cinema/Media/Representation*. Durham: Duke University Press, pp. 157–177.

6

Trading in horror, cult and matricide: Peter Jackson's phenomenal bad taste and New Zealand fantasies of inter/national cinematic success

Harmony H. Wu

Once and future cults

Three of the most anticipated Hollywood-style blockbuster 'event' pictures at the beginning of the new millenium were made far from Hollywood, on New Zealand soil, by New Zealander Peter Jackson. J. R. R. Tolkien's beloved fantasy trilogy *The Lord of the Rings* has been translated to the big screen, the first live action rendering of the epic tale of the battle of good against evil waged by Hobbits, elves, goblins and dwarves in the fantasy realm of Middle-earth. It is also the first time Tolkien's tale has been told in three parts (one film released in 2001, 2002, 2003). Even a year before the release of the first film (*The Fellowship of the Ring*), there was more buzz around these films than any other, and, at the time of this writing, *Fellowship* is one of the top-grossing movies of 2001–2, trailing only the *Harry Potter* powerhouse franchise's first instalment, *Harry Potter and the Philosopher's Stone* (*Sorcerer's Stone* in the USA) (2001). Much of this excitement and box office power is driven by the rabid fans of Tolkien's *Rings* books. International devotees of Middle-earth have erected an estimated four hundred websites (some first posted years in advance of production) parsing every detail of the productions, have made the internet release of the 'teaser' film trailer a record-breaking media event, and have slept overnight on sidewalks to be first in line to see *Fellowship*'s debut theatrical trailer.[1]

Despite the big production gloss and mainstream respectability of *The Lord of the Rings*,[2] before this Peter Jackson was mostly known to cult audiences, at first for his 'low' splatter horror and gore films, and then for his 'high' art house film *Heavenly Creatures*. The *Rings* films are by far Jackson's biggest, most commercially mainstream productions to date – and yet, contrary to usual oppositions of 'cult' and 'mainstream', these anticipated blockbusters, like his earlier

11 The digitally enhanced New Zealand landscape featured in *The Fellowship of the Ring*. With *The Lord of the Rings*, Peter Jackson seems to have permanently traded in bad taste and lowbrow horror for big-budget fantasy blockbusters.

films, are still the site of cult desire, as illustrated by the examples of fan behaviour above. This intersection of 'cult' with both 'low' and 'high' texts as well as with 'mainstream' in Jackson's films is a useful reminder of the need to be attentive to the nuanced articulations of cultism in a variety of locations; an underlying goal of this essay, then, is to dislodge the marginalization of cult as perpetually 'Othered' by the 'center'. Through Jackson's films, I will attempt to trace the currency of cinema, genre, horror and cult aesthetics and cult reception across international borders and hierarchies of taste, and examine how this currency trades in tropes of the nation. A central focus will also be how with Jackson, 'horror' – the usually debased genre – becomes embedded at the centre of cinematic constructions of New Zealand nationality, symbolically and materially, for Jackson has been uniquely successful in parlaying genre and cult 'capital' into international success, and simultaneously using generic and cult idioms to formulate texts of national identity.

High and low horror

Recent critical work in media studies on taste hierarchies has obvious resonance here and informs my thinking about Jackson's cult films. As these arguments are treated elsewhere in this collection, I will only briefly indicate facets of the taste discourse particularly relevant to my discussion. Drawing Pierre Bourdieu's conclusions on taste and class, Jeffrey Sconce has argued that the mainstream's designation of certain cinematic texts as 'aberrant' or 'bad' is part of larger political structures working to reify patterns of cultural power and authority (1995). He concludes, then, that cult (or to use his term, 'paracinematic') fan activity – specifically those cases where reading groups use 'high' cultural capital to read 'low' texts with sophistication – is ultimately an act of resistance against received power hierarchies. Like in Sconce's paracinema, high and low are also mixed in the figure of Jackson as 'cult auteur', with his cinematic roots in bad taste horror and gore, his critically acclaimed art house success, and his current role as architect of international blockbusters – but in this case the mixing of high/low is across the filmography of one filmmaker, raising further questions about the way good and bad taste, high and low aesthetics circulate and intersect.[3] This suggests that cultural legitimacy and illegitimacy can be mutually constitutive and, materially and economically speaking, less hegemonic than might otherwise be presupposed.

Also of importance is horror's special relation to bad taste. Scholars such as Linda Williams (1995), Carol Clover (1992) and William Paul (1994) have argued that, in the hierarchy of genre legitimacy, horror is at the bottom, above only pornography. Bourdieu's important work on taste and class provides insights here, too. Describing the formations of taste, Bourdieu points to a certain corporeal essentialism that is quite suggestive *vis-à-vis* film aesthetics, the horror genre and cinematic hierarchies of taste: 'Tastes are perhaps first and foremost distastes, disgust provoked by horror or visceral intolerance ("sick-making") of the tastes of others' (1986: 192). With 'good taste' located in the act of rejecting that which produces corporeal sensations of disgust and precisely *horror*, it becomes clear why the horror genre is always-already 'low'. The genre that takes its name from the bodily affect has an especially intimate relationship to the substance of bad taste, for its very generic imperatives are to produce exactly the kind of 'visceral intolerance' in which reviled distaste is firmly rooted. It would also seem that horrific forms thus are intractably stuck at the bottom, the 'lowbrow' end, of the hierarchy of genres.

These cult and taste discourses surrounding horror, with their implications of power, center and margins, inevitably circle back to issues of the nation. If a national cinema comes to be known for 'low' texts with cult value, how does this affect the nation, its representation, its cultural image and its political position?

The international currency of bad taste

Peter Jackson's first features – *Bad Taste* (1987), *Meet the Feebles* (1989) and *Braindead* (also known as *Dead Alive*, 1992) – illustrate a particular obsession with the absurd, the comically grotesque and the splatter and gore strains of horror. *Bad Taste* is an alien/zombie film; *Meet the Feebles*, a backstage musical with X-rated puppets; *Braindead*, a zombie film with a staggeringly high body count. All share a comedic sensibility, and all are determined to push the limits of the body, probing the meaty and fluid excesses of corporeal form with a combination of fear and delight. These films, which can be called the 'gross-out trilogy', were all eventually picked up for international distribution, and, though none played in mainstream venues, the gross-out films generated a dedicated, cult audience of gore and splatter fans who were impressed by the extremes to which Jackson decimated, erupted, destroyed and drained bodies of various forms (puppets, zombies, aliens). Each of the films has become a video and midnight movie cult favourite.

Bad Taste has aliens vomit copious amounts of chunky blue spew, which is then consumed by a sickened human. In the film's climax, Derek, played by Peter Jackson himself, slices off an alien's head, dives into its body through the bloody cavity and slices his way out at the other end, declaring, beneath thick layer of sticky ooze and blood, 'I'm born again!' *Meet the Feebles* features a fly tabloid reporter, who gets the sexual scoop on the celebrity rabbit (who hosts the variety television programme 'Meet the Feebles') by rooting around in his fetid toilet and snacking on the contents, while the rabbit's fast-acting venereal disease causes his body to decompose rapidly in dripping wounds and explosions of vomit and pus. *Braindead* also features pus and rotting flesh, and takes the destructive body logic of *Bad Taste* to extremes, depicting a hundred ways to dispatch zombies and abuse the human form – legs are ripped off, a human head is puréed in a blender, a zombie baby burrows through a woman's face from the back of her head. *Braindead*'s *pièce de resistance* is the thirty-minute non-stop parade of zombie dismemberment, culminating in the spectacle of hero Lionel strapping on a

12 Promotional material illustrates how *Bad Taste*'s aims include an all-out assault on mainstream boundaries of good taste and decorum.

lawnmower to pulverize a host of oncoming zombies, until nothing but pulpy bloody flesh remains.

Braindead, *Feebles* and *Bad Taste*'s stock in trade is clearly 'bad taste'. Through the degradation of the screen bodies, the films explicitly traffic in 'sick-making', deliberately seeking viewers' 'vis-

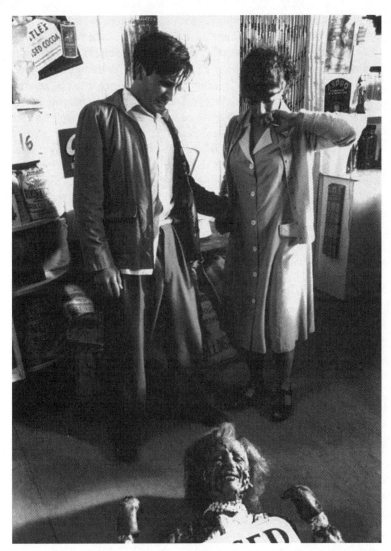

13 Lionel (Timothy Balme) and Paquita (Diana Penalver) regard Lionel's
monstrous mother (Elizabeth Moody) in *Braindead*. Gross-out images such as
the rotting zombies and bloodied bodies of *Braindead* established Jackson's
reputation as a 'Kiwi sicko'.

ceral intolerance'. These films do not court audiences that would see Merchant Ivory's *The Remains of the Day*; rather, they cultivate the very specific cult horror viewing aesthetic, specializing in extremes defined explicitly in contrast to mainstream aesthetics and good taste. Still, even while cult, paracinematic and horror texts are generally debased for their 'bad taste' and loved only by a narrow group of fans, these marginalized texts can also simultaneously translate into very material audiences and financial substance, as indicated by *Variety*'s review: 'This is one of the bloodiest horror comedies ever made, and that will be enough to ensure cult success in cinemas and especially on video. Kiwi gore specialist Peter Jackson goes for broke with an orgy of bad taste and splatter humor. Some will recoil, but "Braindead" wasn't made for them' (1992: 51). Though maligned by arbiters of cultural legitimacy, bad taste films are at the same time potentially valuable to producers, distributors and exhibitors for their niche dollars, especially as cult fans of bad taste and horror are given to serial viewings. This places cult texts and audiences in the possibly conflicted space of being, on the one hand, vilified by the cultural mainstream and, on the other, financially exploitable by the corporations that produce and distribute the dominant media comprising the mainstream that shuns bad taste texts in the first place.

When the bad taste films in question are made outside of the dominant US/Hollywood film industry, 'taste' and 'cult' gather connotations in a larger web of cultural 'value' expressed specifically along terms of national identity. When the squarely Hollywood-centric trade paper *Variety* explicitly labels Jackson 'kiwi', the rhetorical gesture brands not only the director but also New Zealand itself as 'gore-meisters' in the imaginations of industry insiders, critics and consumers. This elision of an entire national identity with the vocabulary of cult aesthetics and genre can be found across a variety of publications: *Onfilm* called Jackson a 'Kiwi sicko' (Doole 1993: 4), *British Modern Review* claimed that, for grossness, 'nobody does it better than the antipodeans' ('BFI Praise' 1994: 12), and a cult film website asserts, 'Peter Jackson has put New Zealand firmly on the map as far as Cult cinema is concerned . . . [*Braindead* is] the best thing that has come from New Zealand since good ol' kiwi lamb chops' (*The Hot Spot*). With these low texts' international cult success, the New Zealand nation itself is mapped and becomes synonymous with cult, horror and bad taste.

This simultaneous inscription of Jackson and New Zealand as purveyors of horror, splatter, bad taste and gore develops out of and reinforces an international perception of New Zealand as an off-kilter land with strange and dark obsessions, an idea explicitly articulated in *Cinema of Unease*, the 1995 documentary on New Zealand cinema (written and directed by Sam Neill and Judy Rymer), which takes the 'off-kilter Kiwi' point of view as its primary thesis.[4] As presumed by *Cinema of Unease* and illustrated in global critical and fan consumption of Jackson's gross-out films, genre, taste and a strange world-view *become* 'nation' – New Zealand itself is genrified, figured as cult object, a site where kooky perspectives and horrific bad taste can be reliably found. In the case of non-dominant, non-Hollywood cinema industries, 'cult' success ultimately can become a question of how the nation is represented on the international stage.

The larger political ramifications of occupying the subordinate positions of these binaries (good/bad taste, high/low culture, mainstream/cult audiences, Hollywood/national cinema) were made visible in a minor scandal after the New Zealand Film & Television Awards bestowed the 'Best Film' honours on *Braindead* in 1993. Awards juror John Cranna, author of short stories and then budding screenwriter, went public with his opposition to the selection of Jackson's film, criticizing *Braindead* as 'a crude horror that makes a mockery of serious film making in New Zealand' ('Integrity and the B.O.' 1993: 8). In Cranna's reading of *Braindead*, the discourses of taste, genre and nation are again implicated in one another, reproducing the international critical conflation of New Zealand with horror and bad taste: the 'bad taste' of *Braindead*'s 'crude' execution of the horror genre, then, reflected *New Zealand*'s own 'bad taste', reaffirming New Zealand's status as second-tier filmmakers on the world stage, and undermining any pretences to cultural legitimacy. Too much revelling in horrific bad taste condemns New Zealand culture industries to perpetual performance of its marginality.

Cranna's is not the only way of looking at the intersection of these hierarchies of taste, power and cinemas, however; 'borders' can be less a rigid wall and more of a permeable membrane, a model which allows for greater moments of exchange between the two sides of a binary. Jackson's gross-out horror films *can* be seen, as in Cranna's view, as ritual exercises in bad taste, repeatedly performing its status as marginalized, an act that only reaffirms the immutability of 'good taste's' position as 'centre'. But alternatively, the films' unapologetic entrenchment in 'gross-out' can be seen also as an exploration of the boundaries of taste in a more active manner (much as Sconce's paracinematic reading practices purposely explore bad taste as a protest against repressive power structures filtered through aesthetic hierarchies of taste).

Instead of conceiving of the hierarchies as fixed, we might see the repeated exercises of 'sick-making' in splatter and gore films as working to deconstruct the very demarcations of 'good taste'. The border thus is not so much a hegemonic barrier as it is a site of renegotiation, a site where new relationships of centre and margin can potentially be re-drafted. And in so far as discourses of national/ international cinema are implicated in the discourse of taste, these aggressively horrific cult films from New Zealand and their trans- gressions of good taste can be read as laying bare, and possibly reconstituting, the centre/margin dialectic that holds other national cinemas – New Zealand national cinema – perpetually subordinate to US/Hollywood hegemony. When a national cinema producing specialized niche titles claims the allegiance of audiences and becomes branded as a reliable source of a particular kind of film, Hollywood's fiercely protected position as centre becomes some- what denaturalized and the inevitability of Hollywood's dominance less apparent.

That Cranna's dismal view of Jackson's horrific bad taste was not widely shared by members of the New Zealand film industry might have had as much to do with *Braindead*'s attention from interna- tional cult fans as with the film's cinematic merits, indicating yet another way of understanding the margin/centre dialectic vis-à-vis genre, national cinema and taste. By doggedly pursuing the niche cult market by pushing the limits of taste and working squarely within genre pleasures, Peter Jackson's gross-out films, it might be argued, afforded him the capital (both economic and cinematic) to transcend the limitations of working in a tiny national cinema in Hollywood's shadow and to reap success that would be otherwise unavailable; Jackson's current role as director of *The Lord of the Rings* suggests that this is indeed the case. First revelling in bad taste to court the marginal audiences, then exploiting the niche dollars of cult cinema, and finally using cult success to vault into 'legitimacy' with big budget, good taste projects, however, is a paradigm that in the end still reaffirms the power dynamics inherent in the good/bad taste discourse. After *Braindead*, Jackson claimed that he would not abandon the horror genre, saying, 'I'm definitely not one of those guys who says they want to stop making horror movies to become a serious filmmaker. I fully intend to remain working in the genre' (Helms 1993: 33). Yet, his claims to generic fealty and his implication that 'serious' filmmaking is the 'Other' of horror filmmaking echoes Cranna's statement that *Braindead* 'makes a mockery of serious film making in New Zealand'. All of this suggests that, while Jackson has made an impressive shift from poverty auteurism in lowly horror to Hollywood-style epic filmmaking with staggering budgets, the dialectic of good/bad taste, high/low culture and Hollywood/national cinema is, while not entirely stable, stubbornly resistant to change. And as far as the taste and the national discourses are intertwined, Jackson's trading in of lowbrow horror for mainstream big-budget fantasy spectacle reiterates a dynamic where the Hollywood model of filmmaking (and its good taste, polished aesthetics and bourgeois ideologies) remains on top.

In exploring the various ways of seeing the dialectics of genre, taste and national cinema, I do not hope to suggest pejoratively that Jackson has 'sold out' to bigger Hollywood budgets. Indeed, Jackson, ostensibly abandoning horror genre filmmaking, at the same time remains decidedly committed to the promotion of New Zealand national cinema, and landing *The Lord of the Rings* on New Zealand shores is the biggest thing to have ever happened to the local film industry.[5] Jackson's follow-up to *Braindead* was *Heavenly Creatures*, his film that is most engaged with issues of New Zealandness and at first glance seems a departure from the horror, gore, splatter and bad taste that marked Jackson's first films. The next section examines *Heavenly Creatures* and its connection to Jackson's gross-out films *vis-à-vis* the emergence of a cult dynamic that still surrounds the film years after its initial release. Discourses of horror and art, cult and mainstream, auteur and genre, national and international cinema, usually conceived in contradiction, intersect in Jackson's films, making it inadequate to consider any one of these paradigms individually; each problematizes the others and must be considered dialogically.

The art of cult

Heavenly Creatures dramatizes the real-life 1954 murder in Christchurch, New Zealand, of Honora Parker, whose life was bludgeoned out of her by forty-seven blows to the head, neck, face and shoulders with a half brick in a stocking wielded by her teen daughter, Pauline, and Pauline's friend Juliet Hulme. Despite the grisly nature of the subject, *Heavenly Creatures* is no grim or gritty 'true crime' flick. Though bookended with the murder, the film is more concerned with the girls' strong personalities and intense pre-crime friendship, their flights of fancy in which they invent complex fantasy worlds (brilliantly rendered with morphing and other computer-generated scenes), their homoerotic explorations, their often vexed family relationships and their class differences. It is a virtuosic film, coursing with visual power and irrepressible kineticism (giddy, gliding camerawork, impeccable production design and imaginative use of computer-generation technology) and driven by stunning debut performances by Kate Winslet and Melanie Lynskey, putting contemporaneous Hollywood films to shame in comparison.[6]

Released internationally in 1994 by Miramax, in the USA the film played on independent and art house screens, accumulating word-of-mouth and critical praise. *Heavenly Creatures* even garnered an Academy Award nomination for 'best screenplay'.[7] The film's emergence as a legitimate, critically acclaimed 'quality' film must be understood as coming out at a time when New Zealand cinema was causing a ripple with more 'highbrow' US viewers as a site of provocative fare associated with the 'art' film, in direct contrast to marginalized cult audiences' perception of Jackson and New Zealand as sites of gross-out horror and gore. New Zealander Jane Campion's international reputation as 'art house' feminist filmmaker had jelled with *The Piano*'s release the year before, with its moody evocations of a woman's patriarchal repression and sexual reawakening.[8] And another New Zealand film, *Once Were Warriors*, directed by Lee Tamahori, was also released to critical acclaim in 1994. The adaptation of Alan Duff's tremendously well-received novel explored domestic abuse and urban poverty through a portrait of a Maori family, with particular focus on the point of view of the adolescent daughter.

At this moment, then, as far as it registered on so-called *legitimate* US film-going consciousness, New Zealand signified smart, chal-

14 Juliet (Kate Winslet) acting out one of the girls' romantic fantasy-scapes in
Heavenly Creatures. *Heavenly Creatures'* release coincided with and contributed
to a new perception of New Zealand cinema as 'arty', and, like Jackson's bad
taste films, developed a cult following.

lenging, edgy and beautiful 'art' films committed to exploring a feminine perspective. *Heavenly Creatures* was promoted and received in
the vernacular of 'art film'; Miramax sold it as a prestige production
and a cinematic achievement – a marketing strategy that was then
becoming Miramax's signature in distributing and marketing 'foreign' films (where 'foreign-ness' itself coupled with exploration of
eroticism – especially homoeroticism – is apparently sufficient to signify 'arty' difference from Hollywood). Peter Jackson's gross-out
cult success was suppressed; most film-goers had no idea that the
director of this 'quality' art film was known to cult audiences as the
'Orson Welles of gore'. When critics acknowledged Jackson's earlier
films, it was only to remark with surprise how much the director had
matured, dismissing the gross-out trilogy as an unfortunate detour
to Jackson's newfound artistry, re-articulating the diametric opposition of the disdained 'lowbrow' of the gross-out films and the 'legitimacy' of *Heavenly Creatures*, with its artfulness and sheen of
quality.

    Heavenly Creatures, with its structurally and thematically sophis-
ticated narrative, fully realized character development, first-rate

15 The real-life Pauline Parker and Juliet Hulme. In opening up interest in the real-life murder of Honora Parker, on which the film *Heavenly Creatures* is based, cult adoration of the film is grounded in the historical and cultural specificity of New Zealand.

performances, and highly developed visual and aural sensibility, does indeed seem a radical departure for Jackson. While these accomplishments were not absent in Jackson's earlier films (and are perhaps most notable in *Braindead*), the overwhelming presence of 'bad taste' in the other films shifts focus away from more conventionally lauded narrative and formal achievements toward the spectacles of ruined bodies. But one of the interesting facets of the film's reception in light of the prior gross-out and forthcoming *Lord of the Rings* trilogies is that *Heavenly Creatures*'s art house success and nods from 'legitimate' critics eventually morphed, like the computer-generated images in the film itself, into an internet-based fan community with cult-like devotion.

One important difference, however, is that fan communities around the *Rings* and gross-out trilogies fit into pre-existing categories of cultism – fandom for the horror genre and for Tolkien's Middle-earth fantasies precedes and exceeds Jackson's films. Alternatively, *Heavenly Creatures*'s cult fan base seems to have grown out of ardent love for the film itself: *Heavenly Creatures* fandom is not part of a larger cult community. That is, for example, one does not come to a cult appreciation of *Heavenly Creatures* because one is a fan of the coming-of-age genre. At the same time, *Heavenly Creatures*'s cultism does fit some discernible features of cult fandom generally.

Jeffrey Sconce (1992) has described two distinct kinds of cult cinephilia, the archaeological and the diegetic: the archaeological cinephile is obsessed with 'collection' and 'artefacts' of cinema, while the diegetic cinephile is invested in a particular universe, an encompassing mise-en-scène offered by a genre (such as the urban landscapes of film noir) or, sometimes, a single cinematic text (such as *Titanic* or *The Wizard of Oz*). *Heavenly Creatures* seems to foster this latter 'diegetic' form of cult cinephilia, wherein fans seek aesthetic delight in the beauty of the girls' friendship and the fantasy-scapes of their books and play-acting. The diegetic cinephile's effort to relive and extend the story universe can take expression as original artwork and creative writing 'inspired' by the film, acts of creation through which the film's story is integrated into the fan's or artist's life (see figures 16 and 17).[9] *The Way Through the Clouds* website provides an example of a fan's imbrication in the diegetic space of *Heavenly Creatures*, as she describes how Juliet's and Pauline's friendship and personalities mirror her own character and relationship with her best friend:

16 Through the act of creating, the film's story is integrated into the artist's life. A fan's interpretation of 'Juliet' and 'Pauline', as played by Kate Winslet and Melanie Lynskey.

> All day I have been thinking about how my best friend Lill and myself . . . are similar to Pauline Parker and Juliet Hulme in the film *Heavenly Creatures* . . . We are remarkably similar in so many ways. An obvious starting point is appearance. Of course we're not exact clones of the girls but we do have similarities . . . I have a very short temper like Juliet that quite often takes me over, and I become easily annoyed . . . I need constant reassurance that Lill will not leave me and I become very jealous very quickly, as Juliet did when Pauline told her about John. Pauline had to reassure Juliet immediately . . . Lill recognises this and does her best to reassure me, as does Pauline . . . When the girls are apart they become incredibly depressed and withdrawn – Pauline cannot eat when Juliet goes into hospital. This is all too familiar! The awful thought that Juliet might die must have been hell for Pauline, and being alone in the hospital without Pauline must have nearly killed her anyway. Juliet writes to Pauline saying 'I miss you and adore you in equal amounts.' How very true. (Gough 2001)

So entangled are the lines of fiction and reality that it is unclear whether the author is reading the film through her life, or her life through the film, illustrating a striking degree of diegetic immersion.

In contrast, cult allegiance to Jackson's gross-out films seems to cleave to the archaeological impulse. In this paradigm, fans of gore

17 A montage of *Heavenly Creatures'* diegetic images extends the film world into the fan world.

and splatter seek to 'collect' and add to their viewing repertoire (what Sconce terms a 'mental checklist') as many severed body parts and buckets of blood as possible; the films and their fetishized body spectacles are part of a larger corpus of related films – they are endowed with cult value only in relation to the larger list of cult films. An expression of the imperatives of this 'checklist logic' is found on web pages for Jackson's gross-out films, where filmographies of other horror, splatter and gore films are frequently posted – panegyrics to horrific bad taste following the 'if you liked *Brain-dead*, then you'll love – ' algebra. Conversely, while fans' *Heavenly Creatures* universe is in its own right deeply intertextual, the cult object of *Heavenly Creatures* fandom ultimately is bounded by the extent of the lives, fictionalized and real, of Juliet and Pauline; there is no readily iterable filmography that can be generated from *Heavenly Creatures*.[10] The gross-out films, in contrast, are a part of a much more expansive cinematic topos, one that includes the horror and splatter cult universe and can extend into matters of production and special effects, other films and auteurs of gore, super-specialized subgenres and the unpredictable and often strange vagaries of personal predilections.[11]

Consistent with the larger discourses on taste and respectability surrounding the differences between the films, the differences between 'diegetic' and 'archeological' cult cinephilia seem to be a matter of form that once again circles the question of 'taste': it is the very bad taste of *Braindead, Bad Taste* and *Meet the Feebles* – their gore, their splatter, their scatology – that the cult cinephile fetishizes. On the other hand, fans of *Heavenly Creatures*, like the girls in the film itself, immerse themselves in the fictional universes offered by the film and prized for their pleasing character, complexity and hermetic completeness – features of classical aesthetic beauty, which is to say, aesthetics valued by 'good taste'.

Historical, national cults

In order to emphasize the differences in cult fandom of *Heavenly Creatures* and the gross-out trilogy and to better dramatize the latter's intertextuality, I have perhaps overstated the closed nature of the *Heavenly Creatures* text. Though its *cinematic* intertextuality is decidedly narrower than the others films', the diegesis proper of *Heavenly Creatures*, its story world, does bleed beyond the border of the frame. That *Heavenly Creatures* is an arresting film is obvious. But it is also based on a terrible, fascinating real story, and diehard fans of the film seem compelled to reckon with the historical matter on which it is based. 'Diegetic immersion' in *Heavenly Creatures*, then, is not simply a matter of subsuming oneself in Jackson's attractive mise-en-scène or reveling in Winslet's and Lynskey's riveting performances; it is also inevitably immersion in the real murder which is the film's referent.

Most *Heavenly Creatures* fan websites, in addition to loving descriptions of the film itself, offer background information on the historical murder and trial. *The Fourth World* website features an exhaustive 500-page dossier on the details of the 'case', such as the social climate of 1950s Christchurch, the professional lives of the girls' parents, the girls' relationships to other teenagers and boyfriends, the trial arguments for the defence and prosecution, and so on. Considerable attention is paid to the film's faithfulness to the historical events, which in one section produces a list of the minute historical details the film got wrong, from timeline aberrations to errors in the number of guests at a family dinner.

This engagement with the 'diegesis' of the historical murder can reach obsessive heights. Andrew Conway became interested in the murder after seeing *Heavenly Creatures*, and, upon discovering that there was little information known about the murdered woman (Honora Parker), set off to research her life. This project manifested itself in 'The "Norasearch" Diary', a detective-like web journal detailing the author's pursuit of the spotty paper trails that might lead to a better understanding of the murdered woman's life. The journal unfolds over the course of a year, as Conway explores Honora Parker's family history and genealogy, the narrative of which consumes him more and more:

> I spend Friday evening in the Green Room with a group of friends: my favourite bar and third home. It used to be my second home, till this Norasearch began. I'm starting to feel a slight unease with the usual acquaintances, bored of the common topics of conversation, half of my mind ruminating on events of ninety years ago, events that are nothing to do with me or my life but which encroach on everything I do, think and feel. I end up talking to Danny because he's the only one present who knows about all of this, the only one there I can tell it to. I update him on everything I've uncovered on the Parkers, which is a huge amount now because the last he heard was our trip to locate 12 Alcester Road. (1999)

As seen earlier with the fan who read her own life and relationships reflected in *Heavenly Creatures*, the author here is also deeply immersed in the story – only this time the filmic diegesis has mutated into the diegesis of history.[12]

Clearly this cult following is not sustained by simple admiration for an excellent film, but rather emerges out of the dense textual layering of the fictionalized representation of Juliet and Pauline, with the real-life narrative and history of the murder; fans of *Heavenly Creatures* are just as much absorbed in the facts of the *real* murder and participants as in the film's *representation* of those real events and persons. Indeed, devoted fans seem specifically caught up in the thrall of the blurred space between fiction and history – reading the history of the murder through fiction, and the fiction of the murder through its history. Cult adoration of *Heavenly Creatures* thus is inextricably interwoven with the locally specific, making cult activity around the film ultimately grounded in the historical and cultural specificity of New Zealand.

Historians Julie Glamuzina and Alison Laurie have argued that, through official and popular discourses of the Parker–Hulme murder which is the subject of *Heavenly Creatures*, the murder has come to function as a New Zealand national cautionary tale, a story used to shore up a specific, patriarchally authored national charac- ter, by condemning the girls' expansive creativity and rumoured les- bianism as deviant, aberrant and monstrous (1991: 111–133). The 1954 murder has become the site of continuing multiple discourses, a screen through which conceptions of national morality, family, motherhood and sexuality are filtered. *Heavenly Creatures*, the only cinematic rendering of the murder (which had previously been recorded, analysed and fictionalized in crime annals, psychiatric books, newspaper accounts, court transcripts, a theatrical play and a novelization), and the cult fascination of the film thus inevitably are part of a larger cultural matrix of New Zealand national identity. Whether *Heavenly Creatures* exacerbates, sustains or disrupts the virulent homophobic subtext of other renderings of the murder cannot be resolved here, yet it must be pointed out that *Heavenly Creatures* has done what no other narrativization or gossip about Parker and Hulme has before – created a significant and vocal pop- ulation that is passionately sympathetic to Juliet's and Pauline's points of view.

Trading in horror and other film fantasies

One might argue that it is precisely in the extreme reading practices of various forms of 'cult' cinephilia that boundaries of high and low are, by turns, most visibly transgressed and insistently reinforced. The cult of *Heavenly Creatures* and the cult of the gross-out films take distinct forms, with differences boiling down to 'art' as opposed to 'splatter', 'quality' in place of 'trash', 'high culture' instead of 'low' and 'good' taste not 'bad'. A simultaneously 'high' and 'low' cult director, Jackson uniquely embodies the construct of the 'cult auteur', revealing how the high modernist conceit of the 'author' is embraced by both high and low taste communities. While the idea of 'low auteurs' is not new, what is different here is that Jackson is *one* director engaging, at different times, both ends of the high/low spectrum, putting into sharper relief the distinctions, as well as the similarities, between the distinct iterations of 'cult' and how these divergent cult practices cling to or jettison accepted notions of high and low culture and 'taste'. Yet for all of the criss-crossing of high and low in Jackson's work, it is also telling that, while the two cult communities of the gross-out trilogy and of *Heavenly Creatures* both rally around the work of one director, cult admiration for one of Jackson's films does not translate into cult fascination with his other films – with few exceptions *Heavenly Creatures* fans do not become fans of the gross-out films and vice versa.[13] This in particular illustrates that while high and low do intermingle in the figure of Peter Jackson, in cult *practice*, there remain divisions between high and low, good taste and bad.

So far in my discussion, the movement between high and low has been on an extratextual level – across Jackson's body of films, the spanning of cultism over disparate texts. But there is one crucial *textual* commonality between the high and low films. *Braindead* and *Heavenly Creatures* are the two films that the different cult communities would claim as Jackson's masterpiece. With Academy-Award-nominated *Heavenly Creatures*, Jackson seemed to have traded the lexicon of horror, gross-out, splatter and bad taste for critical acclaim, prestigious awards and the aura of quality; *Heavenly Creatures* and *Braindead* seem fundamentally at odds. Yet the thematic centres of each film are strikingly similar.

Braindead concerns the meek Lionel, who is trapped in an emasculating and infantilized role of servile care-giver to his ageing, widowed, repressive mother who, like Mrs Bates in *Psycho*, jealously limits Lionel's interaction with the rest of society, particularly young women. When 'Mum' becomes a zombie, Lionel must balance mother-love with increasingly extreme efforts necessary to keep the zombie 'infection' from spreading. Lionel's unhealthy attachment to Mum is given literal expression in the finale of *Braindead*, when the zombie Mum returns, giant-sized, with a monstrous maw and immense drooping breasts, to re-assimilate – literally – Lionel into her womb. As she stuffs him into her belly, which has opened up like a giant mouth, she growls, 'No one will ever love you like your mother!' Lionel cuts his way out of his mother's body from within, spilling out in a torrent of viscera and finally killing her in the process. The matricidal moment enables blood-drenched Lionel to be reborn, unfettered at last from the manacles of mother-love.

Heavenly Creatures opens and closes with the murder of Pauline's mother; the matricide literally frames the story as the narrative flashes back to the blossoming of the girls' friendship. The opening sequence of the film has the manic, sobbing girls running away from the body, just after the murder. When they run into the widescreen close-up, we see blood splattered all over their faces and hair. The murder itself, shown at the end of the film, is shockingly violent and graphic, with close-ups of the dying woman shot from low perspective, blood trickling her face from her matted hair; we see each blow of the brick to her head, and the girls' wildly determined and frightened faces as they swing the brick. While the film as a whole abandons the gross-out aesthetics of his earlier films, in this crucial murder scene – the critical narrative moment from which the rest of the film unspools – *Heavenly Creatures*, like *Braindead* before it, signifies aggressively with the direct language of horror and splatter, not supposedly 'artful' restraint and veiled allusion.[14] And, lest the point be lost beneath the buckets of blood, matricide drives both narratives and the films' most sensational moments of horrific and/ or horrifying spectacle.

The international cult success of *Braindead* led to the New Zealand Film Commission's funding of *Heavenly Creatures*, which in turn was the cinematic calling card leading to Jackson's first Hollywood-funded production, *The Frighteners* (1996), which led ultimately to *The Lord of the Rings*. Jackson's film career illustrates a canny ability to parlay specialized cult films, as well as both high and low films, into mainstreamed commercial viability that does the often tricky job of crossing international borders while still working in a national cinema historically plagued by the dreaded 'brain drain', where homegrown talent seeks better prospects elsewhere. Peter Jackson illustrates that a manipulation of 'cult' and both high and low aesthetics in the intersection of national/international cinemas and audiences works, paradoxically, to make possible a broader international audience, and to engender, through the capital his cult films have secured for him, more wide-scale commercial production on New Zealand soil – as with *The Lord of the Rings*. The cultivation of cinematic expertise, the development of infrastructure, the influx of capital and the international attention Jackson has brought to New Zealand by pulling off this mega-project will by all accounts power the engine of the still infant New Zealand film industry for decades to come. Whatever is in store for the unwritten future of

New Zealand cinema, it is built on the border-crossing cult currency of bloody matricides, breathtaking fantasies and horrific bad taste.

Notes

1 *The Lord of the Rings* was published in three parts in the 1950s – *The Fellowship of the Ring*, *The Two Towers* and *The Return of the King*; two prior animated versions of *The Lord of the Rings* dealt with only sections of the trilogy. Principal photography for Jackson's three films, which were shot simultaneously on location in New Zealand over the course of a year and a half, wrapped on 22 December 2000. The 'teaser' internet trailer was released online on 7 April 2000; its 1.7 million hits in one day beat the previous record held by the internet trailer for *Star Wars Episode I: The Phantom Menace* (New Line 2000). For an example of one of the many *Lord of the Rings* movie fan sites, see the website *Imladris: Lord of the Rings Movie News*. At the end of 2000, E!, the cable television network and website that tracks the contours of pop culture, listed *The Fellowship of the Ring* as number 3 on its list of 'most anticipated' pop culture events of 2001 (Haberman). For a description of Tolkien fans spending the night at theatres to see the theatrical trailer see Gates and Gordon (2001). At the time of revision of this article for publication, thirteen weeks after its initial US release, *The Fellowship of the Ring* has grossed almost $800 million worldwide, according to Variety.com reports on 1 April 2002.

2 *The Fellowship of the Rings* was nominated for a whopping fourteen Academy Awards in 2002, including Best Picture and Director, taking home four awards for the more 'technical' achievements in cinematography, make-up, visual effects and original score.

3 Extrapolating from Sconce's study of the use of 'high' reading strategies for 'low' film texts in paracinema communities, Joan Hawkins has pointed out that high art films can exhibit 'low' or trash aesthetics, and helpfully indicates the coexistence of high and low films within the specialized distribution space of cult cinema catalogues (2000).

4 For a challenge of this view see Roger Horrocks (1999).

5 It should be noted that in spite of the mainstream success of *The Fellowship of the Ring* – winning four Academy Awards and chosen for numerous 'Ten Best' year-end lists – Jackson has not entirely disavowed gross-out aesthetics. In his traditional cameo appearance in *Fellowship*, Jackson belches directly into the camera.

6 Especially considering the minuscule budgets from which Jackson squeezed such high production value and special effects in *Heavenly Creatures* and indeed all of his prior gross-out films.

7 The 'Best Screenplay' category seems specifically reserved for those

non-Hollywood films that clearly warrant accolades, yet somehow do not conform to a broader commercial standard set by the Academy. *Heavenly Creatures* lost to *Pulp Fiction* – which itself was marginalized out of any awards in the 'big' categories.

8 Because of *The Piano*'s colonial New Zealand setting and the exoticized presence of Maori, Campion was at this time still associated with New Zealand national specificity, whereas in future films Campion would become more internationalized, becoming more identified with her 'feminism' than her cultural background, abandoning New Zealand locations and subject matter.

9 An example in another medium: a poem titled 'Ilam' (after the Hulmes' Christchurch estate) appears on *The Way Through the Clouds* website.

10 Of course, the features one is attracted to in the film will suggest a film list. For example, a viewer might have been interested in the 'true crime' aspect of the story, or the lesbianism or the 1950s setting. This then suggests a 'generic' grouping that one can trace. I must also note that Kate Winslet herself comprises her own 'genre' and viewing imperatives. When I started becoming interested in fan activity on the web around *Heavenly Creatures*, Adam Abrams's *The Fourth World* site was the only major presence. After *Titanic* – in which Winslet also starred – *Heavenly Creatures* activity has increased and many (young, female) fans state that they came to *Heavenly Creatures* after *Titanic*, as they were working through Winslet's filmography.

11 One usually finds fan web *pages* on Jackson's gross-out films as part of larger web sites devoted to horror and gore. Except for the handful of *Peter Jackson* fan sites (which include roughly equal attention to all his films, including *Heavenly Creatures* and *The Lord of the Rings*), I have found only one website devoted specifically and exclusively to any of Jackson's gross-out films. (The one gross-out film with its own fan site is *Meet the Feebles* (www.ween.net/feebles/), which perhaps speaks to that film's uniqueness. As a scatological 'muppet' movie, there is no larger, recognizable genre to which it decidedly belongs.) This is in contrast to *Heavenly Creatures* (and *The Lord of the Rings*), which has several websites devoted exclusively to it.

12 In the historical manifestations of diegetic cinephilia surrounding *Heavenly Creatures*, there is an interesting conflation of the diegetic impulse with the archaeological. In these instances, *Heavenly Creatures* fans such as Conway and Porter seek to construct precisely an 'archaeology' of the Parker–Hulme narrative, fetishizing the artefacts (birth certificates, old photos, hospital records) and dimensions (time lines) of history. Although I do not have the space to explore this more fully here, there seems to be a sense in which the diegetic and archaeological forms of cinephilia correspond to how gendered patterns of 'looking' have

been theorized in the cinema. Diegetic cinephilia depends on immersion, envelopment in the text, bespeaking what can be read as emotional 'overinvestment' in the narrative, much akin to how women's relationship to classical Hollywood women's pictures has been theorized. On the other hand, the archaeological depends on the construction of fetishes and the investigative scrutiny that characterizes the fetishistic and sadistic forms of voyeurism theorized by Mulvey as the male viewer's relationship to the screen. The degree to which *Heavenly Creatures* collapses or conflates these impulses and how this interacts with theories of gendered spectatorship clearly warrants more attention.

13 It is sometimes true that fans of the gross-out are also fans of *Heavenly Creatures*; it is rarely true that *Heavenly Creatures* fans (at least the ones on the web) are also fans of *Bad Taste*, *Meet the Feebles* or *Braindead*. A fan on the *House of Horrors* website writes that he became a fan of Jackson's after *Braindead*, then lists all of Jackson's films *except* the 'good taste' films, *Heavenly Creatures* and *Forgotten Silver*. Although most sites or pages for any of Jackson's films will respectfully include a complete filmography, fandom for the two 'kinds' of film in Jackson's oeuvre remains rather neatly separate.

14 Again, see Joan Hawkins (2000) for an examination of larger patterns of 'high' art films employing tropes of 'low' horror.

The author wishes to thank Matt Severson for assistance in obtaining images for this project.

References

BFI Praise for NZ comedy (1994) *NZFilm* (May), p. 12.

Bourdieu, Pierre (1986) The Aristocracy of Culture, in Richard Collins, James Curran, Nicholas Garnham, Paddy Scannell, Philip Schlesinger and Colin Sparks (eds.), *Media, Culture and Society: A Critical Reader*. London: Sage Publications, pp. 164–193.

Clover, Carol J. (1992) *Men, Women and Chain Saws: Gender in the Modern Horror Film*. Princeton: Princeton University Press.

Conway, Andrew (1999) The 'Norasearch' Diaries in *The Fourth World: The Heavenly Creatures Web Site*, www.geocities.com/Hollywood/Studio/2194/faq2/norasearch/nora_99-05-21.html (21 May). Accessed 2 February 2001.

Doole, Kerry (1993) Canada Crits Kiwis, *Onfilm* (April), p. 4.

Gates, David, and Devin Gordon (2001) One Ring to Lure Them All, *Newsweek* (29 January), pp. 60–61.

Glamuzina, Julie, and Laurie, Alison J. (1991) *Parker & Hulme: A Lesbian View*. Ithaca: Firebrand Books.

Gough, Bonnie (2001) Just Heavenly, in *The Way through the Clouds*, htp://heavenlycreatures.cjb.net/ Accessed 26 February 2001.

Haberman, Lia (2000), 2001: A User's Guide, www.eonliine.com/Features/Guide2001/index6.html Accessed 31 January.

Hawkins, Joan (2000) *Cutting Edge: Art-horror and the Horrific Avantgarde*. Minneapolis: University of Minnesota Press.

Helms, Michael (1993) Action Jackson, *Fangoria* (April), pp. 28–33.

Horrocks, Roger (1999) New Zealand Cinema: Cultures, Policies, Films, in Deb Verhoeven (ed.), *Twin Peeks: Australian and New Zealand Feature Films*. Melbourne: Damned Publishing, pp. 129–137.

Integrity and the B.O. (1993) Editorial *Onfilm* (April), p. 8.

New Line (2000) Press Release, www.newline.com (10 April). Accessed 3 January 2001.

Paul, William (1994) *Laughing Screaming: Modern Hollywood Horror & Comedy*. New York: Columbia University Press.

Rev. of *Braindead* (1992) dir. Peter Jackson. *Variety* (25 May), p. 51.

Rev. of *Dead Alive* (1992) dir. Peter Jackson. *House of Horrors*, www.houseofhorrors.com/deadalive.htm. Accessed 21 January 2001.

Rev. of *Dead Alive* (1992) dir. Peter Jackson. *The Hot Spot Online*, www.thehotspotonline.com/moviespot/holly/d/deadliv.htm. Accessed 22 February 2001.

Sconce, Jeffrey (1992) Programming the 'Fringe': All-Night Television and 'Psychotronic' Cinephilia, Paper presented at the Society for Cinema Studies (Pittsburgh).

Sconce, Jeffrey (1995) 'Trashing' the Academy: Taste, Excess and an Emerging Politics of Cinematic Style, *Screen*, 36 (4) (Winter), pp. 371–393.

Williams, Linda (1995) Film Bodies: Gender, Genre, and Excess, in Barry Keith Grant (ed.), *Film Genre Reader II*. Austin: University of Texas Press, pp. 140–158.

Websites

The Fourth World: The Heavenly Creatures Web Site, www.geocities.com/Hollywood/Studio/2194 (Webmaster: Adam Abrams. Dossier by assembled by John Porter), Accessed 29 January 2001.

Imladris: Lord of the Rings Movie News, www.lordoftheringsmovie.com. Accessed 10 November 2000.

Meet the Feebles, www.ween.net/feebles/. Accessed 14 February 2001.

The Way Through the Clouds, http://heavenlycreatures.cjb.net. Accessed 27 February 2001.

7

The making of a cult reputation: topicality and controversy in the critical reception of *Shivers*

Ernest Mathijs

> It will be a sad day when a too smart audience will read *Casablanca* . . .
> But that day will come. (Umbert Eco on *Casablanca*)

Introduction: cult movies and reception

Defining 'cult movies' has always been problematic. Regardless of the genuine weirdness that movies which are considered to be cult present, they also cause discomfort in the field of film studies. This is largely the result of an ambivalent approach to the analysis of cult. Traditionally, discussions of cult are troubled by a double focus on the intrinsic features of the film text *and* on the reception of cult movies, trying to analyse filmic features in order to find an answer how these features make a movie cult, while also dealing with the fact that 'cultist' features are attributed to a film through its interaction with an audience. Inevitably, this either leads to singleminded definitions of cult movies, calling them 'kind of offbeat, kind of weird, kind of strange' (Everman 1993: 1), or identifying a cult film as a film 'that has a passionate following, but does not appeal to everyone' (Cox and Jones 1990: 1), or it leads to ambiguity over what constitutes cult, the text or the context.

In an attempt to go beyond that ambiguity, this essay concentrates on the reception of cult film, and its relation to textual features. When Umberto Eco writes in his famous essay on *Casablanca* that a cult movie must 'provide a completely furnished world so that its fans can quote characters and episodes' (Eco 1986: 198), he suggests a crucial relationship between text and reception, implying that the 'world of the text' interacts with the 'quoting of characters by fans' through intertextual frames, 'stereotyped situations derived from preceding textual tradition and recorded by our encyclopedia' (Eco 1986: 200). Throughout his essay, Eco carefully elaborates on this relationship, insisting that mechanisms in the reception of *Casablanca* may help understand the features of the film. Or to put it more directly: it is essential for the understanding of cult movies to concentrate on exactly which mechanisms govern reception and how they inform the understanding of textual features.

Obviously, not all mechanisms in the relationship between text and reception are of equal importance in defining cult movies. This essay aims to isolate two important mechanisms in specific conditions, namely controversy and topicality in critical reception. Although both are assumed to be important to the reception of films as cult (as becomes apparent from the introductions to the analysis of many 'cult' films, see Mendik and Harper (2000)), they have not yet been analysed as crucial to the process of how critics label a film as cult. To demonstrate their importance, I will research the reception of a film whose discussion by critics and reviewers has undoubtedly influenced (not to say constructed) its reputation as cult, namely David Cronenberg's *Shivers* (1975). I hope thus to indicate where and how critics use the mechanisms of controversy and topicality in making a cult reputation.

In short, this paper argues that, in the particular case of Cronenberg's *Shivers*, the relationship between mechanisms of topicality and controversy in critical reception allows for a consideration of the film as 'cult'. More generally, the paper claims that relations between references to controversy and topicality constitute a framework that guides the reception of films as 'cult' by critics.

The reception of *Shivers*: controversy and topicality

Of all Cronenberg's films up until *Crash*, *Shivers* is probably the most infamous and talked about. It was Cronenberg's first widely distributed commercial feature, but it has also been the subject of several controversies, gaining both notoriety and success. In Cronenberg discourse, it serves as the starting point of the 'Cronenberg Project', the critical interpretation of his work (Haas 1996). Several critics have suggested that the reputation of *Shivers* is the result of a chain of controversies concerning the film (Collins 1996; Grant 2000). This is undoubtedly true, but there is more to it. Although controversy has played an important role as a catalyst, it is also part of, or leads to, a larger framework that regulates the reception of *Shivers*. Moreover, I argue that, in the case of *Shivers*, it is the unique relationship between controversy and topicality that forms the basis of this larger framework. In order to sketch some of the major components that make up this framework, I will focus on topicality (enabling attention for the film), and controversy and 'moral panic' (providing the opposition), but I will also briefly touch upon the mechanisms of auteurist interpretation (creating the 'oeuvre'), and symptomatic interpretation (providing the connection between text and context). I will specifically point to the extensive use of references to structure and design the critics' arguments, and to the curious mix of textual references (including canons and exemplars), seminal references (literature, philosophy), and references to culture (sex, violence) that critics use.

At first sight, the general critical opinion on *Shivers* seems unequivocal: hardly anyone likes the film. Of a selection of twenty-eight reviews from Canada, the USA, the UK, Belgium and France, sixteen are negative, and only six are positive (the rest being classified as 'neutral' in tenor). Moreover, of the sixteen negative reviews, twelve are very negative, and, of the six positive reviews, only three are very positive. Most of these reviews share the same premise and arguments. They appear during the periods when *Shivers* receives local releases, in local publications, and they attempt to evaluate *Shivers* as a film and as a cultural product (an artefact with meaning in society). In making meaning of *Shivers* as a film, most reviews employ textual references to the film itself, while also attempting to compare *Shivers* with similar films, in timing (films that are released in the same period), or in theme (films about similar subjects). These references provide critics the opportunity to like or dislike the film *as a film*, and offer material to substantiate the evaluation. In the reception of *Shivers*, most of the references to other films are introduced on the basis of topical considerations, even when they are designed to deal with the interpretation of *Shivers* as a film. For instance, two UK reviews refer to the then recent film *Towering Inferno* to accompany an argument on the closed character of the community in *Shivers*; two continental European reviews relate to the film's screening the festival of Avoriaz; two other UK reviews link it to *All the President's Men*, which was released around the same period and also carries the motive of paranoia; and several US reviews emphasize the special effects of *Shivers*, connecting it, through make-up artist Joe Blasco, with *The Lawrence Welk Show*. Although designed to comment on *Shivers* as a film, such references also topicalize the film. They link it to particular periods (the time of *Towering Inferno* and *All the President's Men*) and places of release (Avoriaz, the regions that know *The Lawrence Welk Show*), enabling the critic to address his or her specific public and, hence, make his or her review more relevant. The film thus implicitly becomes connected with regional concerns. As long as the references are restricted to serve as tools for interpreting the films as a film, they hardly contribute to a film's cultural impact.

However, when references lose their straightforward connection with the field of film, and invite comparisons with, or considerations on, the relationship between a film and culture, the impact of the film increases. The film then becomes not only topical but also relevant. Evidently, different topical concerns lead to differences in what kinds of references have cultural relevance. It is therefore necessary to analyse the critical reception of *Shivers* within its specific contexts. One such context is, for instance, the notion of 'sex' which is referred to in many *Shivers* reviews. At first instance, references to sex may seem to indicate a certain motive of the film's narrative. Yet, even reviews that do not explore the film's narrative mention it. The reason is obvious: since notions of sex will always exceed the level of textual references because of their cultural resonance, it is evident for critics to point to sexual components in *Shivers*, since it gives their reviews some cultural importance. At the same time, it enables these critics to condemn *Shivers* because it addresses problematic issues. When Vincent Canby calls the characters in *Shivers* 'sex-mad', he is not just referring to the film's narrative, he is also telling us that this film is indecent (Canby 1976).

This implies that many critics deliberately look for references that exceed their textual level, allowing them to construct links to cultural values. When these links involve cultural values around which much discordance exists, as is the case with many references in the reception of *Shivers* (and as is the case with the notion of sex), controversy appears. Like topicality, controversy is regulated by regional concerns, and, since reasons for the deliberate look for references by critics also depend on complicated circumstances, it is necessary to investigate specific instances of *Shivers*' reception to analyse the construction of its reputation. First, I will analyse *Shivers*' release in Canada, to demonstrate the particular relationship between its topicality and the controversy surrounding it. Next, I will elaborate on Robin Wood's reaction to *Shivers*, especially on his strong dismissal of the film. I will pay special attention to the relationship between controversy and topicality, and the use of references to structure symptomatic and auteurist arguments on the film's meaning. Finally, I will analyse *Shivers'* release in Belgium, to provide some insight in how the film was received in a seemingly non-topical environment.

Shivers in Canada

In Canada, *Shivers* gained instant notoriority through one preview, written by Robert Fulford, under the pseudonym Marshall Delaney. Fulford's preview was an initiative of Cronenberg and the producers of Cinepix. They hoped to create a critical climate of goodwill for their exploitation film by allowing a renowned critic to write an exclusive preview, prior to the film's release. Fulford's evaluation of *Shivers* was, however, extremely negative. Its title, 'You Should Know How Bad This Film Is. After All, You Paid For It', leaves little doubt about his view of the film. For Fulford, *Shivers* is the most repulsive, horrible film ever made. Moreover, the fact that the film was co-financed by the Canadian government, through the CFDC, makes it not only bad but also unacceptable. Other critics quickly picked up Fulford's argument. Martin Knelman, in the *Toronto Globe and Mail*, and Dane Lanken, in the *Montreal Gazette*, also published very negative reviews of the film. These reviews created a scandal, leading to parlementary questions, and making Cronenberg (who got to defend his film in the *Montreal Gazette*) a celebrity. In spite of, or thanks to, the commotion *Shivers* quickly became Canada's most successful picture. This success, in turn, generated even more media attention.

The many references to the circumstances surrounding the production and release of *Shivers* (CFDC, financial support and economic success) that dominate these debates are perfect examples of topicalization. Through their use within an argument which initially addresses the film, but rapidly exceeding that level to address the structure of government funding in relation to morally discordant issues, they connect *Shivers* with prior discussions on state funding, and on the *raison d'être* of government support for films that depict sexuality and violence. As a result, they create a controversy, and attribute to *Shivers* an importance it would not have assumed under other circumstances.

Opposing and topicalizing *Shivers* may make it important, but it does not make it a cult film. This also requires using the contextual 'controversial references' on a textual level as well. Such a use is provided by the remarkable reception of *Shivers* in the Canadian film press. Several general film publications, including *Séquences* and *Motion*, published negative reviews of *Shivers*, confirming the negative reception in the general press, but with other arguments. *Shivers* is disapproved of not because of its immorality but because it is a horror film, and does not fit the framework of Canadian film. The genre of the horror movie, and the slasher – or splatter movie in particular, are thought to be American or European. They are dealt with through specific arguments, devised for foreign films, which are very difficult to combine with a consideration of the film as Canadian. The result is that many Canadian film critics tend to dismiss *Shivers* on grounds of its incompatibility with Canadian film (Dowler 1985). Only one Canadian film publication offers an exception to this. In *Cinema Canada*, *Shivers* is enthusiastically received and lauded as a contemporary masterpiece of horror. *Cinema Canada* devotes three articles to the release of *Shivers*. The first is an elaborate essay by Steven Chesley, including an interview with Cronenberg. The second is an open letter from one of *Shivers*' producers, André Link. The third is a review in the regular review section, by Nathalie Edwards. Link's letter contains his reaction to the negative review of Fulford. Though obviously biased, Link interestingly defends *Shivers* by remarking that Fulford's attack on both the film and the CFDC is a typical 'attitude of super criticism of all things Canadian' (Link 1975). For Link, *Shivers* is as Canadian as any other movie from Canada, deserving topical consideration *as a film*, instead of controversy as an example of inappropriate government funding. The articles of Edwards and Chesley contain similar arguments. Moreover, they also include the connection between the text and its reception in their comments. They both mention the Fulford attack, and at the same time emphasize the importance of considering *Shivers* as a film, devoting much space to arguments on the camerawork, editing, sound and, especially, special effects. That *Shivers* is a horror movie (supposedly unacceptable, and not fitting in Canadian film) seems to have no relevance for their opinion. On the contrary, Chesley employs auteurist techniques to show that the film created 'moral panic' because it deals with fundamental issues of culture. As an example, Chesley connects the horror and the controversy with more metaphysical arguments by quoting Cronenberg: '"The true subject of horror films" says David Cronenberg, "is death and anticipation of death, and that leads to the question of man as body as opposed to man as spirit". That's one of the most important aspects underlying Cronenberg's *The Parasite Murders*' (Chesley 1975). Throughout their articles Edwards and Chesley use many such auteurist arguments to identify the form and content of *Shivers* as filmic mediations of personal concerns. That such concerns may have cultural impact does not mean that the film is less a film. While suggesting that critics who concentrated on the cultural role of *Shivers* were unable to understand its true meaning, Edwards and Chesley also connect the contextual references to a textual level, thus placing Cronenberg's 'vision' at the centre of their interpretation.

This practice is not untypical for *Cinema Canada* at the time. Founded by the Canadian Society of Cinematographers in 1972, *Cinema Canada* had been trying to become both a trade paper and a critical reflection on the business. By the middle of the 1970s (at the same time when Cronenberg made his commercial debut) *Cinema Canada* had established itself as a defender of Canadian film as film, and a promotor of innovative film form and content (including genre film). This context not only facilitates an appreciation of *Shivers*; it also makes possible an auteurist interpretation of the themes and motives. The initial negative reports on the film probably only intensified the urge to defend it. It is just this mix of topicality, controversy, and appraisal and auteurist interpretation that got the film its cult reputation in Canada. By linking the controversial aspects of *Shivers* to the intention of the author, the *Cinema Canada* critics succeed in securing *Shivers* a place as an 'fascinating film' even when the initial topicality has been long gone, thus ensuring it a cult reputation (Yacowar 1977; MacMillan 1981; Harkness 1981, 1983).

Shivers and Robin Wood: critical topicality

The reception of *Shivers* in most other countries shows striking similarities with that in Canada. There is an initial dismissal, followed by reconsiderations that use topical references (as well as references to the reception of the film in Canada) as arguments on a textual

level. This strategy does not necessarily require a positive evaluation, but it does need topicality. When this topicality is not achieved
on a regional basis, as is the case with many reviews that appear in
internationally distributed magazines, or with festival reviews, *Shivers* is often connected to arguments on the philosophical discussions
of culture, serving as an example of cultural tendencies. In other
words, whenever regional topicality is unattainable, it is replaced by
'critical topicality', by viewing the film in function of internationally
relevant developments in discussing culture (and film).

A notorious example of this line of reasoning, and one that unintentionally strengthens the identification of *Shivers* as cult, is Robin
Wood's discussion of the film. Wood views *Shivers* in August 1975,
when the film is shown at the film festival of Edinburgh. In a festival
review for *Film Comment*, he mentions the film as part of a series of
exploitation films shown at the festival. He writes:

> The most striking of this year's batch of exploitation movies, by virtue
> of its detestability, was David Cronenberg's *The Parasite Murders* [the
> original name for *Shivers*]. Its derivation is from *Invasion of the Body
> Snatchers* via *Night of the Living Dead*, but the source of its intensity
> is quite distinct: all the horror is based on extreme sexual disgust.
> (Wood 1975 : 26)

Wood initially discusses the film on a textual level, but quickly
exceeds that level to condemn the functions of sexuality that *Shivers*
displays, unfolding his opinion through a mix of references on a textual level (dealing with the film) and topical references to discordant
cultural issues (creating controversy). Likewise, he questions the
motives of the director, especially with regard to the ending, in
which the residents of the appartment building set out to infect the
rest of the world with the parasite, hoping to show that a film with
a 'detestable' attitude towards culture is also a bad film. The topical
background against which this mix of references is situated is not
regional, but 'critical'. By suggesting that *Shivers* is a film that tries
to set back recent cultural achievements (such as feminism, and
sexual liberation), Wood is able to formulate an argument on the
'reactionary' nature and anxieties of horror films from a cultural
perspective, thus legitimizing his connection between films and culture, and reducing *Shivers* to an example of 'detestable' cultural
practices (Wood 1978a, 1978b, 1979a). Significantly, when Wood
returns to *Shivers* in later essays it is always in function of his dis-

cussion of a new framework of criticism. The implicit rhetoric in his Edinburgh review becomes much more explicit in these later arguments. As Wood writes:

> David Cronenberg's *Shivers* (formerly *The Parasite Murders*) is, indeed, of very special interest here, as it is a film single-mindedly about sexual liberation, a prospect it views with unmitigated horror. The entire film is premised on and motivated by sexual disgust. (Wood 1979a: 24)

And further on:

> *Shivers* systematically chronicles the breaking of every sexual-social taboo – promiscuity, lesbianism, homosexuality, age difference, finally incest – but each step is presented as merely one more addition to the accumulation of horror. (Wood 1979a: 24)

These characteristics of *Shivers* are already visible in the Edinburgh review, where their topicality is fuelled by Wood's struggle with the 'Marxist-Freudian' framework (Wood 1976). After he adopts the new critical framework (Wood 1978c), he can reformulate his argument, and show a connection between *Shivers* and contemporary culture, thus grounding his negative evaluation of the film.

There is, however, something odd in Wood's review. Throughout his discussion, Wood employs the same mechanisms of topicality (critical instead of regional) and controversy as the *Cinema Canada* critics in his effort to make his references work on a textual level. Unlike those critics, however, he neglects the reception of *Shivers*, and refuses to call it a cult film. Yet, unintentionally, the matter of reception does appear, even contradicting Wood's evaluation and attributing some positive features to Shivers. Wood's major references are *Invasion of the Body Snatchers* and *Night of the Living Dead*, which already have a cult reputation as canons of the new horror film. By referring to them, even in an attempt to make a negative comparison, Wood invites readers to place *Shivers* within the same tradition, unwillingly attributing to the film some of the qualities these films have (see his use of 'intensity'). He thus solicits his readers to draw extratextual connections between them and *Shivers*, finally allowing them to see *Shivers* as a cult film.

This implication becomes even more clear when Wood's use of the two references is compared to other reviews: most reviews containing references to *Night of the Living Dead* and *Invasion of the Body Snatchers* are far more positive and, importantly, all acknowledge their reception. Charles Leayman writes in *Cinéfantastique* that *Shivers* can be regarded as a trip through 'the historical evolution of the horror film genre as an art form' (Leayman 1976: 23). Leayman elaborates on the structural similarities between *Shivers* and *Invasion of the Body Snatchers*, and he mentions *Night of the Living Dead* (along with *Le Boucher* and *Repulsion*) as references making possible a consideration of *Shivers* as true horror art. In a 1977 reappraisal of *Shivers* in *Cinema Canada*, Maurice Yacowar is even more direct, including an argument on the relationship between *Shivers* and critical reception:

> Cronenberg's film has suffered the same critical disdain that was accorded *Psycho*, *Night of the Living Dead*, *Invasion of the Body Snatchers*. Perhaps serious art in the horror genre must expect to be reviled before it is understood. *Shivers* (by whatever name) will join those classics. If Cronenberg continues to grow this film will rank with *Psycho* as a personal statement. At the very least it will rank with those other two films, as a powerful expression of an anxiety of its day, so deep it hurts. (Yacowar 1977: 55)

Through references to *Psycho*, *Invasion of the Body Snatchers* and *Night of the Living Dead*, Yacowar creates the impression not only that *Shivers* deserves a place among the masterworks of horror (including a reputation as cult), but also that it exceeds particular topicalities (regional or critical). Yacowar's and Leayman's conclusions are as symptomatic as Wood's, but their familiarity with both the reception of the horror genre and Cronenberg's prior reception in Canada allows them to consolidate their argument. Even Wood finally realizes this. When he reformulates his attack on *Shivers*, in the *American Horror* essay, the reference to *Night of the Living Dead* has disappeared, a logical conclusion of Wood's opinion on that film as an example of progressive horror (Wood 1979b). In conclusion, Wood's review shows that the matter of reception not only affects the whole of the film but is also present within specific references, providing much support for the reputation of *Shivers* as cult.

Shivers in Belgium

As the Canadian reception and Wood's criticism show, creating a cult reputation depends heavily upon topicality, and the ability to create (or suggest) a connection between text and context. But even when topical interests are not (yet) available, films can receive cult reputations. *Shivers*' reception in Belgium provides an interesting example hereof. Since the lack of topicality makes it virtually impossible to create opposition (and controversy), Belgian critics force their own frames of reference upon the film. These are largely textual, having no consequences for the film's reputation. In one very important case, however, *Shivers* is forcibly linked with critical topics, and seen as instigation for a new critical practice. This makes the Belgian cult reputation of *Shivers* not just a case of personal critical opinions, but also one of competing kinds of criticism. More importantly, it also demonstrates to what extent cult reputations can be *created* instead of observed.

The initial reception of *Shivers* in Belgium is very negative. Critics quickly dismiss the film as weekday exploitation, not worth much consideration, and without any topical relevance. John Rijpens's review of the film in the weekly magazine *Knack* is typical (Rijpens 1976). The review supposedly deals with *Shivers*' release in Antwerp, but the few arguments it carries are based upon the Avoriaz festival screening. Apparently, Rijpens wrote his review after seeing the film in Avoriaz, and did not make any effort to link it to its Belgian release. Rijpens's major references are to *The Bed Sitting-Room* and *The Final Programme* which were also shown in Avoriaz. Even references to the film's theme are linked with Avoriaz. Rijpens draws attention to *Shivers*' display of sexuality and horror, calling it 'odious' and 'repulsive', like the rest of the 'harvest' of Avoriaz 1976. Other reviews, dealing with the Brussels release, also base their rejection of *Shivers* on the motives of sexuality and horror, without connecting it with local topics.

The only review that tries to go from the textual level to constructing links to discordant cultural values is written by Marc Holthof, and published in the catholic monthly *Film & Televisie*, the most important Flemish film journal. Holthof starts his argument on a textual level. By referring to Cronenberg's previous avant-garde films, he suggests that his work is not restricted to the horror genre. He then considers *Shivers* as a film that transcends its genre, not only depicting horror but also being *about* horror. Holthof writes: 'Cronenberg did not just try to make a film, but has concealed his message in a commercial form. The average viewer will perhaps not notice this, because the film is a very subtle play with the values of the horror film' (Holthof 1976: 36, my translation). This remark operates in two ways. First, it enables Holthof to deal with the film's textual qualities. As a horror film, Holthof links *Shivers* to *Night of the Living Dead*, *Invasion of the Body Snatchers* and *Psycho*, thus placing the film firmly within the canon of modern horror, and also hinting at the cult reputation these films have. Holthof even offers extensive arguments for this. *Shivers*' plot is compared with that of *Night of the Living Dead* and *Invasion of the Body Snatchers*, and Barbara Steele's bath tub scene is considered to be a playful variation on the shower scene in *Psycho*. Second, as a film about horror, Holthof discovers several cues in *Shivers* that deal with horrific values. The theme of sexuality, which has led many critics to reject *Shivers* is, in Holthof's opinion, not mere exploitation but rather a philosophical investigation of the basic elements of the horror tale. Similarly, *Shivers* consciously deals with the antagonistic characteristics of monstrosity in a way different from other horror films. Holthof explains:

> A regular horror film confronts us with horrible alien creatures . . .: our horror is justified, because the monster is invariably 'a bad object'. Cronenberg has cleverly exploited this rule, and has turned its values around: . . . our horror concerns positively a monster, but a very dubious one, since it represents our sexuality. (Holthof 1976: 37, my translation)

For Holthof, the thematic ambiguity of *Shivers*, which he even briefly links with the writings of Wilhelm Reich, makes it an interesting film. The fact that it occurs within a horror exploitation film, at the same time complying and criticizing its genre, both an example of and a reflection upon modern horror, makes it a cult film.

Importantly, Holthof also offers references to the reception of *Shivers*, by mentioning (and emphasizing) the conditions under which he viewed the film. Contrary to other Belgian critics, Holthof's review explicitly links *Shivers* to its screening at the Edinburgh festival instead of the Avoriaz festival. The reference is not incidental: Holthof relied upon the Edinburgh screening (and the information he got there) for his review (Mathijs 1999). As he himself acknowledges, his argument on *Shivers* is heavily influenced by that information and those conditions. Through the reference to Edinburgh, Holthof invites a series of contextual considerations into his argument, concerning both genre and film criticism in general.

Around 1975, the Edinburgh Film Festival tried to distinguish itself from other festivals by trying to combine screenings of contemporary genre films from new directors with treatments of critical issues surrounding those screenings (Wood 1975; Mathijs 1999). While Avoriaz championed films that respected generic boundaries, Edinburgh and its critics favoured films that both complied *and* transcended these limits, operating on intertextual levels. By mentioning this difference, Holthof consolidates his argument, and links it to a critical topicality, making his opinion on *Shivers* relevant. At the same time, his view on *Shivers* becomes symptomatic for a certain kind of thought, influenced by *Screen* and post-structural criticism.

At the time of his *Shivers* review, this topicality is only hinted at. But when Holthof is involved in the start of a new film society, Andere Film, accompanied by a new journal, *Andere Sinema*, in 1978, the relevance of *Shivers* is explicitly acknowledged in several articles that deal with the importance of 'off-Hollywood' genre films, and with the cultural implications of horror films. On 23 March 1979, International Film, a distributor associated with Andere Film, even organizes a special screening of *Shivers* in a small festival (Anon. 1979: 42). Other films that get special releases through International Film include *Night of the Living Dead* and *Eraserhead*. Finally, in 1980, Cronenberg's and *Shivers*' importance for the critical viewpoint of *Andere Sinema* is celebrated in three articles. In the first article Holthof presents an overview of independent 'off-Hollywood' film production (Holthof 1980a). He specifically points to the cultural relevance of such films for the evolution of cinema. Cronenberg is only implicitly mentioned in this article. In two follow-up essays, however, *Shivers* is prominently forwarded as a film that proves the necessity of critical techniques that deal with the relationship between film and culture. According to Holthof, the film shows the topical relevance of modern horror. He writes that 'not only the notion of "good taste" is perverted by horror films; they also unsettle the social order that governs these norms' (Holthof 1980b: 14, my translation).

Through this consideration, Holthof reactivates the implications he only suggested when writing his *Shivers* review. In retrospect, it underlines the importance of his mix of textual and contextual references, and its connection with topicality and reception. Together, these articles place *Shivers* (among other films) at the centre of a topical argument about the future and function of film criticism.

Through this discussion, which, from time to time, still dominates Flemish film criticism, *Shivers* eventually receives critical topicality, leading to its Belgian cult reputation.

Conclusion: critical reception and cult reputations

Throughout my argumentation, the importance of the connection between critics and the film they are reviewing has remained in the background. However, as the case studies show, there appears to be a correlation between the positions critics occupy and their opinion on *Shivers*. In Canada, *Cinema Canada* defended *Shivers* because it allowed them to counter the moral panic surrounding the meaning and financial support of *Shivers*, and carve a space for their own approach. Internationally, *Cinéfantastique* favoured *Shivers* as an example of a genre whose popularity they supported (Clarke 1981). *Film Comment* used Wood's review of the film to take position in recent critical debates. Even if Wood's evaluation of *Shivers* was not positive, his review still strengthened the film's cult reputation. In Belgium, Marc Holthof's review of *Shivers* preluded the new critical viewpoints of *Andere Sinema*. The cult reputation of *Shivers*, then, seems to be at least partially influenced by critical stances. The fact that *Shivers* allowed connections between textual levels and discordant issues in culture enabled critics to create controversy, and made it possible for them to identify themselves against a topical opposition (regional or critical), convincing the critical community of their commitment to good film. By helping *Shivers* receive a cult reputation, these critics secured their own relevance.

The most important conclusion to draw from this is that topicality and controversy are crucial mechanisms in the creation of cult in critical reception. Topicality allows textual references to play a contextual role, and by picking out references that have controversial potential (discordant resonance in culture), critics knowingly (*Cinema Canada*, Holthof) or unwillingly (Wood) use different kinds of topicality (regional and critical) and explicit and implicit references to reception within their arguments to create a cult reputation. This observation permits discussions of cult to move beyond the narrow 'text or context' distinction in considering cult movies, and provide arguments for the ways in which topicality and controversy operate as frames of intertextuality, as Eco calls them (Eco 1986: 200). Evidently, this does not settle the issue of what constitutes cult once and for all. It can, however, improve an understanding of the way cult movies work, as texts *and* with audiences.

Appendix: review corpus

Viviani, Christian (1975) The Parasite Murders, *Positif* 171–172 (July–August), p. 68.

Delaney, Marshall (1975) You Should Know How Bad This Film Is. After All, You Paid For It, *Saturday Night* (September), pp. 83–85.

Knelman, Martin (1975) Parasite Murders, *Toronto Globe and Mail* (11 October).

Lanken, Dane (1975) The Parasite Murders Is Horrible, *Montreal Gazette* (11 October), p. 19.

Lanken, Dane (1975) Writer-Director David Cronenberg Protests the Maniac Tag, *Montreal Gazette* (11 October), p. 19.

Chesley, Steven (1975) It'll Bug You, *Cinema Canada* 22 (October), pp. 22–25.

Link, André (1975) Delaney's Dreary Denegration, *Cinema Canada* 22 (October), p. 24.

Edwards, Natalie (1975) The Parasite Murders, *Cinema Canada* 22 (October), pp. 44–45.

Wood, Robin (1975) New Cinema at Edinburgh, *Film Comment* 11 (6) (November–December), p. 26.

Schupp, Patrick (1976) Frissons, *Séquences* 83 (January), p. 35.

Jackson, Frank (1976a) They Came From Within, *Cinéfantastique* 5 (1), p. 33.

Jackson, Frank (1976b) Parasite Murders, *New Canadian Film* 7 (3–4) (February–March), pp. 33–34.

Shuster, Nat (1976) Shivers, *Motion* 5 (3), pp. 47–48.

Combs, Richard (1976) Shivers, *Monthly Film Bulletin* 43 (506) (March), p. 62.

Sachs, Loyd (1976) They Came from Within, *Variety* 282 (7) (24 March), p. 21.

Leayman, Charles (1976a) They Came from Within, *Cinéfantastique* 5 (3), pp. 22–23.

Leayman, Charles (1976b) Shivers, *The New Statesman* (30 April).

Leayman, Charles (1976c) Shivers, *Sight and Sound* 45 (2), p. 132.

Whitman, Marc (1976) Shivers, *Films Illustrated* 5 (57) (May), p. 330.

Davies, Russell (1976) Superstar Newsmen (incl. rev. of Shivers), *The Observer Review* (2 May), p. 28.

Rijpens, John (1976) The Parasite Killers, *Knack Magazine* (5 May).

Rijpens, John (1976) Frissons (The Parasite Murders), *La Libre Belgique* (15 June).

G., M. (1976) Frissons, *Le Soir* (16 June).

Canby, Vincent (1976) They Came from Within, *New York Times* (7 July), p. 46:4.

Grisolia, Michel (1976) Frissons, *Le Nouvel Observateur* (5 July), p. 11.

Holthof, Marc (1976) Shivers, *Film en Televisie* 230–231 (July–August), pp. 36–37.

Braucourt, Guy (1976) Frissons (Parasite Murders), *Écran* 50 (15 September), pp. 63–64.

Runnells, R. (1977) How Awful is Awful?, *Motion* 6 (3), p. 43.

References

The references also repeat *Shivers* reviews quoted in the text

Anon. (1977) The Night Attila Met the Anti-Christ, She was Schlocked and He was Outraged, *Toronto Globe and Mail* (14 May), p. 6.

Anon. (1979) Festival Programma, *Andere Sinema* 7 (March) p. 42.

Canby, Vincent (1976) They Came from Within, *New York Times* (7 July), p. 46:4.

Chesley, Steven (1975) It'll Bug You, *Cinema Canada* 22 (October), pp. 22-25.

Chute, David (1980) He Came from Within, *Film Comment* 16 (2) (March–April), pp. 36–39, 42.

Clarke, Frederick (1981) Editorial, *Cinéfantastique* 10 (4) (Spring), p. 3.

Collins, Michael (1996) Medicine, Lust, Surrealism, and Death: Three Early Films by David Cronenberg, *Post Script* 15 (2) (Winter–Spring), pp. 62–69.

Cox, Alex and Jones, Nick (1990) *Moviedrome: The Guide*. London: BSS.

Dowler, Andrew (1985) Canadian Gothic, eh? A Glib Overview of Current Schlock, *Cinema Canada* 123 (October), pp. 16–18.

Duynslaegher, Patrick (1983) Griezelnachten, *Knack Weekend* (1 December), p. 67.

Eco, Umberto (1986). *Travels in Hyperreality*. London: Picador.

Everman, Welch (1993) *Cult Horror Films*. New York: Citadel Press.

Grant, Michael (1998) Crimes of the Future; on Crash, *Screen* 39 (2) (Summer), pp. 180–185.

Grant, Michael (2000) Introduction, in *The Modern Fantastic: The Films of David Cronenberg*. London: Flicks Books.

Haas, Robert (1996) The Cronenberg Project: Literature, Science, Psychology, and the Monster in Cinema, *Post Script* 15 (2) (Winter–Spring), pp. 3–10.

Harkness, John (1981) David Cronenberg: Brilliantly Bizarre, *Cinema Canada* 72 (March), pp. 8–17.

Harkness, John (1983) The Word, the Flesh and the Films of David Cronenberg, *Cinema Canada* 97 (June), pp. 23–25.

Holthof, Marc (1976) Shivers, *Film en Televisie* 230–231 (July–August), pp. 36–37.

Holthof, Marc (1980a) Off-Hollywood, *Andere Sinema* 18 (March), pp. 24–31.

Holthof, Marc (1980b) It's Alive, *Andere Sinema* 21 (September), pp. 14–17.

Leayman, Charles (1976) They Came from Within, *Cinéfantastique* 5 (3), p. 23.

Link, André (1975) Delaney's Dreary Denegration, *Cinema Canada* 22 (October), p. 24.

MacMillan, Robert (1981) Shivers . . . Makes Your Flesh Creep!, *Cinema Canada* 72 (March), pp. 11–15.

Martin, Robert (1976) A Canadian Movie Wins at Box Office with a Bloody Tale of Wormy Parasites, *Toronto Globe and Mail* (29 June), p. 29.

Masson, Alex (1994) David Cronenberg: de chair et de sexe, *Première* 213, p. 113.

Mathijs, Ernest (1993) Moraliteit en hedendaagse film: David Cronenberg, *Nieuw Tijdschrift van de VUB* 6 (3), pp. 201–212.

Mathijs, Ernest (1998) David Cronenberg en de horrorfilm, *Nieuw Tijdschrift van de VUB* 11 (special issue) (February), pp. 92–106.

Mathijs, Ernest (1999), Interview with Marc Holthof (23 August 1999 and 24 August 1999), unpublished.

Mendik, Xavier, and Harper, Graeme (eds) (2000). *Unruly Pleasures: The Cult Film and Its Critics*. Guilford: FAB Press.

Moriconi, Martine (1992) Les débuts de Cronenberg, *Studio Magazine* 92 (November).

Portman, Jamie (1976) 'Shivers' Generates Industry Shock Waves, *Ottawa Citizen* (18 March), p. 74.

Renault, G. (1994) Frissons, *Libération* (21 December), p. 46

Rijpens, John (1976) The Parasite Killers, *Knack Magazine* (5 May).

Shuster, Nat (1977) Canadian Filmview, *Motion* 6 (4–5), p. 15.

Wood, Robin (1975) New Cinema at Edinburgh, *Film Comment* 11 (6) (November–December), p. 26.

Wood, Robin (1976). *Personal Views: Explorations in Film*. London: Gordon Fraser.

Wood, Robin (1978a) Return of the Repressed, *Film Comment* 14 (4) (July–August), pp. 24–32.

Wood, Robin (1978b) Gods and Monsters, *Film Comment* 14 (5) (September–October), pp. 19–25.

Wood, Robin (1978c). Responsibilities of a Gay Film Critic, *Film Comment* 14 (1) (January–February), pp. 12–17.

Wood, Robin (1979a) An Introduction to the American Horror Film, in

Andrew Britton, Robin Wood *et al.* (eds.) *The American Nightmare: Essays on the Horror Film*. Toronto: Festival of Festivals, pp. 14–23.

Wood, Robin (1979b) Apocalypse Now: Notes on the Living Dead, in Andrew Britton, Robin Wood *et al.* (eds.) *The American Nightmare: Essays on the Horror Film*. Toronto: Festival of Festivals, pp. 91–97.

Yacowar, Maurice (1977) You Shiver Because It's Good, *Cinema Canada* 34/35 (February), pp. 54–55.

8

The Argento effect

Peter Hutchings

One of the problems in dealing with film and television programmes in terms of their cult status lies in defining precisely what 'cult' means in such a context. Does it simply refer to a congregation of fans or enthusiasts around particular cultural texts, or is there a cult quality within the texts themselves, some property that encourages or facilitates an audience's cultish devotion? Or is it a mixture of the two, the textual and the extratextual, and, if so, what exactly is the relationship between them? Perhaps the main difficulty in pinning down the location of 'cultness' derives from the extraordinary variety of films and television programmes that have acquired cult status over the years, with cultness itself appearing to cut across national borders, traditional generic boundaries and long-established divisions between high and low/mass culture.

This sense of cultness as a kind of moveable feast, as something not bound by traditional cultural categories and hierarchies, is probably what has made it so exciting for fans and, more recently, academics, with both of these groups welcoming the opportunity to 'escape' from the restrictive confines of a normative mainstream culture. Not only does there seem to be a potential here for forging an oppositional politics, for creating forms of cultural resistance to society's dominant values, but there are also possibilities for constructing new communities, for dialogue between erstwhile separated social groups (fans and academics, for instance). The vagueness around what precisely a cult object is has proved very useful in this respect inasmuch as it has permitted the linking together of an array of cultural objects between which otherwise there is no obvious connection. But at the same time that vagueness has arguably vitiated an approach to culture based on notions of cult. Too often it has obscured the specificity of localized 'cult' responses to particular objects in favour of constructing a broader picture of cultural resistance and transgression.

This chapter takes as its subject the responses to the work of Italian horror and thriller film director Dario Argento generated both by fans and by critics, with a particular emphasis on British responses. Argento himself is often presented in fan and critical discourses as someone whose films possess cult status, and in part what I want to do here is consider what such a designation actually means in his particular case. But I also want to see how Argento's films, and the responses to them, relate (if at all) to broader notions of cultness. How useful is 'cult' not only as a way of addressing what is distinctive about Argento but also as an approach to culture generally?

The Argento phenomenon

After a stint as a film critic and a screenwriter (most notably, working with Bernardo Bertolucci on the screenplay for Sergio Leone's classic Italian western *Once Upon a Time in the West*), Dario Argento became a film director in 1970. His first three films, subsequently dubbed 'the animal trilogy' by Argento aficionados, were all psychological thrillers – *L'uccello dalle piume di cristallo* (*The Bird with the Crystal Plumage*, 1970), *Il gatto a nove code* (*Cat o' Nine Tails*, 1971) and *Quattro mosche di velluto grigio* (*Four Flies on Grey Velvet*, 1971). Italian post war genre cinema has often been seen as an imitative cinema, one that reworks predominantly American generic conventions within an Italian context. This is most visibly the case with the spaghetti western but other genres too often looked to American successes for their inspiration. Within this context, Argento's early films were initially seen by British and American critics as spaghetti thrillers, and in particular the work of 'the Italian Hitchcock'. (The term 'Italian Hitchcock' still features in contemporary fan writings on Argento, although very little attempt is made to link Argento's films with those directed by Hitchcock in either thematic or stylistic terms.) As one British critic put it in his review of *L'uccello dalle piume di cristallo*:

> this murder mystery . . . is developed more or less in the classic Hollywood tradition and is all the better for it. Repeated flashbacks to the crucial scene provide ample opportunity for audience participation in true Hitchcock manner, and Dario Argento's direction is well paced

throughout, if occasionally a little overwrought. (*Monthly Film Bulletin*, November 1970: 234)

The extent to which these 'copies' of US originals were inferior precisely because of their imitative nature has preoccupied critical writings on the Italian western, with an increasing tendency there to see these films as both possessing a distinctive national (i.e. Italian) character of their own and having an important place in the history of the western in general (see in particular Frayling 1981). Kim Newman has argued that this is also the case for a wide range of other genres and cycles, including 'horror films, murder mysteries, science fiction movies, superspy thrillers and jungle adventures'. He argues that 'while it is undoubtedly true that many Italian genre films are simply worthless carbon copies with a few baroque trimmings, the best examples of most cycles are surprisingly sophisticated mixes of imitation, pastiche, parody, deconstruction, reinterpretation and operatic inflation' (Newman 1986: 20).

So far as Argento is concerned, it is interesting that some of the early British and American reviews of his first three thrillers noted their derivative nature but also registered their difference from the US 'originals', with particular reference to the films' deployment of spectacle. This is already apparent in the review of *L'uccello dalle piume di cristallo* cited above, with its description of Argento's directorial style as 'a little overwrought'. British and American reviews of *Il gatto a nove code* and *Quattro mosche di velluto grigio* on their original release also remarked upon an increasing reliance on set-pieces and an accompanying diminution of narrative coherence and drive. In a British review of *Suspiria* (1977), Argento's first horror film, Scott Meek summed up Argento's career at that point:

> Ever since *The Bird with the Crystal Plumage* in 1970, Dario Argento's thrillers have been moving away from conventional narrative with plots of increasing absurdity, often full of red herrings that gratify the director's delight in stylistic excess. Similarly, his endings have necessarily become more and more arbitrary, climaxing a series of elaborate set-pieces rather than resolving plot and character. (Meek 1977: 215–16)[1]

Suspiria is significant not only as Argento's first and only major international success at the box office; it also marked the last moment in his career when his films would be widely distributed outside Italy. *Profondo Rosso* (1975), the thriller he made in between

Quattro mosche di velluto and *Suspiria*, received no British cinema release at all and only a patchy release in the United States under the misleading title *The Hatchet Murders*. (Only one of *Profondo Rosso*'s numerous murders actually involves a hatchet.) *Inferno* (1980), Argento's horror follow-up to *Suspiria*, was barely released at all in either America or Britain. *Tenebre* (*Tenebrae*, 1982) – Argento's return to the thriller format – had a brief release in Britain on a double bill with William Friedkin's controversial *Cruising* and appeared briefly in America under the enigmatic title *Unsane*. Subsequent Argento films have been even harder to see, especially in Britain, where the draconian censorship regime inaugurated by the Video Recordings Act of 1984 proved especially hostile to the ultra-violent spectacle upon which Argento's work has increasingly relied. Uncut versions of *Opera* (*Terror at the Opera*, 1987) and *La sindrome di Stendahl* (*The Stendahl Syndrome*, 1996) are, at the time of writing at least, still not legally available in Britain. The vagaries of film distribution in the 1980s and 1990s have not helped matters in this respect, with English-language versions of both *Profondo Rosso* and *Phenomena* (1985) featuring extensive cuts – up to twenty minutes in each case – that relate mainly to story material rather than to scenes of violence and which do not appear to have been made for reasons of censorship.

More recently, the non-availability of Argento's films has been ameliorated by the appearance on DVD and video of complete or near-complete versions. The fact that, thanks to the internet and multi-region DVD players, it is now possible to order such material from abroad and thereby circumvent local censorship restrictions has made it easier than ever before to assemble the complete Argento canon. The interesting thing here is that this material is largely being packaged and marketed around the assumption that Argento's name is already known to the people who will be buying the product (for example, Platinum Media's 'The Dario Argento Collection' on DVD). Given that mainstream film criticism, especially in its journalistic form, has shown little or no interest in Argento's work since the 1970s, it seems clear that this perception that there is a market for Argento relates to, and is itself part of, the development of a particular fan-based following for Italian horror cinema generally throughout the 1980s and 1990s. Similarly, recent publications on Italian horror cinema – most notably the very glossy and extensively illustrated monographs on directors Ruggero

Deodato, Lucio Fulci and Argento himself that have been produced by the British publisher FAB Press – point to the existence of a market niche for what had previously been marginal, illicit and unofficial fan-based activity (see Fenton, Grainger and Castoldi 1999; Thrower 1999; and Gallant, ed., 2000).

The critical and fan response to Argento

During the 1980s and 1990s, Argento fandom tended to be based on the obtaining (usually from other fans) of video versions of otherwise hard-to-see Argento films, with these samizdat third- or fourth-generation copies, sometimes with Dutch or Japanese subtitles, offering the opportunity to view the elusive uncut versions denied to the market by either censors or distributors. (In Britain a few repertory cinemas – notably the Scala in London – also showed this material on the big screen.) Fanzines and other fan-orientated publications in the 1980s and 1990s were similarly preoccupied with what might be termed 'the uncut Argento' and with identifying what had been left out of commercially available versions of his films.[2] In Britain this concern with the depredations of censorship was, and continues to be, intertwined with a critique of the state-imposed censorship embodied in the Video Recordings Act. An early 1990s publicity flyer from Vipco (a British video company that focused its marketing attentions primarily on horror fans), announcing its reissue of a number of video titles that had vanished from distribution at the time of the Video Recordings Act or had been prosecuted under it, made clear what was at stake here. 'In 1984 Big Brother wouldn't let you watch them!' the flyer announced. 'Now it's your decision!' Other than marking some of the forthcoming titles as 'Previously Prosecuted', the flyer does not explicitly reference the Video Recordings Act (which, usefully for the anti-censorship cause, just happened to become law in a year firmly associated with the triumph of totalitarianism); it just assumes that the potential customers reading the flyer will know about it and, more importantly, be against it. As is so often the case in cult culture, an us/them opposition is set up, where 'us' comprises the freedom-seekers demanding the right to see forbidden material, and 'them' the forbidders or disapprovers, here the State, 'Big Brother', but elsewhere the mainstream audience and the censorious, socially conformist values it is deemed to support. Or, as one British Argento internet site recently put it, 'Let's put an end to film censorship and let the adult viewer decide' (*Dario Argento: Master of the Macabre*).

This fannish interest in Argento was part of a broader fascination with Italian horror films evident during the 1980s and 1990s. Like Argento's films, many of these Italian horrors suffered especially badly at the hands of the British censors and thereby, within the context of British culture at least, acquired the marginal status which has been seen by some as a necessary precondition of cultdom. However, cultural marginality in itself is not enough to ensure cult status; not all marginal objects are cult objects. It is also worth remembering here that Argento's marginality has a national specificity to it, relating as it does to the relative inaccessibility (until recently) of both his films and other Italian horror films within particular English-speaking markets. Once one acknowledges this, it then follows that there might be other places where Argento is not so marginal – notably Italy where he appears to be a more mainstream figure whose films attract relatively high budgets and boast the sort of production values associated with 'quality' cinema.

So why did Argento's films acquire a cult following?

As noted above, defining 'cult cinema' is not easy. However, certain ideas about what cult status might entail do recur in various writings on cult. Although these ideas should not be linked together as a composite definition of cultness, an appraisal of them can give a sense of some of the issues at stake here, and especially the way in which cult cinema is often seen in some way or other as separate from the commercial mainstream. A point often made is that cult films are excessive. They offer scenes of spectacle that exceed any narrative function and which go beyond the scenes of licensed or permitted excess found in the mainstream. Or their subject matter, or their treatment of that subject matter, is perceived as excessive, breaching conventional notions of good taste or what is permitted in the mainstream. Often connected with this is a sense of the potential for transgression in cult; cult films transgress and offer a challenge to norms, whether these be the aesthetic norms of commercial mainstream filmmaking or broader social and ideological norms. Cult films also tend to be seen as marginal – in terms of their location within critically disreputable genres such as horror, or marginal in terms of box-office failure, or, with films that were financially successful, marginal inasmuch as they have the capacity to sustain alternative – usually ironic – readings of them. So far as cult responses to films are concerned, these again are seen as going beyond what might be expected of a mainstream response, more devoted, more dedicated, more obsessive.[3]

Most of these ideas can be applied to Dario Argento's films. They are certainly excessive, as some of the journalistic reviews cited above have observed. Extravagant camera movements abound – most spectacularly in the scene in *Tenebre* where a crane-mounted camera travels in one long uninterrupted take from the ground floor of a house, up on to and over the roof and then down to the back part of the house. It would be easy to list a range of other tracks and pans, unusual camera angles and bizarre pieces of editing elsewhere in Argento's films. One might also consider in this respect the excessiveness and spectacle of the scenes of violence that punctuate the films. Elaborate, protracted death scenes are the order of the day, and again these seem to go beyond any narrative-based imperatives. For example, in *Profondo Rosso*, one unfortunate victim is initially terrorized by the sound of a nursery rhyme playing in his flat (a sign that the killer is about to attack); he is then menaced by an automaton doll, hit on the back of the head by a poker, has his teeth smashed in on the edge of a table, and, finally, has a knife driven through his neck into the table beneath (with all of this accompanied by the decidedly idiosyncratic music of Goblin, an Italian rock band whose work features extensively in Argento's post-1975 films and offers yet another source of potential excess).

Argento's films can also be seen as transgressive – transgressive of particular notions of good taste, but also potentially transgressive of certain sexual norms. A number of Argento critics have pointed out how his films focus on ambiguities in sexual and gendered identity (see Hunt 1992; Knee 1996; Mendik 2000). Female characters are masculinized and male characters are feminized, with this sexual ambiguity not just reserved for the ostensibly deviant killer but also permeating the nature of identity itself. To a certain extent, this makes these films comparable with the American slasher film of the late 1970s and early 1980s, which also offers a play with gender identities – although one might argue that Argento's version of this is more self-conscious, more complex and considerably more perverse.[4]

Having said this, it appears that only academic critics have fully engaged with these properties in Argento's work. Given that this way of thinking about cult objects generally has largely been generated by academics themselves, this is perhaps hardly surprising. The fan-produced responses are somewhat different and in certain respects seem to confound some of the more general academic assumptions about cult objects themselves. The first thing to say about these fan responses is that they are remarkably consistent from the fanzines and fan-centred publications from the 1980s through to the websites dedicated to Argento currently on the internet. The second is that the dominant approach to Argento as revealed by these responses is an unashamed auteurism, one which is very much concerned to raise the cultural status of Argento's work. As one fanzine put it back in the late 1980s in its discussion of Argento's critical reputation: 'Why will no-one see sense and recognise talent when they see it, apart from the fans?' (*In The Flesh*, 2, 1989: 15).[5]

In a very traditional auteurist manner, Argento is seen here as someone whose work is interesting because of both the view of the world it offers and the techniques he uses to convey that world. This is often accompanied by a sense of his films' spectacular (i.e. non-narrative) elements, although with a greater willingness to value positively these elements than some of the journalistic reviews cited above. The following indicative quotes, drawn from British and American fanzines, other fan-centred publications and websites, give a sense both of the tone and the content of these accounts:

> The man who mixes Hitchcockian suspense, stunning set-piece murders, high-style furnishings, incredible camera gymnastics and throbbing soundtracks into a fine giallo concoction. (Croce and Miller 1991: 18).

> What, yet another attempted appraisal of the unique cinematic world of Dario Argento – well, yes! (*Necronomicon*, 1993: 15)

> *Suspiria* is a brilliant piece. Argento's skilful utilisation of colour, jagged cross-cutting and subliminally unsettling, unearthly décor, aided by his recourse to the operatic in the maggot shower or the mechanism of death make it so. (www.splatterhouse.net)

> His consistency of vision, his unbridled, deeply-felt passions, and his masterful control of his medium (www.hauntworld.com/under-enter/dario.html)

We seem a world away here from the camp aesthetics associated with some cult movies (notably *The Rocky Horror Picture Show*) or from the more aggressive countercultural manoeuvres associated with what Jeffrey Sconce in an influential article has termed paracinema (Sconce 1995; also see Hawkins 2000). Sconce defines paracinema as 'less a distinct group of films than a particular reading protocol, a counter-aesthetic turned subcultural sensibility devoted to all manner of cultural detritus' (Sconce 1995: 372). While he notes that paracinematic cinephiles 'search for unrecognized talent and long forgotten masterpieces, producing a pantheon that celebrates a certain stylistic unity and/or validates the diverse artistic visions of unheralded "auteurs"', he observes also that a lot of this critical activity is characterized by 'tongue-in-cheek hyperbole' (Sconce 1995: 382). In effect there is a kind of irony at work here as paracinematic cinephiles deliberately and provocatively 'take seriously' films that fulfil none of the traditional and conventional criteria for what makes a good film.

In certain respects, Argento's films lend themselves to being seen in paracinematic terms. Argento himself is not a conventional canonical auteur, he is associated with the horror genre (in some eyes, a low cultural form) and his films – with their weird, convoluted and broken-backed narratives and their obtrusive style – apparently stand at some distance from the Hollywood mainstream.[6] However, Argento fan-writers have tended to avoid the ironies and acute self-consciousness of the paracinematic approach. Instead they make a serious (i.e. non-ironic) case for Argento as a great film artist and litter their articles with frequent references to the director as 'the master'.

Auteurism, looking at popular cinema in terms of the director's vision, was a cutting-edge approach to film back in the 1950s and 1960s, but from the 1970s onwards it has become largely outmoded in the academic study of film. Its exclusive focus on the director as the principal creative agent in cinema has been seen as neglecting the collaborative-industrial nature of film production. In addition, its reliance on very traditional notions of personal artistry, on the artist expressing himself or herself via the work, now seems decidedly old-fashioned. More recent academic accounts of authorship have tended either to use the figure of the auteur heuristically, as a means by which one can address broader non-authorial issues, or have engaged with the industrial agency of the director (see Hutchings 2001).

Certainly the academic approach to Argento has tended to shy away from viewing him as an auteur-director in the traditional sense of that term, as someone who through his talent and his unique artistic vision has somehow transcended industrial constraints. Instead the work is viewed as symptomatic, as a window on themes and issues that do not pertain to Argento alone. This has distinct implications for the way in which those elements of spectacle and other narrative-retarding elements in Argento's films are identified and valued, for here they become associated with what is seen as a systematic undermining of a secure gendered spectatorial position for the films' audiences. In other words, these films are seen to reflect upon and to a certain extent problematize some of the broader enunciative practices of film fiction. So Adam Knee discusses the way in which Argento's work 'forcefully confounds many of the generalizations about relations of gender, power, and spectatorship in the horror genre that have been put forth in film studies', while, similarly, Leon Hunt suggests that Argento's *Opera* raises 'provocative issues in horror spectatorship' (Knee 1996: 213; Hunt 1992: 74). Xavier Mendik, in an extended analysis of Argento's *Tenebre*, argues that the interruption of the narrative by bizarre and (initially at least) hard-to-understand flashbacks has something to do with the primal scene as theorized by Freud, with this having implications not only for the characters in the drama but also for our own relation as subjects to the film itself:

> Once again, the killer's traumatic recollections function to fragment the flow of the narrative. In *Tenebrae*, this scene is both repeated and elaborated throughout the film, producing a series of disruptions which impede narrative progression. These inserts indicate the subject's attempt to work through, make sense of, and thus master, past primal trauma (Mendik 2000: 10)

For the fan-writers, however, such moments of narrative retardation register instead as the most visible instances of Argento's directorial skill and mastery. This leads to discussions of Argento's work that, without necessarily using the term 'art film', nevertheless respectfully treat the films as works of art that are dependent on periodic revelations of the organizing presence of the artist-director. As David Bordwell has put it:

> In the art-cinema text, the authorial code manifests itself as recurrent violations of the classical norm. Deviations from the classical canon – an unusual angle, a stressed bit of cutting, a prohibited camera movement, an unrealistic shift in lighting or setting – in short any break-

down of the motivation of cinematic space and time by cause-effect logic – can be read as 'authorial commentary'. (Bordwell 1979: 59)

There is some basis for considering Argento's work in relation to an 'art film' tradition. Certainly his films not only boast high production values but are replete with the non-narrative motivated elements cited above by Bordwell; they also contain numerous references to high culture, high fashion and art movies themselves (with Michelangelo Antonioni's *Blow Up* an obvious influence on Argento's *Profondo Rosso*). This has been noted by some academic critics, in particular Hunt who considers Argento's work in terms of a vacillation 'between strategies of art cinema and exploitation' (Hunt 1992: 75). Fan-writers, by contrast, tend not to be so interested in exploring apparent tensions between an 'art' aesthetic and commercial-exploitative imperatives. Instead they often take issue with the perception of Argento's work (and horror in general) as low culture or as a 'bad object'. That negative perception of them is seen as emanating from individuals and institutions unsympathetic to horror or to Argento, notably some of the mainstream reviewers and the British censors. An interestingly vitriolic expression of a horror-fan antipathy to British mainstream film criticism can be found in a fanzine called *In the Flesh* (where, incidentally, it sits next to an appreciative article about Argento). The piece is sarcastically titled 'The Barry Norman Guide to Film Reviewing (A Step by Step Guide to Horror)' (*In The Flesh*, 2, 1989: 17). Norman, the BBC's main film reviewer for many years, was often perceived by British horror fans as being biased against horror. 'The Barry Norman Guide' contains the following 'tips'

> Be sure not to actually see the film, as these films can ruin your mind . . . Appear on television once a week and be sure to turn everyone's thoughts against horror . . . Get really pissed off when you see the video and film charts and most of the entries are horror, despite your efforts . . . Sit down, bung a few STEPHEN KINGS on the fire and write another letter to Mary Whitehouse . . . Go to bed and dream that all the directors you've annoyed over the years come to your house and make you watch horror films until your eye-balls explode . . . Come back to life and go grovelling to GEORGE ROMERO for a job in 'BRUNCH OF THE DEAD' (his next film).

It seems from this that the main point of much Argento-fan writing is precisely to establish that his films are in fact 'good objects' and that people who think otherwise, like Barry Norman and his kind, are prejudiced and wrong.

Conclusion

This brief survey of some of the British critical responses to Argento's work has identified a range of attitudes and discourses operating in relation to a number of different institutional contexts – including journalistic film criticism, the academy and fandom. Each of these areas has its own specificity, its own history, its own agendas. For Argento fans, there is clearly the desire to elevate the cultural status of his work. Given the stress in much academic cult-theorizing on the importance of marginality, it is interesting that I was unable to find approval for his marginal status in any fan writing on Argento. Instead one finds a resentment at those forces seen as imposing marginality on Argento, with the British censors and critics a particular focus for this resentment.

By contrast, the recent academic interest in Argento can be seen as part of a broader interest in areas of culture previously left solely to fandom. Although this chapter has not explored this academic work in much detail, it does seem not only that an academic engagement with Argento is distinct and different from the fan engagement with him but also that the academic response to cult culture in general is more heterogeneous and complex than is sometimes supposed. Motivations underpinning this fascination with cult culture involve, variously and in interaction, the desire to interrogate cultural or critical norms through a consideration of 'marginal' cultures, a commitment to a historical inclusiveness (i.e., including material that earlier critical histories had omitted), or a provocative biographical acknowledgement of one's own fandom that is often coupled with an uneasiness about how this might relate to being an academic.

It is hard to put all these approaches – fan and academic – together into a cohesive whole. While they might all engage with areas of culture that are perceived as marginal, definitions and evaluations of the marginal vary enormously. Also, as indicated above, a sense of what is marginal often has a national-contextual specificity, with the 'foreignness' of some European film genres rendering them marginal in markets outside of their country of production. (My non-Italian-speaking status has prevented me from exploring the Italian fan response to Argento. It would be interesting to compare its terms of reference with those of the British response which, along with the American versions, exudes a certain exotic fascination with these foreign objects.) Cult culture emerges from this as something artificial, constructed, a linking together of disparate types of films, television programmes and other cultural texts and responses to those texts, the only common link between which sometimes appears to be that someone somewhere has dubbed them 'cult'. Clearly the growing interest in cult objects within fandom, the academy and the market is a significant cultural phenomenon in its own right and merits further study. However, a more localized investigation of particular aspects of cult culture can – and in the case of Argento does – reveal a specificity of response that in various ways does not fit neatly with more general notions of what a cult response actually entails. It seems from this that although, especially in academic study, the turn to cult objects has proved very productive in bringing into view a range of texts and responses that were previously absent or marginalized, a detailed investigation of those objects and responses necessarily leads to a fragmentation of this area of inquiry. Seen in this way, assigning any film or television programme to the cult category is only a beginning to understanding, not an end in itself.

Notes

1   Meek goes on to see *Suspiria* itself as being both stylistically excessive and imitative, 'Argento's contribution to *The Exorcist* genre'.

2   See, for example, '*Deep Red*. The Missing Minutes!' in *In the Flesh*, 6, 1990, pp. 25–6, and 'The *Opera* Cuts' in *Rats in the Cellar*, 1 (10), January–February 1990.

3   A distinction needs to be made here between cultdom and fandom. Not all cultural artefacts that have attracted a fan following have acquired cult status. For example, one can find numerous internet discussion groups about various crime novelists but, to my knowledge, few if any of these novelists have been seen in terms of cult. Conversely, cult objects often do seem to require a fan constituency. Clearly, having a fan following is an important component of cult culture, but fandom cannot be wholly subsumed within that way of thinking about culture.

4   The sexual politics of violene is clearly an important issue for an understanding of both the slasher film and Argento's work, albeit one which is outside the scope of this chapter. I would suggest here – if only par-

enthetically – that many of the approaches associated with the slasher, both those concerned to attack it for its misogyny and those seeking to explore its ambiguities, don't work very well when applied to Argento's films. I don't want to imply by this that Argento is necessarily a more progressive figure (however one defines that term), merely that his films are different and that any evaluation of these films needs to take this difference into account.

5   It is interesting in this respect that Maitland McDonagh's book *Broken Mirrors, Broken Minds: The Dark Dreams of Dario Argento* is referred to so often in fan accounts of Argento. Although McDonagh's book certainly has academic credentials – based on an academic thesis, an early version of one chapter published in an academic journal prior to the book's publication, an academic tone throughout – it is also the most uncomplicatedly auteurist of the academic accounts of Argento and therefore lends itself far more readily to fan approbation.

6 The fact that Argento's films have primarily been available – in Britain and America especially – on video and subsequently on DVD also brings them closer to paracinema which, as described by both Sconce (1995) and Hawkins (2000), is more reliant on the circulation of video material than it is on seeing films in a cinema.

References

Bordwell, David (1979) The Art Cinema as a Mode of Film Practice, *Film Criticism*, 4 (1), pp. 56–63.

Croce, Bal and Miller, Ken (1991) Deepest Red: An Interview with Dario Argento, *Imaginator*, 7, pp. 18–19.

Fenton, Harvey, Grainger, Julian and Castoldi, Gian Luca (1999) *Cannibal Holocaust and the Savage Cinema of Ruggero Deodato*. Guildford: FAB Press.

Frayling, Christopher (1981) *Spaghetti Westerns: Cowboys and Europeans from Karl May to Sergio Leone*. London: Routledge.

Gallant, Chris (ed.) (2000) *Art of Darkness: The Cinema of Dario Argento*. Guildford: FAB Press.

Hawkins, Joan (2000) *Cutting Edge: Art-horror and the Horrific Avant-garde*. Minneapolis: University of Minnesota Press.

Hunt, Leon (1992) A (Sadistic) Night at the Opera: Notes on the Italian Horror Film, *The Velvet Light Trap*, 30 (Autumn), pp. 65–75.

Hutchings, Peter (2001) The Histogram and the List: the Director in British Film Criticism, *Journal of Popular British Cinema*, 4, pp. 30–39.

Knee, Adam (1996) Gender, Genre, Argento in Barry Keith Grant (ed.), *The Dread of Difference: Gender and the Horror Film*, Austin: University of Texas Press, pp. 213–30.

McDonagh, Maitland (1991), *Broken Mirrors, Broken Minds: The Dark Dreams of Dario Argento*. London: Sun Tavern Fields.

Meek, Scott (1977) Review of Suspiria, *Monthly Film Bulletin* (October), pp. 215–216.

Mendik, Xavier (2000) *Tenebre/Tenebrae*. Trowbridge, Wiltshire: Flicks Books.

Newman, Kim (1986) Thirty Years in Another Town: The History of Italian Exploitation, *Monthly Film Bulletin*, 53:624 (January), pp. 20–24.

Sconce, Jeffrey (1995) 'Trashing' the Academy: Taste, Excess, and an Emerging Politics of Cinematic Style, *Screen*, 36 (4) (Winter), pp. 371–393.

Thrower, Stephen (1999) *Beyond Terror: The Films of Lucio Fulci*. Guildford: FAB Press.

Websites and fanzines referred to in the text

Dario Argento: Master of the Macabre – www.jazzman59.freeserve.co.uk

Imaginator

In the Flesh

Necronomicon

Rats in the Cellar

www.splatterhouse.net

www.hauntworld.com/under-enter/dario.html

Other fanzines or fan-related publications consulted included *Blood and Black Lace* and *Samhain*.

Other websites consulted included *A Fistful of Dario: The Dark Cinema of Dario Argento* (www.en.com/users/tmr/argento.html); *Dario Argento: Master of Colours* (www.argento.vervost.de/argento/index.sht); *Dario Argento: Master of Horror* (www.houseofhorrors.com/argento.htm); *Dario Argento: World of Horror* (http://home.swipnet.se/~w-20851/hemsida/dario.htm); *Dark Dreams: The films of Dario Argento* (www.darkdreams.org/darkdreams.html); *Avete Visto: Dario Argento Page* (www.jmedia.tv/argento/dario.html).

9

Sexploitation as feminine territory: the films of Doris Wishman

Moya Luckett

In 'Trashing the Academy', Jeffrey Sconce explores how cult film consumption articulates a certain remasculinization that ironically inverts cultural hierarchies and the patriarchal tenets they embody (Sconce 1995: 380–8). Most subsequent writings on the topic share his assumptions, somewhat eclipsing the form's traditional affiliation with camp, homosexuality and femininity (Hawkins 2000; Schaefer 1999). Cult film's femininity remains unexplored, figured in largely masculine terms as burlesques of female desire and/or (gutter) divas designed for the queer gaze – an articulation of yet another masculine drama (examples include *Valley of the Dolls*, *Showgirls* and all John Waters' early work). Neither camp nor Sconce's ironic remasculinization can account for the form's essential, even structural, femininity. Sconce's anecdote about Ed Wood wearing a pink bra and panties under his Marines uniform while fighting in Japan in the Second World War does not illustrate (bizarre) masculine transcendence as much as it reveals the inspiration and strength emanating from a latent femininity. This narrative encapsulates the significance of femininity in cult film. Often latent or found in inopportune places, femininity emerges as arguably *the* structuring force in cult films, and, in the process, recasts cinematic interventions into sexual difference.

Doris Wishman, the most prolific woman director of American film in the sound era, is one of cult film's most reknowned auteurs and worked almost exclusively in sexploitation. Her films were originally made for the largely male audiences seeking softcore thrills in rundown cinemas in the cores of decaying American cities. These were essentially homosocial venues, carrying attendant social prohibitions against feminine patronage. None the less, like other softcore directors (notably Russ Meyer), Wishman reworked the form to focus on modern femininity, even recasting the spectacle of the semi-nude woman for female eyes. Contradictory as it seems, sexploitation appears to have been a feminine area within low-budget filmmaking. Other female auteurs included Roberta Findlay, whilst cult action/horror/sci-fi director Ray Dennis Steckler adopted a female pseudonym, Cindy Lou Sutters, for his sexploitation films. Other more heterosocial cult film genres (like educational films, teen musicals (such as *Wild Guitar*), drug films and horror) never had the same feminine authorial presence.

Wishman's career I: the nudie-cuties

Doris Wishman entered New York City's exploitation film industry in 1959 after the death of her husband, directing her first film, the nudist picture, *Hideout in the Sun*, one year later. It made money, launching her in a new career producing films for urban softcore cinemas. According to her website, *Hideout* was among the first nudie films, capitalizing upon recent social transformations and changes in film censorship:

> In the wake of recent court decisions concerning the legality of motion pictures depicting life in a nudist camp, Doris got the idea to make a film that would conform to the law but which, naturally, would attract the attention of more than sunbathing enthusiasts. The result was one of the first films ever produced in the very successful 'nudist' genre of the early 1960s. (www.doriswishman.com/about1.html)

Although this likely overstates her formative role, she made exclusively nudie films until 1965: *Blaze Starr Goes Nudist* (1960), *Diary of a Nudist* (1961), *Prince and the Nature Girl* (1962), *Nude on the Moon* (1962), *Gentlemen Prefer Nature Girls* (1962), *Playgirls International* (1963) and *Behind the Nudist Curtain* (1964). Plot summaries indicate that all these films presented women as protagonists, as subjects with desire, in contrast to the nudist drama and print pin-up eye-candy norm. *Hideout*'s heroine persuades her two bank-robber kidnappers to go to a nudist camp, and, once there, give themselves up. *Blaze Starr*'s movie-star heroine flees to a similar park to escape oppressive career pressures, falls in love with the camp's director, gains a new sense of self and uses it to advance her career. Wishman's nudie films connect women's personal freedom, power and romance to the energizing space of the nudist camp. She takes this trope to its fantastic limits in *Nude on the Moon*, where the planet is harmoniously ruled by naked women.

Wishman's Career II: the roughies

With 1965's *The Sex Perils of Paulette*, Wishman moved into 'roughies', an industry term for darker, more violent, sexploitation dramas of victimized girls forced into sometimes depraved sex. According to Lisa Petrucci, the New-York-centred genre existed as early as 1962's *The Festival Girls* (Michael and Roberta Findlay). Other directors of roughies included Barry Mahon, Joe Sarno, Stan Borden and George Weiss, whose works were distributed by the American Film Distributing Corporation, Distribpix, Sam Lake Enterprises and Wishman's Juri and Mostest Productions (Petrucci n.d.: n.p.). All Wishman's roughies are monochrome (her nudies were in colour) and evidence greater budgetary limitations than her earlier work, repeating footage within and across films and sometimes using out-of-focus shots. As audiences increasingly sought something more hardcore – and as sexploitation faced increasing competition from more explicit European imports – budgets were more constrained (Staiger 1999: 38–74; Wyatt 1999: 105–132). The subgenre's sadistic treatment of women also addressed male concerns about increased feminine power during the mid-1960s, something Wishman inverts to make a statement about women's economic and sexual disempowerment.

Wishman's two most pessimistic roughies, *Bad Girls Go to Hell* (1965) and *Indecent Desires* (1967), feature attractive young blondes entrapped by repulsive men. In the former, a janitor sexually attacks pert housewife, Meg (Gigi Darlene), who kills him in self-defence with an oversized ashtray. She runs from home and the somewhat neglectful (and sexually passive) husband she loves, but, as the film's circular dream narrative makes clear, she cannot escape her crime or her domestic frustrations. *Indecent Desires'* ugly drifter Zeb (Michael Lawrence) finds a ring and a doll resembling glamorous Ann (Sharon Kent) that give him control over her: whenever he touches the doll, she responds, staggered by her sudden erotic responses. When he discovers she has a boyfriend, Zeb's desires descend to violence and he kills Ann by twisting off the doll's head. Most of Wishman's roughies cut this pessimism with humour, optimistic, ludicrous or disconnected subplots or plotless interludes. She inverts stories of female degradation into narratives about men's desire to contain women's ambitions, sexuality and mobility that emphasize her heroine's ambitions and foreground their sometimes brief moments of feminine joy, independence and cameraderie. *Bad Girls'* Meg finds brief moments of comfort as she admires a coat in a shop window, cooks dinner for Al Baines (Wishman's most used actor, Sam Stewart), falls in love with Della Boyd (Darlene Bennett), plays the piano and does acrobatics. *Indecent Desires* comically mutes Ann's sufferings with ludicrous visual juxtapositions that include shots of Zeb lifting up the doll's dress alternating with low-budget 'special effect' images of Ann's nightie rising of its own accord.

Space and style in Wishman's films

Although Wishman's nudie-cutie films focus on the semi-public, semi-private space of the nudist camp as a feminine haven, her roughies explore female desire for a different place – the big city. Wishman's handling of filmic space is different across the genres, as she abandons the nudies' classical exploitation style for something more distinctive. As Eric Schaefer notes, exploitation filmmaking favours long takes, establishing shots and limited scene dissection, ensuring coverage with minimal retakes and at limited cost – the approximate style of Wishman's nudies (Schaefer 1999: 42–95). Her roughies are far more heavily edited, marked by inappropriate and/or bizarre cutaways and odd sound-image-narrative juxtapositions. Sometimes they disregard conventional narrative continuity, exemplifying what Sconce has termed paracinema – a consistently bizarre and inappropriate style where oddly juxtaposed shots, sound and editing alienate spectators from content (Sconce 1995: 372, 388). Low budgets do not entirely account for this style. Instead, Wishman's interventions foreground the texture of space over narrative, her cutaways to paintings, trees, rocks and elements of home decor establishing dialectics of space, desire, consumption and even distraction that are associated with feminine reading protocols.

An early scene from *The Sex Perils of Paulette* illustrates Wishman's paracinematic style and some of its implications. Walking through Central Park, Paulette (Anna Karol) tells her fiancé that they cannot marry because unemployment previously forced her into prostitution. As she speaks, Wishman repeatedly cuts to out-of-focus close-ups of a squirrel running and eating acorns, deflating Paulette's confession. Budgets force Wishman (and other cult filmmakers) to use cutaways to mask unsynchronized sound – a point the squirrel flaunts and undermines. Although not all her cutaways are quite this strange, many work against seamless narrative space while actually requiring more film to be shot – counter to budgetary and representational logic. Her continuity violations are significant because most of the time Wishman edits and selects shots conventionally. Wishman uses the squirrel to lambast Paulette's interpretation of the world, comically inviting viewers to empathize with her, but read her fantasies as naive and unworldly. Simultaneously, it directs spectatorial attention to space, not character or narrative.

Wishman's discontinuous editing has a relatively systematic association with location. Romantic scenes shot in Central Park and interior scenes of seduction and striptease (generally shot in the same two or three apartments) are most heavily and strangely dissected. Central Park is used for romance, for marriage proposals, pick-ups and heterosexual courtship, while scenes of prostitution or men attacking unwilling or disinterested women are shot inside apartments, hallways and stairwells. Exceptions exist: in *My Brother's Wife*, romantic and passionate seductions between Frank and Zita and Frank and Mary occur indoors, as do *Indecent Desires'* love scenes. Wishman maintains greater continuity for scenes where girls have fun, as when female friends dance in *Another Day, Another Man* or *Bad Girls Go to Hell*, and for moments when women initiate and enjoy sexual activity. For example, the scene in *Bad Girls* where Della seduces Meg features just one random cutaway (a brief shot of a clock radio that serves no censorship function and is only minimally disruptive). Wishman's paracinematic editing distances viewers to render heterosexual sexual activity strange, exposing gendered regimes of power and denaturalizing desire.

These distinctive editing strategies are clearly not unintentional. Wishman's audacious and skilful reuse of material across and within films attests to her skill at putting footage together under extremely tight constraints. Identical shots of Darlene Bennett showering appear in *Another Day, Another Man*, *Paulette* and *My Brother's Wife*, while shots of Mary's torso from *My Brother's Wife* serve double duty as shots of prostitute Dolly Desmy (Darlene Bennett) in *Another Day, Another Man*. This recycling is barely noticeable, highlighting Wishman's skill in stretching ultra-low budgets as she uses her limited range of locations and semi-stock troupe of actors to her advantage. Her often-artistic and defamiliarizing compositions, such as her beloved leg and foot shots, further demonstrate her visual skills while providing her with anonymous footage that lends itself to reuse. Once again, her more brazen continuity violations appear intentional, designed to produce a dialectical separation of sound, image and narrative that comment on the diegesis, stimulating laughter and distraction that problematize the spectator's look at images of female degradation and softcore sexual material.

Wishman's shots of standard lamps, house plants, paintings, coffee tables and household ornaments appear to be arranged for a feminine gaze, producing a look that is often at odds with her ostensible goal, the presentation of naked female bodies for men. This disjunction appears near the beginning of *Another Day, Another Man*. Ann has told Steve she cannot have dinner with him that night because her roommate Tess urgently needs to talk to her but narrative suspense is deflated when an upset Tess refuses to speak. Both girls decide they are tired and bizarrely disrobe together in their living room, but titillation is minimised as Wishman does not allow spectators to gaze at either body for long, cutting to plants, the doorway and a painting, a flower arrangement, an ashtray, a clock radio and Playboy lighter combo. While prurient looks are frustrated, the soundtrack delivers important narrative information: Ann warns Tess that Bert is trouble, and asks her why she stays with him. Defensively, Tess says she just can't leave, and also mentions the additional allure of earning $200 a week, arousing further narrative intrigue and the possible thrill of watching Tess prostitute herself. Yet Wishman's disruption of sexual images prioritises female desire and the women's relationship, hinting at the further obfuscation of explicit material to come.

Like her contemporary Helen Gurley Brown, Wishman insists that urban girls' survival depends on self-reliance and hard work (Brown 1962; Radner 1995: xi–xiv; Luckett, 1999a: 75–97). She warns against the dangers of seductive small-town mores that teach women to wait, be passive, dreams for happiness as housewives (Meg in *Bad Girls*, Ann in *Another Day*) or as actresses (Paulette, Dolly Desmy in *Another Day*), demonstrating how they lead to rape, murder and destitution instead. As Wishman shows, these fantasies are so powerful that they can even seduce tough women, like *Another Day*'s Tess, leading them to lose jobs, independence and homes. One of this film's subplots further extends this critique, showing how small-town mores similarly blind men. The girl's pimp, Bert, narrates the story of how he procured the Midwestern Desmy twins (Darlene and Rita Bennett) and young Meg (Gigi Darlene) at NYC's Port Authority bus terminal. Meg 'seemed kind of innocent' to Bert, but Wishman's images show us a brazen, confident girl, dancing with Daisy in a bikini and calmly making dates with clients. Soon, John, Meg's 'hayseed boyfriend', visits and proposes. As Bert's voice-over and Meg's facial expressions both make clear, Meg does not want 'to be a farmer's wife'. After John overhears Meg 'make a date with some guy and mention money', he hits her, calls her a whore (in badly synchronized sound that (deliberately?) ruptures continuity) and leaves. Wishman then uses Bert's voice-over to repeatedly mock John's small-town origins:

> He was from [Meg's] home town, childhood sweethearts, that kind of thing. He'd come to the city to ask Meg to marry him and go back to his farm . . . [After discovering Meg's deception] John was furious. After all that he'd planned. And after that big trip to the city. It hadn't been easy getting away from the farm. And now to find this. Well, he just couldn't believe it, he said. Why Meg had been his big dream from the first moment he'd seen her at the barn dance.

Returning to apologize, John emasculates himself further. The Desmys insist that Meg is not interested in him as both twins playfully jump on to him, smother him in kisses and caresses while laughing and pulling each other off his body. Giggling, they pretend to compete for him, dragging the scared, stiff and stern-faced young man to the floor, rolling over him, pulling off his shoes and overwhelming him with their sexuality. He cannot escape and instead collapses into an almost comatose state of shock as Daisy rolls over his arm, squeezing her cleavage for the camera while her sister extends her long legs. John, the embodiment of passive, subordinate small-town morality, loses his girl while Dolly, Daisy and Meg all transcend their origins and survive. The city becomes the modern feminine provenance, one that comes with its own way of looking, working and its own precarious gendered economics.

Wishman's anti-rural impulse casts her use of Central Park in a darker light. Manhattan's emblematic green space may be its most bucolic, but for Wishman it is also its most deceptive (it also stands in for out of town locales). By associating Central Park with her heroines' utopian ideals, Wishman exposes their domestic fantasies as the products of outmoded, deceptive rural ideology and implicitly endorses urban life for women. Although this systematic use of place is far removed from her earlier nudist park idylls, it none the less underscores the significance of space both for feminine fantasies of the period and for Wishman's own expression of feminine agency and pleasure (Luckett 1999a: 75–97; Luckett 1999b; Luckett 1999c).

Spectatorship in Wishman's films

Even in a genre ostensibly oriented around the male gaze, Wishman asserts the primacy of feminine spectatorship as the hegemonic norm. Arguably the most narratively important scene in her 1960 film *Blaze Starr Goes Nudist* deals with gendered spectatorship in cinema. Our eponymous heroine, a movie star exhausted by the pressures of work and fame, slips into a local cinema to avoid two persistent female fans. Sliding between several middle-aged men, she immediately becomes immersed in an 'educational' nudist camp picture. The mostly male members of the audience are distracted by her chest, framed in a low-cut red dress, and divert their eyes from the screen's naked girls. The sole other woman in the audience glares at her distracted husband before dragging him away. Blaze is similarly annoyed. Her exaggerated head movements and voice-over reveal her attraction to the image and her role as active female spectator, one who will ultimately enact the fantasy of transcending the screen to find her own utopia. She simultaneously offers an avowedly non-Mulvey-esque model of spectatorship, controlling the gaze, glaring back at the men to discipline them, to make them attend to the screen. This scene emblematizes Wishman's investments in female spectatorship and women's investments in looking at female bodies – an intervention that itself suggests another possible audience (and maybe even a feminine/feminist axis) for her sexploitation films. Blaze and the other middle-aged woman are the only two in the audience who appear to understand cinematic etiquette and the rules of spectatorship. They came to watch naked women on-screen.

Blaze Starr is about a woman's irritation with her status as object of the gaze, something that, paradoxically, leads to her adoption of nudity. Wishman and other sexploitation filmmakers (especially Russ Meyer) reframe female (semi-)nudity, using it to articulate women's power and subjectivity. One important implication of their work lies in the way in which they endorse the female look at the topless female body – like Della's look at Meg in *Bad Girls* – just as they present the male gaze as voyeurism, as a perversion, and block its goal: the clear look at the nude female. Wishman's characteristic focus on women dressing (not undressing) rebuffs the male gaze, destroying striptease's pivotal suspense and attendant thrills. Simultaneously it invites a feminine look at both the women's bodies and their clothes, linking nudity with an interest in fashion.

Wishman uses diegetic looks to feminize the male gaze and masculine desire. *My Brother's Wife* constructs the narrative and optical point of view of the duplicitous, seductive and hyper-masculine anti-hero, Frankie (Sam Stewart), using techniques generally reserved for her female characters. She alternates between scenes told from Mary's and Frankie's point of view, both marked by glances at household knicknacks. Her narrative discourse further inverts standard paradigms of male and female desire: housewife Mary wants excitement and sexual thrills while Frankie admires her home decor. Later in the film, Wishman has Frankie walk into the camera to produce an out-of-focus shot that turns the screen black as his figure blocks the light. This technique is reserved specifically for women throughout her films (even in the forthcoming *Bra, Bra Blacksheep*), highlighting their cleavage just as she ultimately blocks visual fulfilment. Frankie is additionally feminized in his interactions with his mistress, Zena, played by Wishman's most frequently used actress, Darlene Bennett. In another striptease variant, Wishman shows a (very tame) male disrobing, underscored through a shot of Frankie's jacket and tie thrown to the floor, an image that reinforces Zena's dominance.

Sexual difference in Wishman's films I: breasts

In opposition to psychoanalytic theories of sexual difference, most sexploitation films position breasts as *the* signifier of sexual difference – especially those directed by Doris Wishman and Russ Meyer. Although censorship is clearly a factor (full frontal male nudity violated most local obscenity statutes), it was not the principal motivation. The breast was the nudist film's *raison d'être*, and the lure of roughies and other softcore films (like Meyer's entire oeuvre and much blaxploitation) oscillated around its veiling and unveiling.

Female power is generally linked to breast size – as in *Beyond the Valley of the Dolls* (Russ Meyer, 1970) and *Foxy Brown* (Jack Hill, 1974) where small breasts highlight marginalization, failure, even utter villainy. The breast is not handled fetishistically but, instead, represents the dominance of the feminine body. If fetishism exists anywhere, it is in the disavowal of, the look away from the straight male body, a figure unable to withstand any non-ironic gendered gaze. Wishman's men exemplify this: they are interchangeable, dimensionless, frequently unattractive, without desire, interiority and ambition (with the exception of some male villains such as lecherous Frankie in *My Brother's Wife* and *Indecent Desires'* drifter, Zeb). In contrast, her women's bodies articulate their power, particularly through their copious, cantilevered cleavages, reaching an apotheosis in her Chesty Morgan films, *Double Agent 73* and *Deadly Weapons*. From Wishman's films to the gender- and sexuality-crossing Z-Man in *Beyond the Valley of the Dolls*, the breast is the sole certain marker of sexual difference. The sudden revelation of Z-Man's identity (from gay man to a masculine heterosexual woman) comes in tandem with his equally sudden acquisition of the small, naked breasts (s)he flaunts during her murder rampage at the end of the film.

Sexual difference in Wishman's films II: the sex change

Like many cult film directors, Wishman hints that masculinity might be improved or normalized through an injection of femininity. The angora-loving Ed Wood blames male dress for problems as varied as baldness (evidently caused by ill-fitting men's hats), depression and suicide in *Glen or Glenda* a semi-crazed logic that reaches its apotheosis in the sex change. Perhaps the cult film's central trope, the sex change combines several of the form's key obsessions: freakish deviation, spectacle, education, cautionary social or moral discourse, sexuality, and a tabloid version of modern science. As cult films overwhelmingly favour male-to-female transformation, the sex change presents the ultimate version of the correction of the pathological male body, the dominance of femininity and the breast's pre-eminent role in defining and revealing sexual difference.

Wishman's sex-change film, *Let Me Die a Woman* (1978), takes documentary form. Although its talking heads and expert, Dr Leo Wollman, M.D., Ph.D., doctor, psychologist, minister, are evidently real, they mostly appear fake. The sleazy cue-card-reading Wollman discusses the therapeutic use of dildoes and points at the sexual characteristics of naked transsexuals with unprofessional relish, while the principal interviewee, Leslie, a Puerto Rican New Yorker, is so feminine that it is hard to believe she was born male. The film opens with Leslie getting out of bed, proclaiming her happiness and putting on earrings, all while swishing her transparent nightdress around her body, her breasts prominently on display. As she dresses, she declares: 'I used to wear baggy shirts, shirts that were concealing. Now I wear things that flatter, that go with my colouring. I love clothes.' After dressing, she checks her reflection, applies make-up and, as the music swells, proclaims 'Last year, I was a man'. This routine yet dramatic opening foregrounds the significance of feminine culture, allies it to normality and stability while offering, again, the spectacle of barely concealed and totally revealed breasts. Narrating her story of sex change and self-discovery, Leslie focuses on her breasts, which, she unscientifically and improbably claims, developed when she was an eleven-year-old boy. Then her chest was 'very, very sensitive to pain. Which later on I found out that when a young girl is developing her breasts at that stage she's very susceptible to pain'. Leslie continually refers to her breasts as natural, referring only once (and then obliquely) to her penis, stating that doctors 'finally removed the disease and left me with my life at last'. Wollman later refers to another transsexual, an ex-Navy carpenter with two children who tried to castrate himself. He failed but emergency surgical intervention brought him what he desired – a female body.

Alongside interviews, demonstrations, graphics and actual male-to-female sex-change footage, *Let Me Die a Woman* includes a short classic Wishman narrative that closely resembles her roughies, albeit in colour. Shot without sound and accompanied by music, it features a young miniskirted woman with long dark hair (identified as Anne Zordie) picking up a man in Central Park. Anne walks, twirls and displays herself in front of a sleazy, middle-aged male, who gives her an approving look. As they enter her apartment, Wishman dollies in on a group of nautical paintings as Anne theatrically retreats behind a curtain. She cuts to Anne's jewellery box, overflowing with cheap, glittery baubles, as the anonymous man pulls off his jacket and grins with anticipation. He draws back the curtain to reveal Anne on her small bed in a black nightie, her head propped up on her arm in a classic sexualized pose of self-display. She tilts her head and initiates the mild sexual contract that, for Wishman, equals prostitution – kissing, undressing and fondling. Anne touches him first, they kiss, and he pulls down her shoulder strap to reveal her breast. Wishman cuts to a reaction shot, showing him gleefully nodding, again underlining the breast's importance. A reverse shot of both breasts follows. Wishman cuts to Anne's nightie falling on the floor, then to a black-and-white pornographic drawing that vaguely resembles an Aubrey Beardsley lithograph, connoting feminine sexual power and decadence. As the camera rotates, the drawing's content remains unclear, although its most prominent components are a woman's head and breast; male genitalia (although present) are difficult to identify. Detouring into near-art-film seriousness, Wishman tints the final shot of the couple red, graphically preparing us for a dissolve to a red carpet as the music swells and the couple's feet hit the ground in slow motion. In stark contrast, the next shot shows a pale smiling Anne in medium close-up, standing against a white wall. This sudden discontinuity separates the sex act and payment, marking the shifting relationship of prostitute and client. A further close-up isolates her hand stretched out for payment, followed by a medium shot of her door as the man exits, smiling to himself as he leaves. In a final act of defiance, Wishman cuts to Anne standing, seemingly towards the door, framed from beneath the waist to her upper thighs. She slowly pulls down her blue underwear, her head descending into the frame to authenticate the shot. She reveals her small male genitalia and turns, as if in a medical film, to display them before exiting. To underscore what we have just seen, Wishman cuts to shots of Anne showering, alternately focusing on her breasts, face and ambiguous genitalia. Once again, a curtain (this time a shower curtain with a bright red graphic print) frames another self-consciously theatrical display of 'female' sexuality.

Wollman subsequently tells us that Anne is saving for a sex change, presumably funded by prostitution. Anne's breasts confirm her evident femininity – as the smile of her client attests – while her small penis is a joke, an element of spectacle, that makes her femininity freakish but does *not* make her a man. Wollman states that Anne is one of 'about 100,000' waiting for a sex change in the US. He later notes that female-to-male surgery is much rarer – about five times smaller. This is perhaps cult film's ultimate feminine affirmation – the male's far greater desire to undergo surgery to become a woman, to exchange a penis for breasts.

Conclusion

It is tempting to speculate about the original reception of Wishman's films. Did her recurrent blockage of sexual spectacle and fulfilment frustrate male viewers? Or were they instead transported to a gendered masquerade where they might share Ed Wood's pleasure in a curative femininity? Is it more likely they simply tolerated boredom and confusion for another glimpse at ample, near-naked breasts and the promise of something perhaps even more explicit? Audiences then and now likely react differently to cult film's dual signifiers of sexual difference – the breast and the sex change – tropes that demand two distinct looks: the former attracts while the latter repels (especially men seeking sexual titillation). While the sex change is rare in Wishman's oeuvre, its look away is formally retraced throughout her work, albeit with a different and kindler emphasis on the material world, allied to a largely unromanticised feminine culture.

The dynamic between looking and repulsion is the core pleasure of many cult film genres, particularly horror, the educational film, the sex hygiene film, the vice and atrocity films (Shaefer 1999: 136–216, 253–289). Unlike most exploitation genres, though, sex-ploitation almost exclusively depends on the compulsive, sexualized look, indicating that Wishman's deflection of this gaze could be her key femininist impulse. But things are not so simple: she also privileges the female gaze and the feminine spectator, aligning the feminine look with the ability to move from detail to totality, the ability to integrate both in interpretation. Her male characters cannot do this, mired in details that limit their ability to synthesize the world, or be good spectators. Examples here include the breasts that distract *Blaze Starr*'s nudie film audience and *Another Day*'s Meg's blonde 'innocence' that fools her hayseed boyfriend John and Bert the pimp, but not the Desmy twins. Naomi Schor observes that details are generally associated with a feminine inability to distinguish between the important and the marginal, something Wishman's work seems to refute as she often uses seemingly random details (as with the Central Park squirrel or the black-and-white etching in *Let Me Die a Woman*) to suggest a bigger picture, one not perhaps visible to the male spectator who seeks only the breast (Schor 1987: 21). Even though many Wishman cutaways are without meaning and remain simply decorative (plants, clock radios, ashtrays), they repeatedly frustrate masculine, goal-oriented ways of seeing. Instead, they correspond with a more feminine look, one allied to a wandering consumerist gaze that has characterized the production of specifically feminine films since at least 1913. In mainstream cinema, at least, such distracted forms of narration have often been associated with 'fragmented, flawed and inherently low-brow' texts, presenting yet another connection between femininity and 'bad films' that certainly requires further investigation (Luckett 1999b: 373).

References

Brown, Helen Gurley (1962) *Sex and the Single Girl*. New York: Random House.

Hawkins, Joan (2000) *Cutting Edge: Art Horror and the horrific Avant-garde*. Minneapolis: University of Minnesota Press.

Luckett, Moya (1999a) A Moral Crisis in Prime Time: *Peyton Place* and the Rise of the Single Girl, in Mary Beth Haralovich and Lauren Rabinovitz (eds.), *Television, History, and American Culture: Feminist Critical Essays*. Durham: Duke University Press, pp. 75–97.

Luckett, Moya (1999b) Advertising and Femininity: The Case of *Our Mutual Girl*, *Screen*, 40 (4) (Winter), pp. 363–383.

Luckett, Moya (1999c) Sensuous Women and Single Girls: Reclaiming the Female Body on 1960s Television, in Hilary Radner and Moya Luckett (eds.), *Swinging Single: Representing Sexuality in the 1960s*, Minneapolis: University of Minnesota Press, pp. 277–300.

Luckett, Moya (2000) Travel and Mobility: Femininity and National Identity in Swinging London Films, in Justine Ashby and Andrew Higson (eds.), *British Cinema: Past and Present*. London: Routledge, pp. 233–245.

Petrucci, Lisa (n.d.) Where Have All The Bad Girls Gone?, *Tease*, 5, n.p.

Radner, Hilary (1995) *Shopping Around: Feminine Culture and the Pursuit of Pleasure*. New York: Routledge.

Schaefer, Eric (1999) *'Bold! Daring! Shocking! True!': A History of Exploitation Films, 1919–1959*. Durham: Duke University Press.

Schor, Naomi (1987), *Reading in Detail: Aesthetics and the Feminine*. New York: Methuen.

Sconce, Jeffrey (1995) 'Trashing' the Academy: Taste, Excess and an Emerging Politics of Cinematic Style, *Screen*, 36 (4) (Winter), pp. 371–393.

Staiger, Janet (1999) Finding Community in the Early 1960s: Underground Cinema and Sexual Politics, in Hilary Radner and Moya Luckett (eds.), *Swinging Single: Representing Sexuality in the 1960s*. Minneapolis: University of Minnesota Press, pp. 38–74.

Vale, V., and Juno, Andrea (eds.) (1986) *Re/Search 10: Incredibly Strange Films*. San Francisco. Re/Search Publications.

Wyatt, Justin (1999) Revising Sexualities in the Marketplace for Adult Film of the 1960s, in Hilary Radner and Moya Luckett (eds.) *Swinging Single: Representing Sexuality in the 1960s*. Minneapolis: University of Minnesota Press, pp. 105–132.

Websites

www.doriswishman.com, 1 September 2001

10

Kung fu cult masters:
stardom, performance and 'authenticity' in Hong Kong martial arts films

Leon Hunt

In *Once Upon a Time in China 3* (Tsui Hark, Hong Kong 1993), legendary martial arts hero Wong Fei-hung/Huang Feihong (Jet Li) has the latest in a series of 'future shock' encounters with technology courtesy of his westernized love interest, Thirteenth Aunt (Rosamund Kwan). Cameras have been the source of some conflict in Parts 1 and 2, but the arrival of the first movie camera in Guangdong is too much for even a Confucian patriarch to resist and soon he is coaxed in front of it to throw some shapes. 'We can teach others kung fu by movie in future', suggests his student Leung Foon with uncanny foresight. But this attempt to marry the Lumière Brothers to Shaw Brothers is not an unqualified success. When the film is viewed, it turns out that a bad case of undercranking has rendered Wong's forms at *Keystone Cops* speed. As Wong's father wonders at his son's phenomenal speed and (more importantly) whether it is genuine, he anticipates the musings of many a kung fu cultist to come. The scene is a typically witty piece of revisionism, synthesizing the Cantonese legend and the 1990s action superstar in what is effectively the first kung fu film. But it also suggests that martial arts legends have had a complex relationship with cinematic technology from the start.

This article has two central concerns. The first is the debate about 'authenticity' which has recurred in English-speaking subcultures surrounding Hong Kong martial arts films and their stars (which I here take to include diasporic talent such as Jet Li, because that is how fan culture still largely sees them). The second is the increasing visibility of technology and special effects in fight choreography, and its implications for a genre with a particular investment in the 'real'. Hong Kong cinema has largely been theorized in terms of the hybrid, the transnational, the postmodern and the postcolonial; none of these is an authenticity-friendly concept. What interests me about the 'authenticity' debate is the way it addresses questions of how technology mediates stardom and performance; also that it is a popular debate about the aesthetics of the performing body that has yet to be fully interrogated by academics. But we must beware of conflating different constructions of the authentic. Although I know of no recent empirical work on Hong Kong audiences, and don't feel equipped to conduct such research myself, my feeling is that the kind of 'authenticity' I am largely discussing here is primarily a western concern. Most recent Hong Kong action has starred Cantopop pin-ups rather than martial artists. In Asian critical and industry debates, authenticity is often linked to questions of identity. For Chiao Hsiung-ping, Bruce Lee's eschewal of special effects and fondness for long-shot/long-take framing testifies to his cross-cultural credentials, a triumph of western 'realism' over 'Oriental fantasies' (1981: 33), while for Ackbar Abbas it provides the key to an 'authentic and heroic Chinese identity' (1997: 29). Although readings focused on Hong Kong's 1997 reunification with China can be simplistic and overdetermined, it seems significant that 'authenticity' has diminished as Hong Kong has embraced a more hybridized, postcolonial identity, both 'Chinese' and not. Ramei Tateishi suggests that the visual pastiche of Jackie Chan's choreography 'could reflect the idea of a disappearing subject of Hong Kong film' (1998: 83). However, Chan remains critical of the 'inauthenticity' of New Wave kung fu films: 'I don't like the *wu xia pian*, the flying, the exaggerated kung fu skills. It's not real. You can make anyone fly like Superman or Batman, but only special people can do my style of fighting' (Reid 1994: 21).

'Authenticity' is a slippery term, but I think it is possible to discern three types of authenticity in popular debates about kung fu films – *archival, cinematic* and *corporeal*. *Archival authenticity* refers to the authenticity of the martial arts themselves – 1970s kung fu films are often valued for displaying recognizable styles (Praying Mantis, Crane, Tiger etc.), while some purists objected to Jet Li's northern *wu shu* being grafted on to southern *hung gar* master Wong Fei-hung.[1] Ron Lim's 'Martial Artist's Guide to Hong Kong Films' (1999) rates movies purely on the basis of the accuracy and execution of their kung fu – in *Warriors Two* (Sammo Hung, Hong Kong 1978), we learn, 'no one . . . does wing chun properly or well' (Lim

1999: n.p.). But this kind of authenticity has its limits – Shaw Brothers films show 'pure Southern Chinese styles' but their fight scenes are 'Slow, slow, slow' (ibid.), clearly in need of a bit of inauthentic flash. *Cinematic authenticity* identifies a desire for transparent mediation, championing long takes and wide framing as a guarantee of the 'real' – 'anyone can be made to look good using tricky camera angles and deceitful editing' (Foster 1999: 15). *Corporeal authenticity* is measured by stuntwork as much as fighting ability, what Ackbar Abbas calls the 'stuntman-as-hero' (1997: 29). By the 1980s, 'pure' kung fu had largely gone out of fashion and Hong Kong action was embracing an increasingly montage-based aesthetic (see Bordwell 1997, 2000). What is left, therefore, is the body itself and what its owner is prepared to subject it to, a logic incarnated most publicly by Jackie Chan doing all (or most) of his own stunts – 'we show only what we can do, what my stuntmen can do' (Logan, 1995: 57).[2] A recent ad for the DVD of *The Big Brawl* (Robert Clouse, USA/Hong Kong 1980) underlines Chan's persona as champion of the 'real' – 'No wires. Just talent.'[3]

The Hong Kong martial arts film has always deployed both cinematic and pro-filmic effects – undercranking,[4] editing 'cheats', trampolines and reverse footage. But special effects became much more ubiquitous in 1990s 'New Wave' films such as *Once Upon a Time in China* (Tsui Hark, Hong Kong 1991), which offered a fast-cut, hi-tech spectacle. The most characteristic feature of these films was their use of 'wirework', allowing performers to take flight, fight in mid-air or on top of precariously balanced objects.[5] Moreover, the montage approach to action meant that non-martial artists could easily be doubled in fight scenes. In *The Bride with White Hair* (Ronny Yu, Hong Kong 1993), neither of the two leads, Brigitte Lin and Leslie Cheung, is a martial artist, but one would never guess from their action scenes. Ackbar Abbas has suggested that the 'real' was now being '"coproduced" by special effects . . . in a new technological and . . . transnational space' (1997: 32). If he slightly overstated the case in pronouncing that special effects were now the stars of the kung fu film, the addition of CGI effects to *The Matrix* (Wachowski Brothers, USA 1999), *Romeo Must Die* (Andrzej Bartkowiak, USA 2000), *Charlie's Angels* (McG, USA 2000) and *Crouching Tiger, Hidden Dragon* (Ang Lee, China/Taiwan/USA 2000) suggests that the genre might now have caught up with his claims. Such developments have not by any means been met with unanimous approval by fans of the genre. The following response to Jet Li's recent Hollywood vehicle *Romeo Must Die* crystallizes their objections:

> the fighting just plain sucks. It sucks because it's all made up, with computers and wire-assisted jumps. Jet Li doesn't need that stuff to show his abilities. In fact, it just worsens the show, because it looks like anyone could do that, hanging from all those wires. (Internet Movie Data Base 2000: n.p.)

However, even *The Matrix* sends out mixed messages about the lure of the 'real' and the 'digital'. Its technical wizardry was central to its claims to innovativeness – according to Manohla Dargis, it created 'a new kind of action hero, one heavily predicated on digital effects' (2000: 23). But this is only half of the story – publicity also made great capital out of Hong Kong choreographer Yuen Woo-ping training Keanu Reeves and other cast members to perform 'real' martial arts stunts.[6] To inject 'Hong Kong action' into a Hollywood blockbuster was, by implication, somehow to authenticate its stars. Ever since Keanu announced, 'I know kung fu', Tom Cruise, Charlie's Angels and The X-Men have been keen to demonstrate that they do, too.

In an ecstatic review of Jackie Chan's *Drunken Master 2* (Lau Karleung, Hong Kong 1994), *The Essential Guide to Hong Kong Movies* observed, 'it will be interesting to see whether Hong Kong directors will now stop over-using high-wire kung fu and return to pull-no-punches action which requires the skill of the actor rather than the director' (Baker and Russell 1994: 47). What is interesting here is the rejection of a certain type of cinematic authorship, a championing of the 'real' over the 'cinematic'. In fact, there has always been a tradition within the *wu xia pian* (martial chivalry film) that prioritized 'authorial' style over performative authenticity – King Hu in the 1960s and 1970s, Tsui Hark and Ching Siu-tung (the Busby Berkeley of 'wire-fu') in the 1980s and 1990s. Hu's leads (Roy Chiao, Xu Feng) were rarely martial artists, although performers (and choreographers) such as Sammo Hung and Han Yingjieh often played the heavies. Hu's oblique visual style was clearly unconcerned with demonstrating whether his performers could really cut it in a fight scene – he has no significant presence in fan appreciations of the genre, because, I suspect, he would be perceived as 'wasting' talent like Hung and Han. If scholarly work on Hong

Kong cinema has been predominantly auteurist, kung fu cultism invests primarily in stars, and, to a lesser extent, choreographers (who may also be stars). Star-auteurs such as Bruce Lee and Jackie Chan are one thing, but when Jet Li turns up in (English-language) scholarly accounts it is usually as a footnote to the *Once Upon a Time in China* series, a series taken to be authored by director-producer Tsui Hark. But fanzines and websites often give greater emphasis to *Fist of Legend* (Gordon Chan, Hong Kong 1994), a remake of Bruce Lee's *Fist of Fury*. While *Fist of Legend* catches some of the same postcolonial resonances as the Wong Fei-hung series, it also works as a vehicle for displaying Jet Li's martial arts skills. Like *Drunken Master 2*, *Fist of Legend* won approval for downplaying wirework and for deploying a wide range of recognizable martial arts styles. Ron Lim gives the film 5 out of 5, and, barring one significant caveat, it seems to provide him with elements of all three forms of authenticity:

> Plenty of Jet Li wu shu, chin na and a slightly more 'street' style (more boxing, Bruce Lee-inspired shuffle feet). Jet and Chin (Siu-ho) perform mi tsung-i, the actual style of the Ching Wu Academy that the film is about. The 'challenge' with (Yasuaki) Kurata is a bit wire-enhanced, as is the finale . . . but not much to complain about as this is wall-to-wall action. (Lim 1999)

Li has divided kung fu aficionados precisely on the grounds of authenticity.[7] *Oriental Cinema*'s pugnacious editor Damon Foster, for example, finds Li's westernized name inadvertently appropriate – 'many of his movies consist of *flight* scenes rather than *fight* scenes' (Foster 1999: 6). *Fist of Legend* has frequently performed the role of 'authenticating' Jet Li, of offering documentary proof of his abilities – 'The fighting scenes are awesome and realistic, "wire-fu" almost nowhere' (Amazon.com 2000). Even Foster, who devoted an entire issue of *Oriental Cinema* to denigrating Li, capitulated to the film's balletic charms.

In *Hollywood East*, Stefan Hammond recalls the audiences who filled London's Scala cinema for kung fu triple-bills:

> When the combatants squared off in their fighting stances, shouts of 'Shapes! Shapes!' would come from the crowd, expressing appreciation for the geometric patterns of robed bodies. An absurd leap or wire effect would be greeted with 'Lies!' but a well-executed manoeuvre would draw the accolade '*Wicked* Lies!' (Hammond 2000: 79–80)

What I find suggestive here is the implication that 'Wicked Shapes' and 'Wicked Lies' are not polar opposites; rather, they co-exist in a more ambivalent relationship and authenticity is valued rather more reflexively than first appears. Kung fu films are often likened to musicals and westerns, but science fiction has been the generic pioneer in blurring the real and the virtual. Both genres hinge in different ways on what Brooks Landon (1992) calls 'the aesthetics of ambivalence', an ambivalence predicated on the paradox of cinematic trickery (accepting the 'fake' as 'real') and a seemingly impossible investment in both documentary realism and fantasy. For a genre about physical skill – as opposed to a genre which is often actually *about* technology – there is of course much more at stake. The 'classic' kung fu film has a documentary tradition of sorts – the theatrical staging of the black-and-white Wong Fei-hung films, the archive of Southern Shaolin styles in Lau Kar-leung's Shaw Brothers classics from the 1970s. The mid-1970s kung fu film went through a distinct 'educational' phase, exemplifying archival authenticity. *Heroes Two* (Zhang Che, Hong Kong 1974), an early entry in Shaw Brothers' Shaolin cycle, is actually prefaced by a ten-minute demonstration film, 'Three Styles of Hung School's Kung Fu', in which stars Chen Guantai, Fu Sheng and Qi Guanjun perform the styles depicted in the film, complete with captions and narration. The narrative of *Executioners from Shaolin* (Lau Kar-leung, Hong Kong 1976) hinges on the minutiae of Southern Chinese fighting styles, on the processes of learning and innovation – callow hero Wenting (Wong Yue) must combine Tiger and Crane to defeat the seemingly invincible *quigong* powers of white-haired, testicle-retracting Bai Mei (Lo Lieh). Jet Li's heroes, by contrast, conflate the historical and the futuristic – the superhuman exploits of *wu xia* novels and serials and the digital motion-capture exploits of console game martial artists. One magazine recently dubbed him 'Bruce Lee for *The Matrix* generation' and there was some expectation that he would appear in the sequels.

And yet if Jet Li is less 'real' than, say, Jackie Chan, he is clearly more than a special effect, which is why *Romeo Must Die* angered some fans by seemingly casting him as Nintendo Li. Wirework at least requires performative skill, and provides a 'warm' analogue alternative to 'cold' digital trickery. 'New technology does have a place in martial arts action cinema', concedes Bey Logan in action-film magazine *Impact*, 'My problems with SFX begin when the genre starts to lose its soul to the machine' (2000: 40). Again, this suggests a kind of reflexive authenticity, a concession to 'Wicked Lies' as long as they do not entirely obliterate the 'real'. But where to draw the line? Somewhere along the way, wicked shapes and wicked lies are bound up with notions of 'aura' and 'presence'.

In 'The Work of Art in the Age of Mechanical Reproduction' (1935/1979), Walter Benjamin places 'authenticity' in a kind of holy trinity with 'presence' and 'aura', each of them always eluding technical reproducibility. 'Aura' is 'that which withers in the age of mechanical reproduction', because technology removes an object (or, in this case, a performance) from the 'domain of tradition': 'The essence of a thing is the essence of all that is transmissible from its beginning, ranging from its substantive duration to its testimony to the history which it has experienced' (ibid.: 852). In this respect, kung fu stars – and stars in general (as Benjamin explicitly argues) – were always in trouble. Numerous hagiographies tell us that Bruce Lee had to be slowed down by the camera – his 'real' speed could not be represented and had to at least be partly taken on (extratextual) trust. When an actor performs live, Benjamin argues, 'aura is tied to his presence', whereas the technological mediation of film takes performance out of the actor's hands – because of the plasticity of editing and different camera set-ups, 'it is composed of many separate performances' (ibid.: 859). *Once Upon a Time in China 3*'s film-within-a-film can be seen as comment both on the 'legend' Wong Fei-hung and on the star Jet Li, both of them losing their 'aura' and presence to the camera. But there are ways of re-synthesizing 'presence', and one can see all three types of authenticity as compensatory strategies. Corporeal authenticity re-synthesizes the 'fabric of tradition'. Cinematic and corporeal authenticity work hardest to convey 'presence', the first concealing (rather than removing) mediation, the second sometimes foregrounding mediation (editing, multi-takes) to guarantee the self-endangering star body. Jackie Chan's films use a much faster editing style than Bruce Lee's – they belong to a more cine-literate phase in Hong Kong cinema – and use other forms of enhancement (undercranking, subtle wirework), but his use of action replays and outtakes re-invent the documentary and inscribe his 'presence' as self-endangerment (Jackie bleeding, Jackie unconscious, Jackie on fire). According to Ramei Tateishi, Chan's stunts ensure 'that the screen is always presenting the authentic subject' (1998: 83).

Bolter's and Grusin's *Remediation: Understanding New Media* provides some ways of thinking about authenticity, aura and presence in the digital age, even if their conclusions are somewhat different from Benjamin's – 'remediation does not destroy the aura of the work of art; instead it always refashions that aura in another media form' (2000: 75). 'Remediation' describes the process whereby a medium 'appropriates the techniques, forms and social significance of other media and attempts to rival or refashion them in the name of the real' (ibid.: 65). This is not simply a linear, successive development, because sometimes media *remediate* each other – films that appropriate aspects of computer games and vice versa, for example. Kung fu films, in the first instance, remediate forms such as Beijing opera (graceful, acrobatic performance) and the storylines, heroic codes and extraordinary feats of *wu xia* fiction. But in recent years, martial arts films and console fight games such as *Tekken* and *Street Fighter* have been engaged in a process of mutual remediation. Kung fu films use wirework and FX to recreate the digital spectacle of hi-tech games, just as those games use motion capture to simulate real martial arts moves and stunts (corkscrew spins, for example), appropriate 'authentic' martial arts styles and even simulate the appearance and style of martial arts stars. *Tekken*'s Lei Wulong is widely taken to be Jackie Chan,[8] even down to his Drunken Master style, but his repertoire also includes Shaolin animal styles (Snake, Tiger, Leopard, Dragon, Crane). Meanwhile, Forest Law couldn't be anyone but Bruce Lee – he has his haircut, his wardrobe, his cocky strut and his repertoire of squawks and shrieks. He even reproduces his *Enter the Dragon* backflip (although, interestingly, that move was originally performed by Lee's acrobatic double, Yuen Wah).[9]

Bolter and Grusin argue that new media have two seemingly opposed, but in fact closely interlinked goals – *transparent immediacy*, which seeks to render mediation invisible, and *hypermediacy*, which foregrounds it (2000: 272). The two are furthest apart in their epistemological sense – one is characterized by invisibility, the other by opacity of mediation (ibid.: 70–71). In this sense, 'Wicked Shapes' offer transparent immediacy, and 'Wicked Lies' a kind of hypermediation. But Bolter and Grusin suggest that each term also has a psychological dimension that brings their effect closer together. Transparent immediacy facilitates a feeling of 'presence', while in the case of hypermediacy the 'experience of the medium is itself an experience of the real' (ibid.: 71). In other words, authenticity (of experience) does not disappear. They cite popular music as an example of hypermediacy which can provide an 'authentic' experience (42). It is also, of course, the site of popular culture's most paradigmatic authenticity debate. For some, 'real' music must involve guitars, must be reproducible 'live', while something recorded on a sampler in someone's bedroom can never be authentic. Yet the latter is central to contemporary subcultural authenticity – the subcultural capital of 'clubbing' lies partly in providing access to some notion of the 'real' (which can be mediated by recreational drugs as well as technology). Martial arts films have had to respond to a similar logic, wherein the 'real' has been refashioned by hypermedia.[10] Bruce Lee's films offer a kind of transparent immediacy – 'presence' and 'authenticity' are guaranteed by the invisibility of his cinematic mediation. Jackie Chan is a much more mediated performer, but is able to re-inscribe his 'presence' in other ways.[11] Jet Li belongs firmly to a digital age (even if only _Romeo_ is literally digital), and is the most visibly mediated of the three, precisely because of the synergy betwen films and games. Computer games are both more and less 'real' than Bruce Lee and Jackie Chan, offering an authenticity and intensity of experience that transparent immediacy might not be able to match. This is evident in some of the 'Who's the Best' arguments which take place between younger and older fans on the internet. For a younger generation of fans, Jet Li clearly _is_ better and more 'real' than Bruce Lee because the hypermimesis of computer games has redefined how a kung fu fight 'feels'. When you are up against the 'vibrating palm' of a Dual Shock Controller, transparent immediacy alone is just not going to cut it.

If we are considering the 'authentic' and the 'real', we need to consider what 'special effects' are, too, a familiar enough question in relation to horror and science fiction, but the martial arts film has not been traditionally thought of an FX genre. Michael Stern has argued that in some ways 'special effects' is a misleading term with its inbuilt implication that 'everything else' is not a cinematic effect of some sort (1990: 67). Nevertheless, degrees of _visibility_ seem to be important in defining the 'special'. He reminds us that _Planet of the Apes_ won an Oscar for its ape make-up while _2001: A Space Odyssey_ wasn't even nominated (ibid.: 66) – were its apes too 'real' or transparent to be 'special'? A similar paradox surrounds the use of wirework in Hong Kong action. 'New Wave' wirework shows us things we know to be 'untrue' – fights on top of ladders (*Once Upon a Time in China*), the shoulders of a crowd (*Fong Sai Yuk*), vertical poles (*Iron Monkey*) or the breathtaking tree-top fight in a vast forest in *Crouching Tiger, Hidden Dragon*. But wires also feature in Jackie Chan's more 'realistic' fights, enhancing moves which at least seem possible. Hong-Kong-based stuntman Jude Poyer explains a sequence in *Thunderbolt* (Gordon Chan, Hong Kong 1995) in which Chan delivers some flying kicks:

> The three kicks are basic ones and wouldn't pose a problem for any Hong Kong stuntman, but a wire is being used to make the technique appear more powerful. If the stuntman performing a jumping kick doesn't have to expend energy to gain height, he can deliver the kicks with more power and more dramatic impact. (Poyer 2000: 217)

One might argue that this is much more of a 'Wicked Lie' than Jet Li's gravity-defying no-shadow kick, but, significantly, that is not an argument that is ever offered.

Probably no kung fu star has come to embody 'authenticity' quite as much as Bruce Lee, even if there is some disagreement over what that authenticity meant – an injection of western realism or an assertion of Chinese identity. And yet paradoxically it is a Bruce Lee film that most radically fragmented the 'presence' of the martial arts star. *Game of Death* was incomplete at the time of his death, and subsequently padded out to feature length with a combination of doubles, shots from his other films and bizarre superimpositions of his face on to a stand-in's shoulders. For Lee cultists, a restored (if incomplete) *Game of Death* is a virtual Holy Grail, but the version released in 1978 was clearly not it. To say that the film synthesized Lee's presence poorly is understating the case – *The Crow* (Alex Proyas, USA 1994) had the technology to do a better job with son Brandon. What is more significant here is that it tried. Rumours have circulated recently of plans to make films using a CGI Bruce Lee, but in fact 'Virtual Bruce' already exists in the form of *Tekken*'s Forest Law. Lee hovers somewhere between a non-presence and a fragmented presence in what is ostensibly 'his' film – he does, however, materialize at his own funeral, a staple scene in the numerous Bruce Lee 'clone' films of the late 1970s. But it is the fight scenes that really complicate matters. The synthesized Lee – choreographed by Sammo Hung – cannot stand in for Lee's presence, but can do things that the star could not. 'He' is more acrobatic, 'he' is a flashier kicker and, because undercranking was more common by the late 1970s, 'he' is faster, too. *Game of Death* is a disquieting film in its dissolution of the star – it is widely regarded as a travesty – but it anticipates some of the practices that would become more central to the genre.

In one of the few essays on performance in Hong Kong action, Greg Dancer detects a mixed response to wirework in Jet Li's films – disappointment that his fights aren't 'real' mixed with excitement over the ingenuity of the wirework itself (1998: 47). Wirework is a reminder that not every aspect of performance can be credited to the performer alone (or at all), but there is a pleasure to be had, he suggests, in 'taking apart' such a performance, in this case wire-spotting (ibid.: 48). I must confess to some identification with these wire-spotters, although my own obsession is with stunt doubles – I am a fan as well as an academic and so entitled to be a little bit obsessive. Doubles are more potentially damaging to the martial artist's 'aura' than special effects could ever be because an aura mediated by technology needs somehow to reassure us of the unity of the star presence – as Dargis puts it, the star body has become 'the last stand of the real' in the age of digital reproduction (2000: 20). There is a now-you-see-him-now-you-don't quality to some Jet Li fight scenes, plenty of evidence of his grace and speed but just as much that his double can do pretty much everything he can and maybe one or two things he can't. This sets me off on my own search for wicked shapes and wicked lies (DVD has made me much worse, another way in which technology impacts on the genre). Part of me wants my kung fu idols to be authentic, especially when they are as charismatic and glamorous as Jet Li. I get enormous pleasure from confirming that a particularly impressive move was actually performed by Jet. And yet another part of me knows that the authentic kung fu star belongs to history, or perhaps to myth, that martial arts films simply do not need their stars to be trained martial artists any more, and that the kung fu cult master was always partly the magnificent creation of technology and choreography.

There is a scene in *Romeo Must Die* where Jet Li finds himself surrounded by the villains. In one 'continuous' take, he leaps in the air, rotates horizontally in midair to kick each opponent in turn, reverses (there is no other way of putting it) on to a ledge and then hops down to deliver a couple more kicks. There are more than wires holding Jet up here – three separate shots were digitally combined to achieve this state-of-the-art and yet breathtakingly silly effect. Moments later, he is using a fire hose as a rope dart, twisting and spinning in graceful, balletic circles – even the overzealous editing cannot disguise the fact that here is the star doing what Keanu Reeves and Tom Cruise just cannot. Investing in authenticity flies in the face of some historical-cultural particularities about Hong Kong cinema and – more problematically – wants to keep it pure, profilmic, by implication 'primitive'. But it clearly remains central to cult consumption, and therefore to some of the meanings these transnational texts have taken on. And sometimes all it takes is a martial artist and a firehose to keep this pleasurable myth in circulation.

Notes

1 The differences between Northern and Southern Chinese *kung fu* are popularly encapsulated in the phrase 'Northern leg, Southern fist'. The north was flat and open, thus the emphasis on high and flying kicks (supposedly to remove opponents from their horses). The south was marshy, more crowded and (in the case of Guangdong) built up, thus the emphasis on solid stances and fighting styles adapted to enclosed spaces. From this description, 'Southern fist' may sound less cinematic, but the climactic alley fight from an earlier Wong Fei-hung film, *Martial Club* (Lau Kar-leung, Hong Kong 1980), offers spectacular proof to the contrary. *Wu shu*, a national sport in the People's Republic of China, draws mainly on Northern styles but also incorporates gymnastic performance.

2 Sometimes corporeal authenticity can compensate for other deficits. (Jimmy) Wang Yu, a popular action star until Bruce Lee displaced him, is generally regarded as a poor martial artist, an exponent of what some fans call 'swingy arm style' – 'agonizingly long fights with flailing arms' (Lim 1999). But for some cultists he retains a gritty authenticity through his dangerous stunts and no-nonsense scrappy fighting. See *Oriental Cinema* 19 (2001), 'The Jimmy Wang Yu Issue', or my own 'One Armed and Extremely Dangerous: Wang Yu's Mutilated Masters', in Xavier Mendik (ed.), *Shocking Cinema of the Seventies* (London: Noir Publishing, 2001).

3 Many Chan fans were angered by Wong Jing's heretical action-comedy *High Risk* (Hong Kong 1995), which features an action star clearly modelled on Chan. 'Frankie' (Jackie Cheung) is renowned for doing his own stunts, but is represented as a drunken buffoon who relies on his stuntman and bodyguard, Kit, to compensate for his own diminished abilities. To add insult to injury, Kit is played by Jet Li, who has made little

secret of his use of stunt doubles (not to mention wires). Given that Chan and Li represent diametrically opposed approaches to fight scenes, *High Risk* is more interesting (and more fun) than its cynical packaging (*Die Hard* meets industry in-fighting) might suggest.

4 Hong Kong filmmakers often shoot fight scenes at twenty-two frames per second or less – 24fps is the 'normal' camera speed (Bordwell 2000: 209). This speeds up the fight (when projected) without making it look as comical as *Once Upon a Time in China 3*'s film-within-a-film, and can give sequences a preternatural precision and velocity.

5 Chinese martial arts films have a long history of using wires to make characters fly or perform 'weightless' leaps. Primitive wirework can be traced back to Shanghai-produced films such as *The Burning of the Red Lotus Monastery* (Zhang Shichuan, China 1928), but became much more sophisticated in post-1980s Hong Kong films such as *Once Upon a Time in China*. Wirework has recently been incorporated into western action films and television, especially those films that have used Hong Kong choreographers (*The Matrix, Charlie's Angels, Romeo Must Die*).

6 Interestingly, the two most technically advanced science fiction films of 1999 featured martial arts. *Star Wars Episode I: The Phantom Menace* (George Lucas, USA 1999) featured virtual sets, virtual characters (the universally loathed Jar Jar Binks) and the sort of state-of-the-art effects one would expect from a glorified toy manufacturer such as Lucas. But for Jedi-sceptics such as myself, nothing matched the glorious *wu shu* spins performed by Darth Maul (Ray Park) – the film's most memorable spectacle was firmly in the realm of the 'real'.

7 Jet Li/Li Lianjie is a Beijing-born, former Mainland *wu shu* champion – as a teenager, he performed to Nixon at the White House in 1974. Li began making films in the early 1980s, but initial success was shortlived until Tsui Hark cast him as Wong Fei-hung, at which point he became one of Hong Kong's top action stars and Jackie Chan's nearest rival – Li could act as well as fight and possessed an intriguingly quiet charisma. If his *wu shu* medals at one level authenticate him, there are purists who question whether *wu shu* (designed for performance, not combat) is a 'proper' martial art. Early films such as *Martial Arts of Shaolin* (Lau Kar-leung, Hong Kong/China 1986) and *Dragon Fight* (Billy Tang, Hong Kong 1988) show how fast and agile Li can be, even without the aid of wires – some regard them as his 'best' films, but they were not commercial successes. Li is less enamoured of painful injuries than Chan – he was extensively doubled for *Once Upon a Time in China* after breaking his ankle, and stunt doubles seem to have proliferated in his historical 'wire fu' films. Modern-day films such as *Bodyguard from Beijing* (Yuen Kwai, Hong Kong 1994) confirm that he can still, as the fans put it, 'bust-a-move'.

8 Jackie Chan now has his own game, *Jackie Chan: Stuntmaster* (Radical/Sony Playstation, 2000), a mixture of adventure and platform game rather than the tournament beat-'em-up of games such as *Tekken*. Rumours have circulated recently that Chan will play Lei Wulong in the *Tekken* film.

9 Something very interesting is going on around 'aura' and 'presence' when stills of that backflip ar reproduced (as they often are) as images of 'Bruce Lee'.

10 Although my own focus is primarily on western fandom, I don't mean to downplay more culturally specific factors in Hong Kong cinema's mixture of the authentic and the technologically mediated, namely its hybridised or postcolonial 'identity'.

11 David Bordwell's formalist work on Hong Kong action (1997, 2000) underlines both how hypermediated it is and how central corporeal 'presence' (eye-popping stunts) is to its kinetic effect.

References

Abbas, Ackbar (1997) *Hong Kong: Culture and the Politics of Disappearance*. Minneapolis: University of Minnesota Press.

Amazon.com (2000), Customer reviews of *Fist of Legend* DVD, www. amazon.com/exec/obidos/ts/dvd. . .8NS/ref=pm_dp_ln_v_6/102-3499426-3434568.

Baker, Rick and Russell, Toby (1994) *The Essential Guide to Hong Kong Movies*, London: Eastern Heroes.

Benjamin, Walter (1931/1979) A Small History of Photography in *One-Way Street*. London: NLB, pp. 240–257.

Benjamin, Walter (1935/1979) The Work of Art in the Age of Mechanical Reproduction in Gerald Mast and Marshall Cohen (eds.), *Film Theory and Criticism*, New York and Oxford: Oxford University Press, pp. 848–870.

Bolter, Jay David, and Grusin, Richard (2000) *Remediation: Understanding New Media*. Cambridge, Mass. and London: MIT Press.

Bordwell, David (1997) Aesthetics in Action: Kung-Fu, Gunplay, and Cinematic Expressibity in Law Kar (ed.), *Fifty Years of Electric Shadows*. Hong Kong: Hong Kong International Film Festival/Urban Council, pp. 81–89.

Bordwell, David (2000) *Planet Hong Kong: Popular Cinema and the Art of Entertainment*. Cambridge, Mass. and London: Harvard University Press.

Chiao Hsiung-ping (1981) Bruce Lee: His Influence on the Evolution of the Kung Fu Genre, *Journal of Popular Film and Television*, 9 (1), pp. 30–42.

Dancer, Greg (1998) Film Style and Performance: Comedy and Kung Fu from Hong Kong, *Asian Cinema*, 10 (1), pp. 78–84.

Dargis, Manohla (2000) Ghost in the Machine, *Sight and Sound*, 10 (7), pp. 20–23.

Foster, Damon (1999) Jet Li, *Oriental Cinema*, 16, pp. 2–25.

Hammond, Stefan (2000) *Hollywood East: Hong Kong Movies and the People Who Make Them*. Lincolnwood (Chicago): Contemporary Books.

Hunt, Leon (1999) Once Upon a Time in China: Kung Fu from Bruce Lee to Jet Li, *Framework*, 40, pp. 85–100.

Internet Movie Data Base (2000), User comments for *Romeo Must Die*, http://us.imdb.com/commentsShow?165929.

La Valley, Albert J. (1985) Traditions of Trickery: The Role of Special Effects in the Science Fiction Film, in George Slusser and Eric Rabkin (eds.), *Shadows of the Magic Lamp: Fantasy and Science Fiction Film*. Carbondale: Southern Illinois University Press, pp. 141–158.

Landon, Brooks (1992) *The Aesthetics of Ambivalence: Rethinking Science Fiction in the Age of Electronic (Re)Production*. Westport and London: Greenwood Press.

Lim, Ron (1999) The Martial Artist's Guide to Hong Kong Films, www.ronlim.com/martial1.html#anchor98800.

Logan, Bey (1995) *Hong Kong Action Cinema*. London: Titan.

Logan, Bey (2000) Casting Electric Shadows, *Impact*, 102, p. 40.

Poyer, Jude (2000) Aiyah! That Had to Hurt, in Stefan Hammond, *Hollywood East* (Lincolnwood (Chicago): Contemporary Books), pp. 203–231.

Reid, Craig R. (1994) An Evening with Jackie Chan, *Bright Lights*, 13, pp. 18–25.

Tateishi, Ramei (1998) Jackie Chan and the Re-invention of Tradition, *Asian Cinema*, 10 (1), pp. 78–84.

Stern, Michael (1990) Making Culture Into Nature in Annette Kuhn, (ed.), *Alien Zone: Cultural Theory and Contemporary Science Fiction Cinema*. London and New York: Verso, pp. 66–72.

11

'Sharon Stone, Screen Diva': stardom, femininity and cult fandom

Rebecca Feasey

Bad Movies We Love was published in 1995. This book is a compilation of film reviews that had been published previously in the popular film magazine *Movieline*, and its authors are Edward Margulies and Stephen Rebello, writers who have published largely non-academic books for a mainstream readership but who also have claims to cultural legitimacy. Edward Margulies, for example, has been the executive editor of *Movieline* but is also the co-author of '100 Best Movies', in which he and his co-author, Virginia Campbell, attempt to identify and analyse the greatest movies ever made, films that include *Queen Christina* (1933), *Citizen Kane* (1941), *Vertigo* (1958), *Raging Bull* (1980) and *The Unbearable Lightness of Being* (1988) (Margulies and Campbell 1995: Online). Similarly, Stephen Rebello has written for a number of mainstream popular magazines such as *GQ*, *LA Style* and *Movieline* but has also written some well-respected studies of Hitchcock – *Alfred Hitchcock and the Making of Psycho* (1998) and *North By Northwest* (2002) – and has co-written the volume *Reel Art* with Richard Allen, a major academic known for his contribution to the philosophy of film (1992).

However, if these authors had previously written celebrations of major films and respected directors, *Bad Movies We Love*, as its title suggests, celebrates those movies that are simply downright 'bad'. In this way, the book displays a particular cult sensibility in its celebration of the 'bad' movie (for work on the 'bad' movie see Telotte 1991; Sconce 1995; Schaefer 1999; Hawkins 2000 and Jancovich 2002). However, although most work on the 'bad' movie concentrates on low-budget or independent filmmaking, the films that make up *Bad Movies We Love* are, by and large, examples of big-budget mainstream Hollywood filmmaking.

Consequently, this book does not represent the whole of the cult movie 'experience', but rather a specific, if important, strategy of cult reading and appropriation. These movies are appropriated as fun because they operate as objects of ridicule: they are films that are not just bad but 'those big budget, big star, big director aggressively publicized fiascos that have gone wonderfully, irredeemably, loveably haywire' (Margulies and Rebello 1995: xvii). This cult strategy is, as Jancovich has argued, similar to Commoli's and Narboni's 'category e films' or 'films that seem at first sight to belong firmly within the ideology [of mainstream filmmaking] and to be completely under its sway, but which turn out to be so only in an ambiguous manner'. As they put it: 'The films we are talking about throw up obstacles in the way of the ideology, causing it to swerve and get off course. The cinematic framework lets us see it, but also shows it up and denounces it' (Comolli and Narboni 2000: 199).

This kind of celebration of the 'bad' movie (as the movie that shows up the working of mainstream filmmaking) can be seen in Sconce's contribution to this volume, but, although Sconce's strategy works to deconstruct cinematic norms, the celebration of bad movies within *Bad Movies We Love* does not threaten cultural hierarchies but works to reaffirm them. As with other elements of cult movie fandom, Margulies and Rebello celebrate the 'weird and wonderful' – the strange and exotic (Vale and Juno 1986 and Ross 1989) but, as we have seen, they still continue to privilege legitimate filmmaking. They do not reject or invert standards of good and bad taste, but rather distinguish between the 'good bad' movie and the bad movie which is simply bad. Some films are therefore 'special bad movies', movies that are 'fun bad', 'jaw-droppingly astoundingly bad' (Margulies and Rebello 1995: xviii). In other words, there is a special category of movies that are celebrated on the grounds that they are 'so bad that they are good'.

However, the celebration of these films is not innocent, but relies on and reaffirms existing cultural hierarchies (see Bourdieu 1998). In other words, the authors' taste for these movies is also based on a distaste for other movies and more particularly the tastes of those social groups with whom those films are associated. In the process, the authors set themselves up as privileged readers, with special access to films, against the 'ordinary' film viewer. As they comment, the films that they like are those 'that means you guffaw when you see one' (Margulies and Rebello 1995: xviii), but this reaction is not associated with everyone. On the contrary, they point out that while 'you' are laughing at the film 'you're surrounded by dolts who are actually sitting in polite silence' (ibid.: xviii). Most viewers are therefore seen as "suckers" and the success of mainstream films is not a guarantee of their quality but evidence that Hollywood has "fooled 'em again"' (ibid.: xviii). Furthermore, the 'polite silence' of the 'ordinary' viewers identifies them as passive and is distinguished from the 'guffaw' of the cult viewers, which identifies them as active. The latter, it is suggested, resist and reject the film while the former passively accept and consume it.

However, as has often been pointed out, the passive viewer is also routinely associated with femininity (Huyssen 1986; Hollows 2000, Read 2000). Indeed, the 'dolts who are actually sitting in polite silence' are claimed by Margulies and Rebello to be the kind of audience that would be 'wondering whether or not Julia Roberts will be killed by her co-star' (Margulies and Rebello 1995: xviii). The choice of Julia Roberts here is particularly telling given her status as the queen of the 'chick flick'. The audience who care about her fate are therefore presumed to be predominantly female. Of course, the authors don't simply dismiss female-orientated filmmaking: they also single out films such as *Days of Thunder* (1990) for ridicule. But these films, it is suggested, are directed at an audience of teenage boys, an audience that is made up of individuals who are presumed to be not only unsophisticated but also implicitly anxious about their masculinity: they are not properly or fully masculine. However, the majority of the films that Margulies and Rebello discuss are associated with female genres and audiences: for example, there is a particular emphasis on the musical and the melodrama.

In this way, the authors present themselves as discerning viewers and address themselves to what is presumed to be a discerning reader. They therefore emphasize the exclusivity and inaccessibility of many of the materials that they discuss, and the reader is told that they 'won't find every bad movie we love at your corner video and laser disk store' (Margulies and Rebello 1995: xix). Readers are advised not to 'overlook your local [television] listings as a guideline to locate hard to find gems which you can tape for posterity' (ibid.: xix). The volume also informs the reader that many 'of our favourites are available for rental by mail' (ibid.: xix) and they provide information about specialist outlets. Such hard-to-find films are therefore positioned against the 'bad bad movies' that have 'polluted' the world, movies that are familiar with 'anyone who's been to their plex anytime recently' (ibid.: xvii). Bad bad movies are therefore seen as both ubiquitous and hence easily available.

This essay will therefore provide an analysis of this volume, but one that concentrates on its handling of Sharon Stone, a star who not only receives a chapter all to herself but who also wrote the foreword to the book. In the process, the book provides different images of Stone, although it is concerned mainly with her early career. Rather than concentrate on her star status, which had been established a couple of years before with the phenomenal success of *Basic Instinct* (1992), the authors invite the reader to 'revisit the career milestones that made the beauteous towhead what she is today' (Margulies and Rebello 1995: 135). In this way, the authors establish *Basic Instinct* as the context for a humorous retrospective on Stone's career: 'Before Sharon Stone came on strong as the leggy, scene-stealing stinker in the otherwise forgettable *Basic Instinct*, she had honed her craft in some real stinkers' (ibid.: 135).

These comments also highlight the specific concerns of the authors. Stone is presumed to be not only a bad actress but also one who is defined by her body and hence assumed to be dumb blonde: she is a 'leggy [. . .] beauteous towhead' or a 'gorgeous dim bulb' (Margulies and Rebello 1995: 135). When her acting is mentioned it is referred to as a 'tour de farce' (ibid.: 138), and she is often dismissed as incompetent, mannered and overblown. Her success is therefore attributed to her looks and particularly her supposed penchant for parts involving 'lots of sex and acres of bare flesh' (Andrews 1994: 78). In other words, she is an actress whose appeal is presumed to depend on her status as an object of sexual display.

However, Sharon Stone is presented not simply as an object of sexual exploitation but as someone complicit in her own exploitation and hence an exploitative figure herself. However, as we will see, while this position was often used to present Stone as an active and intelligent Hollywood player who maintained power and control over her own career, Margulies and Rebello present her as a passive victim but one who is blamed for her own victimization. For example, although they sneer at *Action Jackson* (1988) and refer to it as the kind of movie in which women 'exist to be naked, dead, or both' (Margulies and Rebello 1995: 136), they do not use this as the basis for an attack on the gender politics of contemporary Hollywood cinema but project such problems on to female stars such as

Stone who is derided for being a 'nudity-friendly vamp' (ibid.: 138). In other words, the authors do not suggest that it is the sexual politics of the industry that is at fault but rather the female performers who conform to its demands.

In the process, the authors rely also on the familiar association of femininity with passivity, artificiality and superficiality. As Hollows points out, feminine beauty is often associated with artifice and superficiality and hence used to associate masculinity with authenticity and substance:

> The ways in which men have been associated with the 'rational' world of production and women the 'irrational' world of consumption . . . structures many negative accounts of fashion [and beauty practices]. Many theorists who are anti-fashion draw on these critiques of mass consumption and mass culture . . . Within these critiques women's investment in what is seen as the shallow, trivial and irrational world of fashion is used to associate femininity with shallowness, triviality and irrationality (and vice versa). (Hollows 2000: 137–138)

Women are therefore seen to lack intelligence and internality – they are seen as other-directed and objectified while men are independent, individualized and self-possessed.

This chapter will therefore examine the various ways in which Sharon Stone's early career is made to mean within the book and the ways in which it operates in relation to discourses of femininity. The next section, for example, concentrates on the authors' account of *King Solomon's Mines* (1985) and the ways in which Stone is presented as a classic dumb blonde starlet. The following section then moves on to their discussion of *Scissors* (1991), a film that the authors ridicule precisely for its pretensions. In this film, Stone is required to turn in a psychological portrayal of a 'twenty-six year old virgin', and she is ridiculed for not relying on her sex appeal and for attempting to act.

Finally, the article will examine Stone's own voice within the book and the ways in which she challenges the authors' presentation of her. If the authors present her as an object to be laughed at, Stone presents herself as self-conscious and active by laughing at herself. In other words, she refuses the role of the unselfconscious object but, in the process, she is implicitly required to distance herself from her own femininity – to make herself 'culturally one of the boys' (Thornton 1995: 104). As a result, the article will demonstrate the gendered dynamics of these specific forms of cult movie fandom and the homosocial use of femininity as an object of otherness that is used to secure and legitimate masculinity (Hollows, this volume, pp. 35–53).

King Solomon's Mines (1985)

In 1985, CAA (the Creative Artist's Agency) was representing Sharon Stone and it announced that it had waved its commission to realize her ambition to star in the African jungle adventure, *King Solomon's Mines*. The film was modelled on the success of the Indiana Jones series, and Stone played the female sidekick, Jesse Huston, to Richard Chamberlain's male hero, Allen Quartermain. The film and its sequel, *Allen Quartermain and the Lost City of Gold* (1987), bankrupted Canon Pictures, but Margulies and Rebello declare that Stone is 'enjoyably terrible – unlike her co-stars who're just plain terrible' and claim that the film is an 'expensive, trashy . . . jungle adventure' (Margulies and Rebello 1993: 136). In this way, their celebration of the film is indistinguishable from contempt and the terms of this contempt, are gendered. The film is presented as extravagant, self-indulgent and tasteless; qualities that have frequently been linked to femininity. Indeed, as we have seen, women's association with the sphere of consumption is often equated with self-indulgence, weakness, destructiveness, waste, triviality and irrationality – qualities that are not only associated with femininity but are used to privilege masculinity through an association with benevolence, productivity, creativity, substance and rationality (Hollows 2000: 114).

If the film provokes laughter, it is therefore clear that we are not supposed to be laughing with its creators but 'laughing at them' (Margulies and Rebell, 1995: 137). To some extent the problems are blamed on the script, which is described as 'going nowhere' and requires the leads to 'swap pathetic witticisms' (ibid.: 137). However, these witticisms also raise another issue. Margulies and Rebello make special mention of a scene in which Chamberlain tries to instruct Stone on how to handle the throttle of a plane by yelling, 'It's right there between your legs, pull on it!' (ibid.: 137) At another point, they refer to a scene in which a tribe of cannibals place the stars in a huge cooking-pot and Chamberlain says to Stone, 'Did anyone tell you you look ravishing with onions in your hair?' (ibid.: 137)

The significance of these references is that they highlight Margulies's and Rebello's preoccupation with Stone's body in this film. Here the humour of the film is focused on Stone's body itself as the key signifier of bad taste. They seem almost completely uninterested in the casual racism of the scene with the cannibals, and virtually obsessed with references to Stone's hairdos and make-up. At one point, they tell the reader to keep 'your eyes peeled during the scene in which a spiked ceiling is closing down on the pair, who stand neck deep in water, and Stone's hair color and coiffure change completely' (Margulies and Rebello 1995: 137). Here the humour is less about the inconsistency of the filmmaking than about the inappropriateness of Stone's hairstyles.

Indeed, Stone's make-up and hairdos are identified as the most ridiculous element in the film, a film in which its leads 'battle Nazis', deadly snakes, giant spiders, quicksand, tribal priestesses, hilarious hair and make up jobs' (Margulies and Rebello 1995: 137). In other words, the stars are 'at sea' not only because of the hopelessness of the script but also because of the inappropriate glamorization of its leading lady, who is referred to as 'an improbable archeology student' (ibid.: 137). No argument is actually provided for why she is so 'improbable' but the implication is clear: Stone is mere eye-candy and a women who looks like that could never be intellectual.

Scissors (1991)

If Stone is dismissed as a 'bimbo' in *King Solomon's Mines*, she becomes an object of ridicule in *Scissors* for trying to act. For Margulies and Rebello, Stone cannot win. If she is ridiculed as a 'nudity-friendly vamp' (Margulies and Rebello 1995: 138), she is presented as even more ridiculous when she attempts to go it 'fully clothed', and they question whether 'the same millions [that went to see her in *Basic Instinct*] would be willing to put in their time' to see her in such a role (ibid.: 138). Furthermore, her role in *Scissors* is made to seem even more ridiculous in that she is supposedly 'wittily cast against type as a twenty-six year old virgin' (ibid.: 138). However, the wit here is presumed to be entirely unintentional, and the film and its star are presented as hilarious precisely because of their seriousness.

Stone is therefore derided for 'keeping a straight face while playing impossible scenes' (Margulies and Rebello 1995: 138). The problem, it is suggested, is not simply that she can't act but that she doesn't even seem to be aware of how awful she and the film are. This, of course, does not stop them from attacking her performance, which, as we have seen, is dismissed as a 'tour de farce' (ibid.: 138). It may be a role that Stone takes seriously and sees as an 'opportunity' to demonstrate her dramatic skills, but the performance that she turns in is presented as ludicriously overblown and over the top. In one scene, it is claimed, she 'freaks out, hilariously, and faster than you can say *Gaslight*' (ibid.: 138), while in another she is supposed to be 'under hypnosis' and 'repressing some sexual trauma involving her stepfather, her mother, and a puppet of a little pig (don't ask)' (ibid.: 138).

Despite her efforts and the film's content, her performance is dismissed as overblown and mannered and therefore crucially lacking in psychological realism. Certainly, as the reference to the 'puppet of a little pig' makes clear, the problem is not just Stone's performance but the fact that the psychology in the film is all 'mumbo jumbo'. However, it is the sheer absurdity of the material that provides Margulies and Rebello with such pleasure. The film is not just about people trying to drive Stone's character 'stark, raving mad', it drives 'us' as an audience mad (Margulies and Rebello 1995: 139), and results in a film that is itself 'crazy', a film that is 'weird and wonderful' like other cult classics. In addition to the 'puppet of a little pig', Stone's character 'works temp jobs but lives in a stadium-size, high-rise apartment surrounded by antique dolls' (ibid.: 138), and the details of the plot, it is suggested, defy not only belief but also logic. If it is the pretensions of the film that are therefore derided, this is made abundantly clear in the reference to it as a 'tacky *Repulsion* rip off' (ibid.: 138). Here the film is chastised for its attempt to emulate a work of 'art house' horror (see Hawkins 2000) while producing a film that is not only supposedly artless but even exploitative.

In the process, it is therefore *Basic Instinct* that is not only seen as the film that 'proved [that] millions enjoy spending time in the dark' with its leading lady (Margulies and Rebello 1993: 138) but is consequently presented as the crucial intertext for Sharon Stone. However, while popular, critical and cult discourses all present this erotic thriller as a crucial intertext, they present Stone in very different ways. The mainstream film industry frequently associates her sex appeal with the bygone glamour of classical Hollywood and often explicitly the Hitchcockian ice-princess. In this way, they try to distinguish the star from the stars of direct-to-video erotic thrillers such as Shannon Tweed and Sharon Whirry. However, in *Bad Movies We Love*, the authors present Stone as a cult movie goddess specifically through her association with the contemporary erotic thriller, an association which is emphasized by references to her roots in a tacky and disreputable back catalogue.

From image to word

If Margulies and Rebello present Sharon Stone as a 'dim bulb' who is blissfully unaware of how ridiculous she really is, Stone presents herself very differently in the foreword to the volume, an introduction in which she clearly presents herself as sharp and witty precisely by laughing at herself. She claims that Margulies and Rebello, 'these bad, bad men', had asked her to 'write something about their book', a book in which she had 'heard they had slammed me' (Margulies and Rebello 1995: xivi). On the one hand, she presents her situation as hardly unique. It is claimed that 'practically everyone else in Hollywood' was also a target within the book, and bad movies are simply the standard fare of Hollywood, 'the big bad town we all love' (ibid.: xivi). On the other, she also presents herself as being special. The authors not only asked her to provide an introduction but when she said, 'You're *not* kidding, are you, bad men?' they answered, 'Oh, no, my pretty, in fact you have your own *chapter*' (ibid.: xivi). This exchange not only demonstrates that she was singled out for special mention within the book, but it is also written in a self-mockingly childlike tone. The authors are 'bad, bad men' and she is the wide-eyed innocent, 'my pretty'. As a result, the authors are made to sound like the fairytale wolf as it prepares to eat Red Riding Hood, but Stone is setting this scenario up to dismiss it.

It is her own 'big bad ego' which 'couldn't resist looking into it', and her response to the book is also suitably assertive. Rather than the demure, cringing and passive 'dolts' who care what happens to Julia Roberts in a film, she is able to 'laugh and titter and guffaw' (Margulies and Rebello 1995: xviii), to share in the joke with a robust and masculine sense of physical self-possession. It may be 'other chapters' that make her laugh the most, but she is able to laugh at herself when reading her 'own chapter' (ibid.: xivi). Nor is there any sense of lingering resentment. She confirms that the authors 'really do love these "bad" moves', and informs us that she is 'darn glad that they do' (ibid.: xivi).

There are two reasons for this gladness. On the one hand, Stone is often represented as someone who unashamedly pursues that which provides her with enjoyment, and she has frequently claimed that she likes to play the Hollywood bad girl because it gives her 'more freedom . . . and more fun' (Thompson 1994: 12). On the other, she is also often presented as a workhorse, someone who is serious about her work and willing to put in the commitment and the effort to make a project happen. She is anything but the temperamental female star of Hollywood myth. As a result, she presents herself as someone who appreciates the book not only because she enjoys a laugh as much as the next person but also because 'we try just as hard when we make a "bad" movie as when we make a "good" movie (Margulies and Rebello 1995: xivi). Even if a movie is bad, she appreciates that someone is able to derive pleasure from the work that she has put in, whatever the nature of that pleasure.

This also allows her to perform a little sleight of hand, and she calls into question the very distinction between good and bad movies. 'After all,' she asks, 'what makes a movie "good"?' and she precedes to tell us: 'It's "good" because you enjoy it, because it made you laugh (at it or with it) or scream or cry or howl or remember or forget or just simply to escape within it' (Margulies and Rebello 1995: xivi). In other words, she questions the distinction between good and bad, not to challenge existing cultural hierarchies but rather to argue that a movie is good so long as it provides pleasure. In this way, she is able to justify her own films: 'That's why I make them anyway, "good" or "bad" (ibid.: xivi). She therefore instructs the audience to 'have some fun' and use the book as a guide to future film viewing: 'Look inside these pages, rent a video, pop some popcorn, and laugh and love' (ibid.: xivi). And finally she thanks the reader 'for going to the movies' (ibid.: xivi).

In this way, Stone presents herself first and foremost as a professional, a person who understands that she is doing a job and will work with whatever resources are available to her. Consequently, the self-mockery found in her introduction is not unique to this volume but can be found throughout the press coverage on her. Indeed, in September 1993, the same year that *Bad Movies We Love* was published, an interview with Sharon Stone in *Empire*, a popular British film magazine, was accompanied by a piece entitled, 'Know

Any Beautiful Blondes'. In the piece, Sharon Stone 'guides you through the highlights of her back catalogue' and archly begins the description of each film with the line 'I played a beautiful blonde . . .' (Stone 1993: 92–3). In her description of *King Solomon's Mines*, for example, she comments: 'I played a beautiful blonde with a really bad hairdo who worked for Cannon Films. I think that says it all' (Stone 1993: 93). Similarly, in her description of *Scissors*, she claims: 'I played a beautiful blonde who was trapped alone in an apartment. It'll be the next Rocky Horror Picture Show' (Stone 1993: 93).

This self-mockery is therefore used to distance herself from these roles and to present herself as being fully self-conscious when making them. In other words, the humour allows her to present herself as being fully in control, as simply exploiting the system to get ahead, rather than being a victim of it. However, in the process, she is forced to distance herself from her own femininity, and to participate in the othering of the 'ordinary' dumb blonde. Her femininity simply becomes a performance, something she uses to get ahead, and she is therefore often figured as a masculine women or a dominatrix. The quotation from Stone on the front of the September 1993 issue of *Empire* is: 'Since becoming famous I get to torture a better class of man . . .'. In other words, she asserts herself to be 'culturally one of the boys' and her self-consciousness, self-possession, control, intelligence and determination remain opposed to the figure of the feminine other, the dumb blonde.

Conclusion

As we have therefore seen, Sharon Stone's image is shaped in relationship to discourses of femininity and the ways in which these are ranked and valued within cultural hierarchies. Stone may be celebrated by the collection over stars such as Julia Roberts, but this is precisely because she represents the lowest of the low within the hierarchies of Hollywood femininity, the 'nudity-friendly' dumb blonde.

However, as we have also seen, Stone's image is not fixed but has a multi-accentuality, which means that in other contexts the actress is privileged as a female star who is sharp, intelligent and in control of her own career. Unfortunately, this presentation also involves an othering of the 'dumb blonde'. In other words, Stone and others are able to raise her value but only by distinguishing herself from the figure of the dumb blonde, a strategy that only works to affirm the worthlessness and contemptability of this figure of femininity.

Consequently, we have seen how much certain forms of cult movie fandom are predicated on a homosocial othering of femininity and hence how much these forms of fandom are a boy's game. This is, of course, to claim not that women cannot participate within it, but rather that to do so they must distance themselves from, and disavow, their own femininity. They must convert femininity into an object of otherness and ridicule and hence become 'one of the boys'.

References

Andrews, S. (1994) Wits Out for the Lads, *Empire*, 59 (May), pp. 76–81.

Bourdieu, P. (1998) *Distinction: A Social Critique of the Judgement of Taste*. London: Routledge.

Comolli, J. L. and Narboni, P. (2000) Cinema/Ideology/Criticism, in Joanne Hollows, Peter Hutchings and Mark Jancovich (eds.), *The Film Studies Reader*. London: Arnold, pp. 197–200.

Hawkins, J. (2000) *Cutting Edge: Art-horror and the Horrific Avant-garde*. Minnesota: University of Minnesota Press.

Hollows, J. (2000) *Feminism, Femininity and Popular Culture*. Manchester and New York: Manchester University Press.

Hollows, J., Hutchings, P. and Jancovich, M. (eds.) (2000) *The Film Studies Reader*. London: Arnold.

Huyssen, A. (1986) Mass Culture as Woman: Modernism's Other, in T. Modleski (ed.), *Studies in Entertainment: Critical Approaches to Mass Culture*. Bloomington and Indianapolis: Indiana University Press.

Jancovich, M. (2002) Cult Fictions: Cult Movies, Subcultural Capital and the Productions of Cutlural Distinctions, *Cultural Studies*, 16 (2), pp. 306–322.

Margulies, E. and Rebello, S. (1995) *Bad Movies We Love*. London and New York: Marion Boyars.

Read, J. (2000) *The New Avengers: Feminism, Femininity and the Rape-Revenge Cycle*. Manchester and New York: Manchester University Press.

Rebello, S. (1992) *Reel Art: Great Posters from the Golden Age of the Silver Screen*. London: Abbeville Press.

Rebello, S. (1998) *Alfred Hitchcock and the Making of Psycho*. London: Marion Boyars.

Rebello, S. (2002) *North by Northwest*. London: St Martin's Press.

Ross, A. (1989) *No Respect: Intellectuals and Popular Culture*. New York:

Routledge.

Schaefer, E. (1999) *'Bold! Daring! Shocking! True!' A History of Exploitation Films, 1919–1959*. Durham and London: Duke University Press.

Sconce, J. (1995) 'Trashing' the Academy: Taste, Excess, and Emerging Politics of Cinematic Style, *Screen*, 36 (4) (Winter), pp. 371–393.

Stone, S. (1993) Know Any Beautiful Blondes?, *Empire*, 51 (September), pp. 93–94.

Telotte, J. P. (1991) *The Cult Film Experience: Beyond All Reason*. Austin: University of Texas Press.

Thompson, D. (1994) *Sharon Stone: Basic Ambition*. London: Warner Books.

Thornton, S. (1995) *Club Cultures: Music, Media and Subcultural Capital*. Oxford: Blackwell.

Vale, V., and Juno, Andrea (eds.) (1986) *Re/Search 10: Incredibly Strange Films*. San Francisco: Re/Search Publications.

Internet references

Margulies, E., and Campbell, V. (1995) The 100 Best Movies Ever Made (in English), in *Movieline:Online*, December 1995, www.movieline.com/reviews/bestlist.shtml, 25 April 2002.

12

The importance of trivia: ownership, exclusion and authority in science fiction fandom

Nathan Hunt

In discussions of fandom, either fans are denigrated for their obsession with apparently useless trivia or else their concern with this information is valorized as a form of radical cultural criticism. For example, in his classic study of fandom, Jenkins discusses these positions in his opening chapter '"Get a Life!": Fans, Poachers, Nomads' (Jenkins 1992: 9–49). The chapter begins with an anecdote about an appearance by William Shatner, star of cult television show *Star Trek*, on the comedy sketch show *Saturday Night Live*. On the show, Shatner appears in a sketch in which he plays himself at a fan convention where, appearing in front of overweight, bespectacled and Spock-eared fans, he is bombarded by demands for trivia about *Star Trek*. This information is presented as useless and trivial, with fans demanding to know the combination to Captain Kirk's safe and arguing over the cabin number of minor character Yeoman Rand. Finally, driven to distraction, Shatner yells 'Get a life, will you people? I mean, I mean, for crying out loud, it's just a TV show!' (Jenkins 1992: 10). Jenkins's point here is that the sketch reproduces popular depictions of fans as sad and pathetic, lacking a grasp of reality and obsessed with the unimportant. (For other discussions of the negative image of fandom see Jensen 1992.)

Jenkins uses this sketch to foreground and explain the position against which the rest of his book argues. He rejects the idea that fans are obsessed with useless and trivial knowledge but, in the process, he ends up trying to validate fan knowledge as part of a supposedly radical activity of 'textual poaching'. In his desire to assert that fan knowledge is not unimportant, he avoids any association with the term 'trivial' and is forced to suggest that fan knowledges are therefore never about apparently 'trivial' details. However, fan magazines such as *SFX* sell precisely because they provide fans with access to various forms of knowledge, knowledge that is not always as significant as Jenkins might imply. For example, a recent *SFX* article discusses *Star Wars, Episode II: Attack of the Clones* and it opens with the information that the musical score for the movie is 125 minutes long and was recorded by 110 musicians and a full choir (*SFX*, 90, April 2002: 21). Other recent articles have also been preoccupied with discussions of Ewan McGregor's beard (*SFX*, 89, Spring 2002, Star Wars Episode II Spoiler Guide: 9). Similarly fans engage in the exchange of information in the readers' letters pages of fan media. For example, a recent *SFX* 'Letter of the Month' identifies references to the movie *Toy Story* (1995) in the SF television series *Farscape*, and it points out that in one episode the villain Scorpius has the name 'ANDY' written on the bottom of his shoe (*SFX*, 86, January 2002: 11).

However rather than denigrate fans for their obsession with trivia or trying to present these knowledges as vital acts of symbolic resistance, this article will demonstrate the ways in which trivia work as a form of cultural capital within fandom. It concentrates on the coverage of one SF film, *Star Wars Episode I: The Phantom Menace*, within one publication produced for SF fans, *SFX*. In the process, it will examine how trivia operate to establish the ownership of SF texts. Through their use of trivia, fans lay claim to having special access to, and hence dominion over, specific texts owing to their supposedly superior knowledge of them. Second, the article will analyse how this position is used to define and police the borders of fandom. Trivia are used to establish who is an insider and to declare others to be outsiders who do not have the right to participate within fandom. Third and finally, it will explore therefore the role of trivia in producing, maintaining and negotiating hierarchies within fandom.

In the process, the article draws on Sarah Thornton's work on British dance club cultures. Her study examines the relationship between fan cultures and the mainstream, and Thornton objects to the unqualified use of the term 'mainstream' in studies of fandom: 'Inconsistent fantasies of the mainstream are rampant in cultural studies' (Thornton 1995). Instead Thornton proposes a model in which the mainstream is not a real tangible culture but a construction of fandom. Fan cultures construct images of the mainstream in order to produce a position of difference. 'They carry around images of the social worlds that make up club culture. These mental maps, rich in cultural detail and value judgement, offer them a distinct "sense of [their] place" but also a sense of the other's place' (Thornton 1995: 99). As a result, this opposition between fandom and the mainstream is never stable but is constantly renegotiated by fans in their efforts to define and police its boundaries (for other discussions of this relationship see Jenkins 1992; and Jenkins and Tulloch 1995).

However, if trivia serve specific functions within fandom, we need to distinguish them from other claims about trivia. For example, in her exploration of gossip as a form of cultural discourse, Mary Ellen Brown posits a model of gossip as a subcultural discourse of resistance and affirmation. For Brown, gossip provides a sense of belonging to communities of women through resistance to masculine ideology. In her view, gossip is neither the phatic, empty chat that popular dismissals suggest, nor is it the extension and internalization of masculine ideology and oppression as many scholars have claimed. Instead gossip provides a way of establishing bonds through common points of interest to members of a specific culture (Brown 1994). By implication, however, gossip also performs an exclusive function: if gossip bonds women, it also excludes the discourses of masculinity. Brown's study essentially uses the same approach as Jenkins's does: it distances gossip from implications of triviality by valorizing it as a process of ideological resistance. However, Brown's work still makes possible a useful comparison with the study of trivia within science fiction fandom. Within this area of fandom, trivia are also used to create a sense of inclusion through shared knowledge, but they are also used to exclude outsiders, to produce and maintain the boundaries of the subculture. In other words, although Brown's study places gossip in a largely nurturing and affirming environment, trivia also function within a highly competitive and hierarchical environment within fandom.

Trivia and fan media

As we have seen, a large proportion of fan media is devoted to the dissemination of trivia (see Jenkins and Tulloch 1995 and Jancovich and Hunt, forthcoming), and fan magazines such as *SFX*, *Starburst* and *Dreamwatch* are dominated by news and articles about films and television, particularly new films in production. The information in these publications takes a variety of different forms such as gossip, reports on forthcoming science fiction films and television shows, opinion columns, picture previews and articles about specific productions. These reports provide details about directors, stars, scriptwriters, budgets and even plots.

First published in 1995 by Future Publishing, the magazine *SFX* is one such publication and, according to its own publicity, it is now Britain's best-selling science fiction fan publication. Regardless of the accuracy of this claim, the magazine is certainly successful on a national level, with the average circulation, by April 2002, of over 37,000 copies.[1] The magazine is published monthly and found on the shelves of most high-street newsagents in the UK alongside other successful SF and fantasy magazines such as *Starburst* and *Dreamwatch*. Appealing to a largely young male readership, the magazine has moved from relatively small sales as a quirky and colourful fan publication to a much higher level of distribution, along the way acquiring a more 'glossy' higher-quality finish and seemingly moving towards an older but still male-orientated readership (for a more extensive discussion of the gendering of magazines see Winship 1987; Hermes 1995; Nixon 1996; Jackson, Stevenson and Brooks 2001). Like most magazines, *SFX* is divided into sections, including reviews, articles, editorials and a letters page. There is in particular a concentration on forthcoming movies within the large news and gossip section of the magazine called 'Strange Tales'. This section is the most clearly centred on the provision of trivia and it includes a large number of sub-sections such as 'Development Hell', which looks at films delayed in production. The magazine even has regular columns dedicated to trivia about forthcoming productions, particularly features on the new Star Wars movies: 'Star Wars Rumour Roundup' and 'Tremors in the Force'.

However, it is important to remember that *SFX* is not a fanzine: fanzines are usually produced by fans and distributed on a small scale usually for very little, if any, financial profit. *SFX* on the other hand is a profit-orientated publication, owned and distributed by a large publishing company. This parent company Future Publishing, also publishes more 'mainstream' magazines such as *Total Film*, a big-budget film-orientated publication similar to *Empire*, and *T3*, a publication devoted to electronic consumer items.[2] None the less, like the fanzines, *SFX* is written and edited by self-confessed SF fans. Of course, such media cannot provide direct evidence of fan cultures. They are, after all, commercial publications created to make money. Indeed, despite *SFX*'s frequent claims to be written 'by fans, for fans', many readers disagree with its content, style and reading of SF texts, as is often evidenced within the magazine's letters page. There is, of course, a danger in conflating the opinions and claims made by professional journalists who write the magazine with fandom itself. These kinds of problems have been acknowledge within many studies of audience reception (see Staiger 1992; Urrichio and Pearson 1993; Allen and Gomery 1985 and Klinger 1994), but they do not necessarily invalidate the use of such media. Even direct audience responses are not without their problems. As Ien Ang's influential study of *Dallas* fans shows, audiences are aware of the way that their comments can be perceived and judged. Their comments are never a simple reflection of their actual experience but are always shaped by the specific social contexts within which they comment (Ang 1985; Bacon-Smith 1992; Barker and Brooks 1998) Evidence never speaks for itself but must always be subject to interpretation that takes into account its specific conditions of production.

However, if used carefully, media such as *SFX* can provide us with valuable insights into the cultures within which they circulate. Indeed, these media are often immersed in the subcultures to which they sell themselves. Readers often aspire to be journalists, just as the journalists themselves profess their allegiances to various fan factions and were themselves readers of fan media. In addition, while the fans and journalist often disagree, journalists themselves often engage in public conflicts in much the same ways that fans do. Indeed, as Thornton demonstrates, fan media are 'instrumental in the congregation of [fans] and the formation of subcultures' (Thornton 1995: 121). In other words, as Jancovich has argued, fan cultures 'are themselves brought together, and a sense of "imagined community" is produced and maintained, *through* the media' (Jancovich 2002: 318).

Fandom and ownership

The release of *Star Wars Episode I: The Phantom Menace* in July 1999 was a significant event for SF fandom. As the long-awaited 'prequel' to the legendary *Star Wars* franchise of *A New Hope* (1977), *The Empire Strikes Back* (1980) and *The Return of the Jedi*

(1983), the film was always going to be a significant event for SF fans because of the canonical status of its predecessors. On its release in both the US and the UK, the media was rife with stories of fans sleeping outside cinemas overnight to be the first in the queue and paying to see another film only to leave after the *Episode I* trailer.

As a result, *Episode I* was not just a significant event for the SF fan community, and this proved highly significant within the fan community. The release of the movie was a major cinematic event for film fans more generally, and *Episode I*, like its predecessors, showcased not only spectacular special effects but also the use of groundbreaking cinematic technology in digital filming techniques.[3] The film was also to be a significant event for many less regular moviegoers and, alongside the less aggressively publicized *The Matrix* (1999), *Episode I* was the event movie of summer 1999 and attracted record-breaking audiences (see Kramer 2001). Pre-release articles about *Episode I* covered everything from the soundtrack to the costumes, and these articles appeared, often long before the film's release either in the UK or the USA, in a range of publications not directly associated with the SF genre. Articles and information appeared in everything from television guides to movie fan magazines such as *Empire* to lifestyle publications such as *The Face* and 'new lad' magazines such as *Loaded* and *FHM*.[4] As such, in 1999, two SF movies found enormous popularity among more mainstream audiences.

This mainstream popularity created a paradoxical problem for fandom. On the one hand, such enormous popularity confirmed the importance of SF as a cinematic genre. However, at the same time, such popularity threatened fandom's position of difference from, and opposition to, the mainstream. As Thornton explains, subcultures fear the popularization of their culture because such popularity negates their sense of difference (Thornton 1995). As a result, *The Phantom Menace* became a site of struggle for ownership for fandom, and so placed fan media in a difficult position. Unable to praise the film without the danger of associating its tastes with those of the mainstream, and yet, at the same time, unable to denigrate the film without undermining fan investment in it, *SFX* chose to claim ownership of only certain elements and readings of the film. In doing so, certain elements of the film were rejected and associated with the mainstream. In other words, the magazine claimed ownership of the film through a supposedly superior textual and extra textual knowledge of the film, and this ownership was itself used to distinguish the magazine's appreciation of the film from that of mainstream publications.

In its discussions of the film, *SFX* went to great lengths to draw attention to the cultural significance of the film. It was particularly concerned with the film's box-office record-breaking status.

> As *The Phantom Menace* blitzes the stateside box office, toppling cinematic records in spite of a barrage of critical sniper fire, the buzz is already beginning on *Episode II* . . . At presstime, *The Phantom Menace* had toppled *The Lost World*'s record of the most successful opening day in screen history. While Steven Spielberg's dinofest took $26,1 million on the Sunday of Memorial Day weekend 1997, *Episode I* bagged a gross of $28,542,349 in its first 24 hours. (*SFX*, 53, July 1999: 3)

The use of box-office figures here are intended to demonstrate the irrefutable status of the movie as one of the most significant cinematic events of all time. Interestingly, these statistics are rather selective in their use. The article ignores the industry-favoured standard of using the opening *weekend* figures (which would have placed *The Lost World* higher) in favour of using the opening day in order to heighten the importance of *Episode I*. The article also attempts to defend *Episode I* against bad press. Negative critical reception is tellingly referred to as 'critical sniper fire', carrying all the connotations of malevolent, destructive criticisms that are an attempt to sabotage the film's success.

However, fandom's claims to ownership of the movie were not without their problems, and certain aspects of the movie proved extremely contentious. The character of Jar Jar Binks, for example, received a barrage of criticism from fans and fan media. Jar Jar Binks was an alien character who was remarkable to the extent that his screen appearance was partially generated through CGI (Computer Generated Imaging) technology: throughout much of the movie, the creature's face is superimposed on to an actor's body. There was some unease both inside and outside of fan media that such a prominent character was generated largely by a computer,[5] and many fans tried to distance themselves from the character while maintaining a claim to rightful ownership of the film. In other words, this character was used to establish fandom's supposed difference from the mainstream. Binks was identified as the mainstream appeal of the movie, and the character was denigrated in reviews and articles in order to demonstrate that both the magazine and fandom were resistant to the mainstream.

The magazine therefore took issue with Jar Jar Binks's meaning within the film. One particular article, for example, picked up on the alleged racial stereotyping associated with the Binks character: 'African-American studies professor Micheal Dyson questions his "stereotypical elements . . . The way he spoke, the way he walked"' (*SFX*, 54, August 1999: 14). A reference was also made to a similar opinion expressed in *The Wall Street Journal*. However, what is at issue here is not whether Binks is a racist stereotype, but rather that he was seen by fans as a cynical marketing ploy aimed at children. In both this article and other reports, the character is referred to in exactly these terms. He is compared to the Ewoks from the preceding movie *The Return of the Jedi* (1983), another aspect of the Star Wars franchise that came in for a great deal of criticism from fans. However, it is also claimed that, by comparison, 'The Ewoks had it easy' (*SFX*, 53, July 1999: 9), a claim that alludes to a rather humorous article in the previous issue that had complained about the Ewoks as a marketing ploy:

> You cannot deny that the Ewoks were a merchandiser's dream. They were cute and fluffy and, with their more than faint resemblance to teddy bears, a sure-fire hit. The soft toys flew off the shelves, there were spin-offs . . . Kids loved them . . . They were designed purely to make money, and hold little resonance with the rest of Lucas' vision. (*SFX*, 53, July 1999: 9)

The reference to this previous article also performs another function. The article assumes a pre-existing knowledge of trivia, and this self-referential aspect of trivia serves to exclude any non-fans who would not be familiar with these debates, thus maintaining the exclusive boundaries of fandom.

By denigrating Jar Jar Binks and the Ewoks, *SFX* is able to make a case for fandom's position as the arbitrator of what is 'good' and what is 'bad' about the film – for example, what is an authentic and integral part of 'Lucas' vision' and what is an inauthentic and alien to that vision. By implication, 'good' science fiction is presented as serious and adult, while 'cynical marketing' and 'children's characters' are that which constitute 'bad' science fiction. If a pun may be excused here, the real 'phantom menace' for many fans is the spectre of the mainstream that threatens to undermine their claims for the quality of science fiction. Furthermore, the magazine consolidates the right to make these distinctions through appeals to the arbiters of culturally legitimacy. They make reference to an academic (a professor no less) and to one of the most respected newspapers in the United States. Such references to legitimate culture are far from unusual in fan media, and fan discourses have been deeply rooted in the academy historically (Fiske 1992; and Jancovich and Hunt forthcoming). However, *SFX* allies itself not only with the academy but also with other subcultures. Another piece of trivia contained within the same report notes the objections of rap artist Stormtroopa, who had released a track entitled 'Jar Jar Binks Must Die'.

What is most interesting in these references is that these attacks on Binks all share the same basis, an objection to mass-marketing and racial stereotype. What are taking place therefore are subtly shifting cultural associations. *SFX* uses legitimate culture and other subcultures to demonstrate a broad range of cultural capital whilst at the same time taking care to marginalize or exclude the tastes of the mainstream as represented by Hollywood and the 'ordinary' consumer, and what is at work here is a process of distinction. Furthermore, it is the image of science fiction fandom that is at stake. Certain knowledges and tastes are associated with science fiction fans, and others are not. SF fans, it is claimed, are critical and discerning and hence they understand both legitimate culture and authentic subcultures. However, these preferences also place them in opposition to 'children's films' and the commerciality of the franchise as represented by Binks and the Ewoks.

However, just as this article draws upon numerous authorities to legitimate its opposition to the mainstream, the mainstream itself remains a wildly eclectic and amorphous entity into which many different ideas are collapsed. Children's movies, femininity, consumerism and Hollywood all become interchangeable and so demonstrate just how vague, intangible and 'phantom' this menace really is. The complexity of some of these negotiations can be seen in the discussions about George Lucas that feature in the magazine. At some points, Lucas is valorized as the champion of the independent filmmaker. Within these accounts, he is characterized as working outside of the mainstream (i.e. outside Hollywood). However, at other times he is presented as the megalomaniac of marketing, 'selling out' for merchandising profits and betraying science fiction fans with the profit-motivated likes of Jar Jar Binks. These criticisms extend even beyond the content of the movie into a critique of his distribution methods.

> These include a no-advertisement clause and a demand that all trailers shown should not exceed a total of eight minutes. With Fox reputedly booking up two minutes, that leaves only six minutes for other films. Some are reconciled to this, but others are not too happy. 'A lot of what they're doing is wrong. It's too bad that a movie that should have been so much fun has turned into such a headache.' Said one disgruntled exhibitor. (*SFX*, 52, June 1999: 18)

There is also, of course, an inherent contradiction in these oppositions to commercialism. A major part of fan culture is consumption, with the watching of movies and the purchasing of books and other merchandise constituting an integral and indeed central aspect of fan activities. As a commercial publication, *SFX* is highly consumer-orientated, but again this contradiction is negotiated through its supposed opposition to the mainstream. The consumption of fandom is valorized by presenting fans as discerning consumers, or made ironic through self-deprecating and self-conscious humour. In contrast, the mass consumption of the mainstream is denigrated whether or not the object of consumption is actually the same.

Authority and economy

As Allen and Gomery argue, extratextual publications serve an agenda-setting function in which the magazine does not necessarily tell the reader what to think, but rather provides fans with frameworks for discussion (Allen and Gomery 1985). Indeed, readers of *SFX* are well aware of the function that the magazine serves in providing them with the discourses and knowledges necessary for participation within fandom. However, as I have already stated, trivia differ from Brown's model of gossip through their use in competitive discourses.

From a purely pragmatic point of view, the publication's role as supplying trivia about forthcoming films, publications and events makes it economically viable. Fans buy the magazine with the intention of entertaining themselves. This seems fairly obvious, but the question must be asked: Why this magazine? Why any magazine at all, when trivia are available from other sources such as the internet and word of mouth? The reason for this is contained within the importance of subcultural capital in fandom. Trivia are a vital component in the economy of fandom, and the fact that *SFX* as a publication has access to large amounts of in-depth industry information places it in a position of wealth in this economy. Fans of course want to possess this capital in order to define and maintain their fan status.

An example of this process can be found in the reports on the production processes behind film (and television) productions. *SFX* includes interviews and information about scriptwriters, producers and special effects teams in addition to the star- and director-orientated trivia that tend to be privileged by some other magazines such as *Empire*. For example, the constant references to Joss Whedon's role not only as the creator of *Buffy the Vampire Slayer* but also as a scriptwriter for other texts such as the films *Alien Resurrection* (1997) and *Se7en* (1995) demonstrates the magazine's expertise in the area of information and also justifies its attention to *Buffy* through its creator's qualifications as a major player in Hollywood science fiction.

The investment in information about forthcoming films is particularly evident given that the history of a film in production is often followed over lengthy periods of time. *The X Men* (2000), for example, had been followed since its early pre-production talks:

FILM: **X-Men**
SCRIPT: **Ed Solomon**
DIRECTOR: **Bryan Singer**
STUDIO: **20th Century Fox**
POSSIBLE RELEASE DATE: **Christmas 1998**
Apparently this heady combination of alienation metaphors and pop-culture is already making the big guns slaver in anticipation . . . And, yes, it probably will have Wolverine in it. (SFX, 26, June 1997: 10)

This pre-production report on the possibility of the comic *The X-Men* being made into a film was published in June 1997 and demonstrates that the publication is not concerned just with the stars or director but also with the scriptwriter, the studio and others involved in a production. This kind of reporting demonstrates *SFX*'s ability to deliver information that fans would be unable to find elsewhere (apart from similar publications such as *Starburst* or

Dreamwatch). This not only carries importance as a marketing strategy; it also demonstrates the superior knowledge of the writers – superior knowledge that define *SFX* as authentic and expert.

The marketability of this expertise is evident also in *SFX*'s overwhelming coverage of *The Phantom Menace*. One issue devotes a full nine pages simply to 'behind the scenes' trivia, providing reports on everything from locations to costumes. The largest report within this section concerns the action scenes of *Episode I* and it demonstrates the ways in which notions of authenticity and expertise are constructed through trivia.

> Lucas conjured up a three-way battle between Darth Maul, Obi-Wan and Qui-Gon. But it was up to Nick Gilliard, a renowned stunt coordinator, who was chosen to design and choreograph these key sequences and develop a martial art that could be applied to the swordsmanship skills of the Jedi. . .
>
> 'I figured that since the Jedi had chosen a lightsaber, they'd have to be really good at it,' says Gilliard. 'So I took the essence of all the great sword fighting techniques, from kendo through sabre, epee and foil, and flowed them together' . . . Initially hired to hone the new techniques with Gilliard, martial arts expert Ray Park won the role of Darth Maul when Lucas and producer Rick McCallum reviewed rehearsals of Gilliard and Park kicking ass. (*SFX*, 54, August 1999: 51)

Authenticity and expertise are central here on two levels. First at the level of publication: the report demonstrates the magazine's expertise in obtaining quotations and in-depth information about the production of the film. Second, within the agenda of the report, expertise and authenticity are used to validate the interests of fans in the movie. Whilst Jar Jar Binks is 'bad' SF because it is mainstream and profit-motivated, action scenes and lightsaber battles are 'good' SF because they are an authentic display of real martial arts skill, designed and executed by experts.

These discourses contradict many critical and popular discussions of fandom that denigrate fans by labelling them as lacking in critical skills, emotional distance and reason (Jensen 1992). Indeed, fandom is preoccupied with distancing itself from these negative images, and many of the articles published in *SFX* are designed to prove exactly the opposite: that the authenticity of the real fan is defined through their discerning taste and critical distance.

If critical distance serves to define inclusion and exclusion from fandom, it also helps to define the hierarchies that exist *within* fandom. This process relies also on a construction of the mainstream, and, whilst struggles over the status of individual texts are common, there remain some reading modes that are unacceptable. For example, disliking canonical texts is both common and acceptable but only so long as those dislikes are framed as competitive contestations. Conversely, liking texts for the wrong reasons such as the adoration of stars or the enjoyment of aspects tainted with the mainstream (Jar Jar Binks and the Ewoks) is unacceptable and the expression of these opinions are put down and ridiculed.[6]

As a result, hierarchies within fandom do not go unchallenged, but the struggles within fandom tend to be conflicts over precise rankings rather challenges to the practice of ranking itself. For example, the infinitely varied subdivisions of fan culture that pledge allegiance to *Star Trek*, *The X-files*, *Dr Who* or even *Thunderbirds* are involved in constant competition to establish the validity of their own opinions over those of others and even against the magazine. The letters pages of fan media provide a forum or 'arena' for exactly these kinds of competition in which the main weapon is trivia. For example, one letter to *SFX* defends Jar Jar Binks from the attacks discussed above by drawing attention to other stock characters and elements in the movies, and by trying to demonstrate greater knowledge of the *Star Wars* movies:

> What are the politically correct critics of Jar Jar Binks if not stereotyped examples of the killjoy chattering classes whose critical clichés are repeated . . . by lemmings, zombies, do-gooders and hate-mongering shit-stirrers alike?

> If Jar Jar is a racial stereotype then what the hell is C-3PO if not a subservient stuck-up-the-ass yellow bellied British butler from the 1930s . . .

> So what if the Evil *Empire* is British and that the Emperor sounds like Mr Granger from Grace Brothers or that the virgin mother is Swedish . . . (*SFX*, 59, Christmas 1999: 33)

Here the defense of Binks is precisely presented as a virtual 'throwing down of the gauntlet', a challenge offered by a combatant eager to prove himself or herself, not the *faux pas* of a naive and ignorant consumer.

However, this is not to imply that these discourses are purely competitive and without the sense of affirmation that has been attributed to gossip. These competitions require competence in the necessary discourses of trivia and, as such, are open only to SF fans, i.e. people with the competences to engage with the debates taking place. As a result of this, however combative, these debates still centre on a form of interaction but one that is specifically constructed to exclude the non-fan. However, given that someone who had no investment in these debates would probably not be reading the magazine, these debates are less designed to exclude a constructed other who is never really present than to demonstrate the exclusivity of fandom itself.

Conclusion

As we have seen, within fandom trivia are neither a worthless currency of fan obsession nor the product of radical cultural criticism. On the contrary, trivia are important exactly because its value can be recognized only by insiders. Their possession is therefore a form of cultural capital through which fandom is able claim special access to, and knowledge of, specific texts and groups of texts and, in so doing, to make claims to ownership of them. In the process, they also enable fans to distinguish themselves from the 'phantom menace' of the mainstream consumer, and so present themselves as discerning, rational and cultured. Finally, trivia are also used in competitive struggles within fandom in which different sections of fandom not only vie with one another for status but also provide a sense of affirmation and solidarity through masculine contests of homosocial competition (Hollows 2003).

As a result of these processes trivia are a form of cultural capital and, as in any other marketplace, they are a commodity that can be turned into economic capital. In essence, then, the information or trivia contained within fan media are currencies used in a combined economic and cultural exchange. Fans buy the magazine to acquire competences, competences that, in turn, provide the necessary currency for acceptance and participation within fandom.

Notes

1 These figures are from the publisher's own sitehtp://futerenet.com but derive from independent surveys provided by ABC.
2 I am not of course suggesting that these publications represent a real and tangible mainstream, but rather that they cater to distinctly less specific audiences than a strictly genre-based title such as *SFX*.
3 The importance of the Star Wars franchise to cinema technology is discussed in more detail in Allen (1998).
4 I use these categories rather loosely when in fact the cultural status of these magazines is as complex as that of *SFX*; see Jackson,Stevenson and Brooks (2001).
5 This negative reception is in itself the result of complex issues of authenticity that surround the use of CGI to alter or replace the role of actors in films. For example there was some concern over the 'macabre' use of CGI to complete *The Crow* (1994) after its star Brandon Lee died during filming, while the similar use of CGI to add Oliver Reed posthumously to scenes in *Gladiator* (2000) seemed to have met little objection. Yet neither of these met with the criticism levelled at Jar Jar Binks in *Episode I* or the photo-real CG 'actors' of *Final Fantasy: The Spirits Within* (2001). On the other hand the use of CG to aid the processes of more traditional animation seen in modern Disney films or to create the 'unrealistic' characters of *Toy Story* (1995) is positively received.
6 Such practices point to a distinct gender bias in the economy of fandom, a bias based on a series of questionable assumptions about the gendered reading of texts that underpins many of the discourses of subcultural economy. For more extensive readings of the gendered construction of fandom see Constance Penley (1997), Radway (1984) and Hermes (1995).

References

Allen, Michael (1998) From Bwana Devil to Batman Forever: Technology in Contemporary Hollywood Cinema, in Steve Neale and Murray Smith (eds.), *Contemporary Hollywood Cinema*. London and New York: Routledge, pp. 109–129.

Allen, Robert C., and Gomery, Douglas (1985), *Film History: Theory and Practice*. New York: McGraw Hill.

Ang, Ien (1985) *Watching Dallas: Soap Opera and the Melodramatic Imagination*. London: Methuen.

Bacon-Smith, Camille (1992) *Enterprising Women: Television Fans and the Creation of Popular Myth*. Philadelphia: University of Pennsylvania Press.

Barker, Martin, and Brooks, Kate (1998) *Knowing Audiences: Judge Dredd – Its Friends, Fans, and Foes*. Luton: University of Luton Press.

Bourdieu, Pierre (1984) *Distinction: A Social Critique of the Judgement of Taste*. London, New York: Routledge.

Bradley, Marion Zimmer (1985) Fandom: Its Value to the Professional, in Sharon Jarvis (ed.), *Inside Outer Space: Science Fiction Professionals Look at their Craft*. New York: Frederick Ungar.

Brower, Sue (1992) Fans as Tastemakers: Viewers for Quality Television, in Lisa A. Lewis (ed.), *The Adoring Audience: Fan Culture and Popular Media*. London and New York: Routledge, pp. 163–184.

Brown, Mary Ellen (1994) *Soap Opera and Women's Talk: The Pleasure of Resistance*. Thousand Oaks and London: Sage Publications.

Cline, Cheryl (1992) Essays from *Bitch: The Women's Rock Newsletter with Bite*, in Lisa A. Lewis, (ed.) *The Adoring Audience: Fan Culture and Popular Media*. London and New York: Routledge, pp. 69–83.

De Certeau, Michel (1984). *The Practices of Everyday Life*. Berkeley: University of California Press.

Dickinson, Roger, Linne, Olga, and Harindranath, Ramaswami (eds.) (1998) *Approaches to Audiences: A Reader*. London: Edward Arnold.

Ehrenreich, Barbara (1983) *The Hearts of Men: American Dreams and the Flight from Commitment*. New York: Doubleday/Anchor Books.

Fiske, John (1989) *Understanding Popular Culture*. London: Unwin Hyman.

Fiske, John (1992) The Cultural Economy of Fandom, in Lisa A. Lewis (ed.), *The Adoring Audience: Fan Culture and Popular Media*. London: Routledge, pp. 30–49.

Hermes, Joke (1995) *Reading Women's Magazines*. Cambridge: Polity.

Hollows, Joanne (2003) The Masculinity of Cult, in Mark Jancovich, Antonio Lazaro, Julian Stringer and Andrew Willis (eds.), *Defining Cult Movies: The Cultural Politics of Oppositional Taste*. Manchester: Manchester University Press.

Jackson, Peter, Stevenson, Nick and Brooks, Kate (2001) *Making Sense of Men's Magazines*. Cambridge: Polity.

Jancovich, Mark (2002) Cult Fictions: Cult Movies, Subcultural Capital and the Production of Cultural Distinctions, *Cultural Studies*, 16 (2), pp. 306–322.

Jancovich, Mark and Hunt, Nathan (forthcoming) The Mainstream, Distinction and Cult TV, in Roberta Pearson and Sara Gwenllian Jones (eds.), *Worlds Apart: Essays on Cult Television*. University of Minnesota Press, forthcoming.

Jenkins, Henry (1989) Star Trek Rerun, Reread, Rewritten: Fan Writing as Textual Poaching, *Critical Studies in Mass Communication* 5 (2), pp. 85–107.

Jenkins, Henry (1992) *Textual Poachers: Television Fans and Participatory Culture*. London and New York: Routledge.

Jenkins, Henry and Tulloch, John (1995) *Science Fiction Audiences*. London: Routledge.

Jensen, Joli (1992) Fandom as Pathology: The Consequences of Characterization, in Lisa A Lewis (ed.), *The Adoring Audience: Fan Culture and Popular Media*. London: Routledge, pp. 9–29.

Klinger, Barbara (1994) *Melodrama and Meaning: History, Culture, and the Films of Douglas Sirk*. Bloomington and Indianapolis: Indiana University Press.

Kramer, Peter (2001) 'It's aimed at kids – the kid in everybody': George Lucas, *Star Wars* and Children's Entertainment, *Scope: An Online Journal of Film Studies*, December, www.nottingham.ac.uk/film/journal.

Nixon, Sean (1996) *Hard Looks: Masculinities, Spectatorship and Contemporary Consumption*. London: UCL Press.

Penley, Constance (1997) *Nasa/Trek: Popular Science and Sex in America*. London and New York: Verso.

Sconce, Jeffrey (1995) 'Trashing' the Academy: Taste, Excess, and an Emerging Politics of Cinematic Style, *Screen*, 36 (4), pp. 371–393.

Staiger, Janet (1992) *Interpreting Films: Studies in the Historical Reception of American Cinema*. Princeton: Princeton University Press.

Radway, Janice A. (1984) *Reading the Romance: Women, Patriarchy, and Popular Literature*. Chapel Hill: University of North Carolina Press.

Thornton, Sarah (1995) *Club Cultures: Music, Media and Subcultural Capital*. Oxford: Blackwell.

Urrichio, William, and Pearson, Roberta (1993) *Reframing Culture: The Case of the Vitagraph Quality Films*. Princeton: Princeton University Press.

Winship, Janice (1987) *Inside Women's Magazines*. London: Pandora Press.

13

Art, exploitation, underground
Mark Betz

> Being a Catholic, guilt comes naturally. Except mine is reversed. I blab on ad nauseam about how much I love films like *Dr. Butcher, M.D.* or *My Friends Need Killing*, but what really shames me is that I'm also secretly a fan of what is unfortunately known as the 'art film.' Before writing this sentence, I've tried to never utter the word 'art' unless referring to Mr. Linkletter. But underneath all my posing as a trash film enthusiast, a little-known fact is that I actually sneak off in disguise (and hope to God I'm not recognized) to arty films in the same way business men rush in to see *Pussy Talk* on their lunch hour. I'm really embarrassed. (Waters, 1984: 108)

Writing in the mid-1980s, trash filmmaker John Waters opened his essay 'Guilty Pleasures' with the paragraph above. On the one hand, Waters's admission of furtive trips to the art house to see films directed by Ingmar Bergman, Alain Resnais, Marguerite Duras, Pier Paolo Pasolini and other prominent European film directors of the 1960s and 1970s provides early evidence of the leveling of high/low distinctions in aesthetic culture that has since come to be considered a key aspect of postmodernism. And it is in precisely these terms that contemporary scholars of visual and media culture who advocate such a levelling have received and interpreted Waters's words – for example, Andrew Ross, who felt a decade ago that only 'Waters could be capable of brilliantly confessing, in the most complete inversion of taste possible, to the guilty pleasure he experiences in watching art films' (Ross 1989: 154). On the other hand, reading Waters's words almost two decades hence, I cannot help but be struck by their appropriateness for anyone working in the field of film studies today – especially for anyone who likes or even works on European art cinema of the 1960s and 1970s, as I do. Perhaps 'inversion' is just the right word to indicate how the high/low culture dismantling project has proceeded *vis à vis* art cinema. For it is not so much that poststructural theory and postmodern culture have eliminated the distinction between the two as it has inverted them.

This situation has partially to do with the historiography of European art cinema of the 1950s and 1960s. This historiography, when it ventures occasionally outside the rubrics of auteur or national film movement under which practically all work on art cinema is written, has generally considered and represented its object as a heroic, modernist response to Hollywood global domination in economic and/or aesthetic terms (Armes 1976; Kawin 1978; Kolker 1983; Bordwell 1985; Sorlin 1991; Orr 1993). Such work tends to emphasize the stylistic and industrial differences between European art cinema and Hollywood cinema, while acknowledging that those differences were in the late 1960s incorporated into a new Hollywood model of artisanal and youth-oriented cinema. The heyday of European art cinema is thus tied historically to its alterity to American commercial cinema, with all that entails for the current historicisation of its stylistics and cultural impact. In short, the state of art cinema scholarship has been stuck in the same rut for decades.

The moribund situation is very much the result of the shifts in taste culture that have characterized academic film studies' theoretical reorientations from May 1968 on – Althusserian Marxism and semiotics, psychoanalysis and feminism, queer theory, postcolonialism, cultural studies and cult. None of this is meant to decry current scholarship and historical work on long-ignored sectors of film culture like cult, such as Eric Schaefer's history of American exploitation films and Joan Hawkins's study of art-horror and cross-over reception. Hawkins finds compelling correspondences between the oppositional positioning that both paracinema fans and art film cinephiles take to Hollywood cinema, correspondences borne out in contemporary cult film fanzines and mail-order video catalogues that list cheek-to-jowl what film studies has traditionally considered radically opposed high and low forms. Her focus on horror 'as perhaps the best vantage point from which to study the cracks that seem to exist everywhere in late twentieth-century "sacralized" film culture' provides an important account of genre hybridity and taste culture formation and negotiation (Hawkins 2000: 28). One of the many interesting features of Schaefer's study is his periodization, which situates the ascension, apogee and declension of classical exploitation between the years 1919 and 1959. For 1959 is also the year of the first cresting of the French New Wave and of the New Italian Cinema, a crucial marker in art cinema historiography for the beginning of its high modernist phase with films such as *Hiroshima mon amour* and *L'avventura*. Indeed, among the many factors Schaefer notes as contributing to the decline of classical exploitation, it is the rising popularity of European art cinema and the inauguration of the American sexploitation film in the late 1950s by the likes of Russ Meyer, whose *The Immoral Mr Teas* prompted an avalanche of imitators, that are crucial to my understanding of the intersections between art and exploitation cinema at the level of both marketing and audiences (Schaefer 1999: 331–339). I would like to compli-cate the historical issue of these high and low cinemas of the 1960s by arguing that they proceeded not simply as parallel alternate modes of film practice, but as shared discourses and means of address.

In some respects I am not saying anything new. As early as 1959, Arthur Knight was rallying against the characterization of art cinema as elitist and for 'eggheads' only, suggesting that the chief distinction between art and exploitation houses 'would seem to lie in the demitasse of black coffee served in the lobby of the snootier establishments. For make no mistake about it, the art house operators – may their tribe increase – are in business just as surely as their competitors who feature *Mr. Rock and Roll, I Was a Teenage Werewolf*, or *Garden of Eden*' (Knight 1959: 24). Two years later, Pauline Kael weighed in with a rant of her own, a baroquely argued yet sincere jeremiad on how 'the educated audience often uses "art films" in much the same self-indulgent way as the mass audience use Hollywood "product," finding wish fulfilment in the form of cheap and easy congratulation on their sensitivities and their liberalism' (Kael 1961–62: 5). Although is by no means clear just what Kael wants from audiences instead, she does draw fine similarities between nudie magazines' imaging of the female body and those of the more elegantly laid-out French publications found on the coffee tables of artists and professors. These early attempts to locate the growing exhibition and patronage of European art films in America within the lower rungs of the nation's contemporary cultural consumption were subsequently lost in the flood of art film criticism that sensed in its object the opportunity to legitimate the cinema as art.

Lost perhaps, but not quite forgotten. Virtually all of the scholars who have written on art cinema as a movement or as a field of textuality mention the degree to which sexual frankness and 'adult' displays of sexuality are constituent elements of European art cinema's appeal. Linda Williams, for example, has recently commented that 'One of the most important aspects of the New Wave was the prevalence of love stories in which what took place in the bedroom was as important as what took place everywhere else' (Williams 1996: 491, 495). And Peter Lev, writing on Euro-American cinema, instructively points out that it was neither Fellini nor Resnais but Brigitte Bardot – whose *And God Created Woman* flouted conventional morality and 'shocked and exhilirated 1958 audiences' with her unapologetic nudity – who was the 'leading personality in the breakthrough of foreign art films to larger audiences in the United States. Explicit sexuality became expected in foreign films, to such an extent that "foreign film", "art film", "adult film", and "sex film" were for several years almost synonyms' (Lev 1993: 13). But what makes Lev really representative of art cinema historiography is his next sentence: 'More interestingly, many of the successful foreign imports of the period were not merely explicit but thoughtful, sophisticated works as well'. This 'yes, but' gesture regarding sexploitation and art cinema is ubiquitous in scholarly work on the latter, and its precedents extend back to the first serious explicators of art cinema. Also consistent across the board is the notion that the conflation in the US of sex and adult-oriented material with foreign or art films was a post-Bardot phenomenon. Although the focus of my research concerns art cinema in its high modernist phase in the 1960s, I will begin with its predecessors in the period immediately after the Second World War and into the 1950s in order to offer a re-view of that subject as well.

What really motivates the work of which I am here providing a sketch is a desire to revitalize the study of art cinema on the one hand, and on the other to make use of the kinds of extratextual materials that are so much a part of current film and media historiography. I will concentrate in this article on publicity materials, more particularly US distributors' pressbooks. I have so far looked at a hundred or so of these books, which range in length and size from a single two-sided 10 inch by 12 inch sheet to much larger and more elaborate bound or stapled booklets of up to fourteen pages in length. Variously called Merchandising Manuals, Showman's Manuals, Exhibitor's Showman's Manuals, or Showman's Campaigns, these pressbooks are divided into various sections: plot synopses and credits pages, box-office promotion sections of stills and unauthored 'articles' extolling the films' merits, exploitation and merchandising hints and tie-ins, and ads and accessories that exhibitors can use or buy to market the films in local newspapers and theatre fronts and lobbies. What I found throughout these pressbooks, particularly in the varied ad slicks from which the theatre owner can choose for newspaper publication, was a frequent concentration on the imaging of sexuality, especially female sexuality, as iconic markers of the films' purported content.

In Joe Burstyn's and Arthur Mayer's 1947 pressbook for *Open City* (Figure 18), blocks of textual praise for the film were balanced with less lofty sentiments and imagery that built up the sexual angle: hints at lesbianism, 'violence and plain sexiness' link the marketing of this film in uncanny ways to that of American exploitation films of the same period: the image of the young woman with hiked skirt or black bra or both appears in every ad in the book. In a subsequent Mayer Burstyn pressbook for *The Bicycle Thief*, a film that would seem to provide considerably less possibility for sexually charged exploitation, the ad slicks uniformly synecdoche by the bare leg of a woman astride a bicycle being whisked off her feet by a male rider whose fedora has just blown off his head, suggesting whirlwind courtship and fast-paced romantic comedy. The tagline that comes to my mind when I look at these ads is: 'The Bicycle Thief: He'll steal your heart!' If the success of Italian neo-realist films such as these with American audiences was due in no small part to their ad campaigns (as several have suggested; see for example Elsaesser 1994: 25), then that success cannot be separated from a conflation of sex and art that is so consistent a feature of post-Bardot art film reception.

Foreign films, especially Italian 'rosy neo-realist' films with their female leads adorned in peasant rags barely containing their voluptuous forms, and French Tradition of Quality historical films and costumers featuring women in various stages of bosom-emphasizing dress and corseted and stockinged underdress, were popular import items throughout the 1950s. The ad slicks for these types of films lose no opportunity to display women as licentious or exhibitionist. It is the films of this era of 'imported Euro-skin', as Eddie Muller and Daniel Faris have called it, and starring Michele Morgan, Martine Carol, Gina Lollobrigida, Sophia Loren, and especially Bardot, that really pushed through European cinema's appeal to a growing

18 Admat excerpt from
Mayer–Burstyn pressbook for
Open City, 1947

American audience (Muller and Faris 1996: 56–61). The films of the young Ingmar Bergman were similarly marketed and received: exploitation pioneer Kroger Babb handled Bergman's first major success in America, released in 1955 as *Monika The Story of a Bad Girl* and accompanied by an ad campaign that featured Harriet Andersson in several breast-thrusting poses. And even as recognised and respected a purveyor of film art as Jean Renoir is implicated in this tendency in the American pressbook for his film *French Can Can*, marketed by the United Motion Picture Organization as *Only the French Can*, where once again the image of a seated woman with bared leg or a silhouetted figure in high kick is everywhere present.

Equally popular import items into the USA in the middle 1950s were British comedies of the *Carry On* or Dirk Bogarde *Doctor* series, as well as the subtle comedic pantomime films of Jacques Tati. Comedy or lightheartedness is signified in the ads for these films through the use of obviously drawn figures as opposed to the photographed or otherwise realistically rendered human figures of dramas, humanist or costume. The characters of comedy imports of the period often appear in ad slicks as two-dimensional, silhouetted or cartoonlike forms. In the case of *Mr Hulot's Holiday*, distributed in the US in 1954 by GBD International Films, the familiar pose of the avuncular title character – erect, rigid, hands-on-hips – appears on the front cover of the pressbook, gazing off the page with characteristic aplomb. In the ad mats, however, Mr Hulot is bent forward and stooped down in order to provide an occasion for a composition implying male voyeurism and female near-nudity or exhibitionism (Figure 19). Such an explicit set of Mulveyesque looking relations are repeated throughout the ad campaigns for American burlesque and nudist camp films of the same era, as well as for the first wave of nudie-cutie films (see Muller and Faris 1996: 82–83; McCarty 1995: 39). Indeed, the choice of 'Lucky Pierre' as the theatrical moniker for Chicago entertainer Billy Falbo in the 1959 sexploitation film of the same name is in this context a highly motivated one that draws upon and extends the general impression of naughtiness, nudity and comedy that appear in the ad campaigns of the French films that preceded it throughout the 1950s – like the Renoir film of 1956, the American nudie-cutie *The Adventures of Lucky Pierre* can do, too, what only the French can.

The ad campaigns for French and Italian art films in the 1960s that are my focus rework the tropes of their predecessors and ratchet

19 Ad mat excerpt from G. B. D. International Films pressbook for *Mr Hulot's Holiday*, 1954

them up a notch or two. The oversized and elaborate Exhibitor's Showmanship manual for *Boccaccio '70*, distributed in the US by Joseph E. Levine in 1962, is one of the more overtly exploitational, which is not inappropriate considering this omnibus film's status as a blatant, producer-generated attempt to cash in on the commercial success of three marketable Italian directors and their previous actresses. The exaggerated size of Loren, Ekberg and Schneider in relation to De Sica, Fellini and Visconti throughout the book's pages implies the degree to which female stars are perhaps more marketable images than the names of the artists directing them at this stage of art film patronage in America; most definitely it indicates as well the kind of monstrous or unrestrained female sexuality that is the theme of the film's three episodes (Figure 20). But even in a European film as commercially driven as *Boccaccio '70*, art and high culture nevertheless perform dual duty in the packaging: the arcing curtains and the tagline 'The first 3-act motion picture ever presented!' not only point towards the episodic organization of the film but also suggest a stage tradition that the film never works into its diegesis. Within the film itself, the only link to the theatre is the separation of stories by sliding cards announcing the end of each act and the beginning of the next. For any patron of the theatre who has seen *Boccaccio '70*, the theatrical signifiers present in the distributor's marketing materials would appear decidedly disingenuous.

There is another possible reading, another possible audience being addressed by these ads, however. Those curtains so clearly delineated on the left side of the film's ads, that cartoonlike woman using the 'B' of the film's title to shield her denuded form from full frontal view, those title cards within the film slid in and out of place by a female, cut-out animated hand and forearm announcing the act viewers will next witness: all are explicit elements of burlesque shows and films following the Second World War. Although burlesque films had by the time of *Boccaccio '70*'s release in 1962 been pushed off the exploitation circuit by the nudie-cutie, it is none the less striking the degree to which the ads for the popular European import adapt iconic elements from the burlesque film ads as illustrated in Eric Schaefer's work on the genre (Schaefer 1999: 303, 308, 313): larger-than-life, shapely women reaching or looking directly out towards the seated male spectator, the mobilization of woman-as-spectacle, the prominent place afforded the female performer's name as marketing device. Whether one considers the *Boccaccio '70* ads, then, as shrewd examples of audience cross-marketing, or as a conscious deployment of culturally legitimate theatrical signifiers and an unconscious residue of a different, and culturally less legitimate, stage tradition, the degree to which they condense high and low codes of visibility and identification is indicative of much of what I have seen throughout my research. Clear-cut distinctions between high and low are difficult to establish in most marketing materials for European art films in this period. They are quite fluid and porous texts.

20 Ad mat excerpt from Joseph E. Levine's Exhibitor's Showmanship manual
for *Boccaccio '70*, 1962

Nonetheless, some general shifts do appear. One is that films from France from the mid-1950s to the late 1960s often refer explicitly in their ads to their status as national products, thereby stating their potential racinesss. Likewise, the high-cultural iconographies and connotations become less and less evident as the exploitation quotient is upped. The French–Italian coproduced omnibus film *The Seven Deadly Sins* was accompanied in its Washington, DC, run in 1952 by an elegant brochure that emphasized in its text 'the superb artistry of its actors and directors' but promised through its images entertainment of an adult nature. The libretto for this film is informative, it assumes a certain familiarity with the directors so scrupulously listed in the credits for each episode in its inner pages, it mentions that the feature will be preceded by 'Pastoral', conducted by Leopold Stokowski, filmed by Mary Ellen Bute. No mere entertainment, *The Seven Deadly Sins* and its presentation at the World Playhouse is a cultural event. But the stylized silhouette of a curvaceous woman that is the brochure's icon (and that, in the inner pages, assumes poses and guises connoting classical figures of Hellenic beauty) points towards that other lure of art cinema for international audiences, especially American ones: tastefully visualized sex or nudity. Ten years later, the US distributor's largest ad image for another Franco-Italian coproduction, *7 Capital Sins* (Figure 21), promises 'a new look at seven old sins . . . that are not strictly French!' The French New Wave is here at its crest, but the protested appeal of this film is universal. As in the 1952 brochure, a stylized female figure sells the film, but in this case there is no hedging, no careful balance between cultural capital and sexual commerce. No longer classical in her proportions and attire, this modern woman obliges the (male) viewer to enter into the world of a film that is 'not strictly French!' Unlike the cover image of the previous version, there is no snake coiling around the woman's body – Eve has already fallen into sin, now it's Adam's (the viewer's?) turn. The relationship between French cinema and playful licentiousness is not simply produced here: it is *assumed*.

The ad campaigns for European art films of considerably higher artistic pretensions tend to dispense with drawn or cartoonlike representations of women and opt instead for photographic representations. It is commonly claimed that the young heterosexual couple is the focus of New Wave cinema, and much of the imagery in the American distributor's manuals for the films of this period and

21 US distributor's ad mat for *7 Capital Sins*, 1962

movement centres on the modern couple. The sense of fun or comedy is replaced in the ads for many of the 'serious' films from both eastern and western Europe at the turn of the 1960s by an altogether more grim conception of romantic coupling with clear melodrama elements. And it is certainly true that many of the art films of this period depict what was received as more realistic portrayals of romantic or married life than that offered by Hollywood films of the same era. Overwhelmingly, the visual emphasis in these ad slicks is on the face and expression of the woman character in the film gripped by anomie or doubt, her gaze directed out of frame to imply thought or apprehension. The view provided of the male, on the other hand, is always obscured by the foregrounded face of the female, and often his secondary yet necessary presence is indicated simply by the back of his head. For films such as *Hiroshima mon amour*, *L'avventura* and *The Cranes Are Flying*, the ads are' more or less appropriate indices of the subject matter, which concentrates on a modern female protagonist, her hesitations and actions as she enters the terrain of modern romance, the risks involved in that undertaking. But the fluidity of this visual trope is striking in its deployment in the 1960 Zenith International pressbook for *The 400 Blows* (Figure 22), the ad mats for which all contain an image grab from the only instance of heterosexual embrace in the film, when Antoine Doinel spots on a Paris street corner his mother with a man not his stepfather, and relocates that moment to the seaside locale that ends the film, a geography of ambiguous possibility for the troubled youth and his search for identity, freedom and maternal acknowledgement. Trepidation is here borne in the mien of an adolescent boy rather than an adult woman, and indeed the film is centrally concerned with Doinel's complex relationship to his mother. But the ads for *The 400 Blows* also overwhelmingly imply an adult male/female romantic affiliation that is quite simply not a predominant element of the film's narrative. My point is not so much that the ad is misleading as it is that the New Wave couple and modern romance are hallmarks of European art film marketing in the USA, and that they extend to films marginally concerned with the subject.

The heterosexual couple trope is often taken to the point of passionate or violent coupling in ads for other art films of the 1960s. In the case of the Lopert Pictures campaign for *The Night* (*La notte*) (Figure 23), the image of Marcello Mastroianni forcing himself upon Jeanne Moreau implies the kind of overdetermined spectacle that to my eye overpowers the message of the text. What is new about this motion picture as it appears in these ads seems to be its ability not to provoke thought and emotion in the spectator as much as to image provocative sexual embracing that might for some patrons arouse a more visceral form of feeling. The passionate ravishing or violent rape of the women in the pressbook imagery for art

2 col. x 50 lines—(100 lines)   Ad Mat #202

2 col. x 25 lines—(50 lines)   Ad Mat #203

22 Ad mat excerpt from Zenith International pressbook for *The 400 Blows*, 1960

23 Ad mat excerpt from Lopert Pictures pressbook for *The Night* (*La notte*)

films such as *The Night, Rocco and His Brothers, Where the Hot Wind Blows, Woman in the Dunes* and others are of a piece with those used for the juvenile delinquent American and wayward youth European sexploitation films – or nudie roughies – that were at this time sharing the same newspaper page for ad space (see Muller and Faris 1996: 94–99, for examples). The visual and temporal relationship between European art and American sexploitation cinemas in the 1960s, at the level of their marketing, is more thoroughly interdependent and mutually informing than one might assume from the historiography on art cinema.

In this respect, the 1959 marketing campaign for Louis Malle's *The Lovers* goes to considerable lengths to capitalize on the rapturous possibilities of the foreign or art film. Jeanne Moreau is pictured in medium close-up from the side, her head reclined and buried in pillows, neck arched, eyes closed, lips parted, right hand clutching the sheets by her head, as a man's disembodied left hand tightly grasps her by the wrist. In textually informing the potential patron of this French film that what is being imaged in the ad is 'her moment', the line separating the art from the sexploitation film disappears completely. The climax of *The Lovers*, like that of the Hedy Lamarr film *Ecstasy* some quarter-century earlier, is female orgasm, plain and simple. What is remarkable here is that the female money shot so immodestly imaged in the ad for *The Lovers* is well ahead of the curve of the wave of similarly marketed arty Scandinavian softcore sex films such as *Swedish Wedding Night* and *I, a Woman* that washed across American art house and grindhouse screens in the mid-1960s, and is considerably ahead of the curve for American hardcore.

I plan to undertake more and concerted research into other areas of exhibition and reception of postwar European art cinema, especially industrial research on histories of specific distribution companies and networks (Grove Press and Joseph E. Levine's Avco-Embassy, pre-eminently). But there are other relations at play within the art/exploitation nexus – censorship discourses and litigation, case studies of art theatres and other forms of art film exhibition, audience demographics and fan culture – and I would like in my final pages to gesture towards these as fruitful and fascinating avenues of inquiry. Although Roger Corman's move towards theatrical distribution of European art films with his establishment of New World Pictures in 1973 is perhaps the most famous example of an intersection between art and exploitation at the catalogue level of theatrical distribution, it is not without precedent. Corman started as an exploitation director for American International Pictures and developed later into a producer and distributor of both exploitation and art cinema fare. The opposite career trajectory was followed by the softcore art film proponent Radley Metzger: between 1956 and 1970 his Audubon Films distributed in America some twenty-six sexploitation films from France, Spain, Japan, Italy, Sweden and Denmark, including a compilation film by his own hand, *The Dictionary of Sex*, and the huge success *I, a Woman*. In the same period he directed six erotic films to supplement his catalogue, and from 1973 to 1983 concentrated almost exclusively on making hardcore features under the pseudonym Henry Paris. And even earlier, the Times Film Corporation advertised on the back page of its pressbook for *Wild for Kicks* (*Beat Girl* in the UK), a 1960 AIP-style exploitationer fusing elements of rock 'n' roll, teenage rebellion, sex and violence, and fast cars, other titles available for rental, whose 'wide appeal will satisfy the preferences of audiences everywhere' (Figure 24). Art films all, Louis Malle's *Frantic*, Claude Chabrol's *Leda* and René Clement's *Purple Noon* here share common space with *Wild for Kicks*. The representational codes of the images used to promote these films to exhibitors, even here on the back page, are congruent with those of the ads I have shown whose audience is potential moviegoers: female melodrama, voyeurism and exhibitionism, horizontal heterosexual clenching.

Where all of this meets the American underground film movement of the same period is in both the law courts and the movie theatre itself. The prosecution of *Flaming Creatures* in 1964 coincided with that of other underground movies. Kenneth Anger's *Scorpio Rising* had been charged with obscenity and tried by a court in Los Angeles on the basis of a few frames of an erect penis; Shirley Clarke's *The Connection* was banned for the naked portrayal of drug use and the repetition of the word 'shit' (as slang for heroin); Jean Genet's *Un chant d'amour* (completed in 1951, but shown for the first time in America in 1963) was also banned for the frontal nude shots of prison inmates. Other titles, such as Barbara Rubin's *Christmas on Earth* and Carolee Schneeman's *Fuses*, were targets of occasional attacks by watch groups and authorities, but managed to stay clear of the courts. It is only in the pages of censorship history that I have seen art, exploitation, and underground cinemas occupy

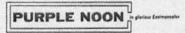

24 Back page of the Times Film Corporation pressbook for *Wild for Kicks* (UK title *Beat Girl*), 1960

the same scholarly space, yet even here they tend to be segregated into different conceptual categories and accorded differential weight that has little to do with the specifics of their litigation and everything to do with their varying statuses on the scale of taste culture. American nudist camp and nudie-cutie films such as *Garden of Eden* and *The Immoral Mr Teas*, underground films such as *Flaming Creatures*, and *Scorpio Rising*, Scandinavian softcore sex films: all of these challenged US censorship laws equally as much and in similar ways as the 'prestige' European and American films (*The Miracle*, *The Moon is Blue*, *Pinky* etc.) that dominate the postwar history of the US Production Code.

It is clear as well that in the major urban exhibition outlets of New York City, Los Angeles, Chicago, Cleveland, Washington and other large American cities in the 1960s, these films at times shared not only the same representational codes of marketing and the same police lockup shelves, but also the same exhibition space and quite heterogeneous audiences. In his 1965 publication *Foreign Films on American Screens*, Michael F. Mayer, son of the pioneer European art film distributor and exhibitor, lists in an appendix some fifty-one New York City theatres then screening foreign films. From the cursory perusal I have taken of New York advertising in the period, the indications are that there is considerable and at times simultaneous cross-programming of European art and sexploitation, and American sexploitation and avant-garde films in New York City theatres throughout the 1960s and early 1970s. The pages of the local newspapers advertising the current film offerings, like the *New York Daily News* of 4 October 1967 (Figure 25), tend to cluster art, underground and sexploitation ads on the same page in a top-down fashion, but the bleed across the three is none the less readable in both scansion and location: the World 49th Street Theater showing two new adult films with names too saucy to print, for example, also figured prominently as a venue for underground films and mid-level European art films. While New York City was clearly a privileged site for the distribution and exhibition of exploitation, art and underground films in the 1960s, I would nevertheless predict that the exploitation/art correspondences that I have emphasized throughout this article are less tied to regional specificity than the underground connections I have put forward at its end. Only more research into this aspect of taste culture and genre hybridity will determine whether this prediction holds true.

In 1981 Michael Silverman presented a fascinating paper at the 'Cinema Histories, Cinema Practices' conference at the University of Southern California; as published three years later, his paper is concerned with the financing and production of the neo-realist film *Riso amaro* (*Bitter Rice*, 1948), directed by Giuseppe De Santis. In his conclusion, Silverman posits that the director

> was faced with the inevitable choice – accept American money and influence or not make the film at all. Lacking institutional support from the left, De Santis and the others initially involved in the project accepted the compromise. Even a mildly symptomatic reading of the film today easily reveals the moments of investment and diversion, the capital outlay revolving around and anchored in the body of Silvana Mangano. (Silverman 1984: 43)

25 Local film advertising, the *New York Daily News*, 4 October 1967

From what I have been recovering in the marketing of European-produced films distributed in US in the 1950s and 1960s, Silverman's compelling conclusion needs to be readdressed in light of another circuit of commercial and scopic exchange that complicates the historiographic divide between European art and American capital. It is in examining the reception of art cinema that a much richer picture of its international history might be envisioned. At the very least, it offers an opportunity for some of us no longer to feel so guilty.

Note

All images are courtesy of George Eastman House. I am grateful for the extensive access I was accorded to the Eastman House's pressbooks collection.

References

Armes, R. (1976), *The Ambiguous Image: Narrative Style in Modern European Cinema*. London: Secker and Warburg.

Bordwell, D. (1985), Art-Cinema Narration, in *Narration in the Fiction Film*. Madison: University of Wisconsin Press, pp. 205–233.

Elsaesser, T. (1994), Putting on a Show: The European Art Movie, *Sight and Sound*, 4 (4) April, pp. 22–27.

Hawkins, J. (2000), *Cutting Edge: Art-horror and the Horrific Avant-garde*. Minneapolis: University of Minnesota Press.

Kael, P. (1961–62), Fantasies of the Art-House Audience, *Sight and Sound* (Winter), pp. 4–9.

Kawin, B. F. (1978), *Mindscreen: Bergman, Godard, and the First-Person Film*. Princeton: Princeton University Press.

Knight, A. (1959), For Eggheads Only?, in R. Hughes (ed.), *Film: Book 1 – The Audience and the Filmmaker*. New York: Grove, pp. 24–32.

Kolker, R. P. (1983), *The Altering Eye: Contemporary International Cinema*. London: Oxford University Press.

Lev, P. (1993), *The Euro-American Cinema*. Austin: University of Texas Press.

McCarty, J. (1995), *The Sleaze Merchants: Adventures in Exploitation Filmmaking*. New York: St Martin's Griffin.

Mayer, M. F. (1965), *Foreign Films on American Screens*. New York: Arco.

Muller, E., and Faris, D. (1996), *That's Sexploitation!! The Forbidden World of 'Adults Only' Cinema*. London: Titan.

Orr, J. (1993), *Cinema and Modernity*. Cambridge: Polity.

Ross, A. (1989), Uses of Camp, in *No Respect: Intellectuals & Popular Culture*. New York: Routledge, pp. 135–170.

Schaefer, E. (1999), *'Bold! Daring! Shocking! True!': A History of Exploitation Films, 1919–1959*. Durham: Duke University Press.

Silverman, M. (1984), Italian Film and American Capital, 1947–1951, in P. Mellencamp and P. Rosen (eds.), *Cinema Histories, Cinema Practices*. Los Angeles: University Publications of America, pp. 35–46.

Sorlin, P. (1991), *European Cinemas, European Societies 1939–1990*. London: Routledge.

Waters, J. (1984), Guilty Pleasures, in *Crackpot: The Obsessions of John Waters*. New York: Vintage, pp. 108–115.

Williams, L. (1996), Sex and Sensation, in G. Nowell-Smith (ed.), *The Oxford History of World Cinema*. London: Oxford University Press, pp. 490–496.

14

Midnight sex-horror movies and the downtown avant-garde

Joan Hawkins

The 1980s–1990s saw the emergence of a US and cultural formation which, for want of a better term, I am identifying as late twentieth-century avant-garde. Many of the filmmakers discussed here (David Wojnarowicz, for example) self-identify as 'artists' or 'experimental filmmakers', filmmakers primarily interested in film or video as artistic media irrespective of their 'entertainment' value. Others, such as Larry Fessenden and Abel Ferrara, simply regard themselves as 'independent', narrative filmmakers who attempt to maintain some measure of independence from Hollywood studio control and funding. At least two of the directors have also done commercial work, and make no distinction between it and their more experimental production. Collectively these filmmakers and their fans represent what Raymond Williams would call a 'cultural formation', an affiliation 'not based on formal membership or any sustained collective public manifestation, but in which there is *conscious association or group identification*, either informally or occasionally manifested' (Williams 1982: 68).

What draws these cineastes and cinephiles together is a common urban lifestyle, a shared commitment to formal and narrative experimentation, a view of the human body as a site of social and political struggle, an interest in radical identity politics and a mistrust of institutionalized mechanisms of wealth and power. Politically, they run the gamut from anarchist to libertarian. Many of them have roots in the punk underground. They find literary parallels and, occasionally, inspiration in the works of J. G. Ballard, Louis-Ferdinand Céline and William S. Burroughs, and are theoretically indebted to the writings of Georges Bataille, Jean Baudrillard, Gilles Deleuze, Michel Foucault, Félix Guattari, Karl Marx and Friedrich

Nietzsche. They are self-reflexive in their use of and allusions to
both film history and film theory; in terms of cinematic style, they
seem to draw equally from the dream-inflected imagery of surrealism, the non-Hollywood narrative tradition of European art cinema
(which David Bordwell has characterized as being marked by a dis-
ruption of classical Hollywood's reliance on cause and effect, and by
lack of closure, 1979: 56–64), and the avant-garde traditions of
Yvonne Rainer (who specializes in politico-feminist narratives which
are frequently disrupted by theoretical discussion delivered in direct
address to the camera) and Andy Warhol (especially his extensive use
of long takes and real time). But they also borrow heavily from 'low'
culture – erotic thrillers, horror, sci-fi and porn – and the adjectives
most frequently used to describe their work are 'dark', 'disturbing',
intelligent', 'provocative' and 'quirky'.[1]

The first downtown films[2] – Alexis Krasilovksy's *Blood* (1975) and
David Lynch's *Eraserhead* (1976) – appeared in the mid-1970s, but
the impetus for a new underground cinema really took hold in the
1980s when, as Robert Siegle notes, the US economy 'turned mean'
(1989: 9). In the face of recession and, later, the threat of an AIDS
pandemic, some US artists and filmmakers began moving downtown: to the East Village in Manhattan, the warehouse district in
Chicago, the South of Market area (SOMA) in San Francisco,
depressed areas where rent was cheap and studio space was available. Once there, they got day jobs and lived in what Chris Kraus has
called 'independent poverty' (1997: 196) so that their real energy
could go into cultural production. The cultural products they made
reflected the neighbourhoods they inhabited – burned-out areas
which stand, Robert Siegle writes, 'as one of the most potent demys-
tifiers of the illusions in which most of us live' (Siegle 1989: 1). It
was the neighbourhood itself which provided a sense of artistic
cohesion, and it is perhaps for that very reason that both the artists
and the work they produced were labelled with geographic epithets
– 'downtown', 'East Village', 'SOMA'.

In addition to being united by a sense of community or place, the
filmmakers are also united by a clear sociopolitical agenda. Like the
Dadas and surrealists, they attempt 'to shake up reified relations'
(Siegle 1989: 3) both in the art world and in society at large. Their
work challenges received ideas about gender, race, class and sexual
preference; it attempts to destabilize the existing social order
through direct intervention in that social order's spectacle. But

downtown artists are not naively utopian. They know 'no structure will escape reification, no legislation fail to repress and normalize, no specification avoid replacing the 'reality' it was intended to approach' (Siegle 1989: 3). Despite these odds, however, downtown artists persist 'in a sort of hit-and-run guerilla action' designed to make the consumers of their art confront the skeletons in our cultural closet (Siegle 1989: 3). In film, this often takes the form of disturbing documentaries and non-fiction cinematic essays. Jennifer Montgomery's *Home Avenue* (1989), for example, is a seventeen-minute non-fiction film, shot on a quiet street, in a nice neighbourhood. Walking along the street, 8 mm camera in hand, the filmmaker retraces the events of a night when she was raped at gunpoint, not far from her parents' house. 'It is mock TV news', Bill Nichols notes – referring to the often inappropriately 'perky' tone that many US newsreaders habitually adopt as they inform the listening audience that violence continues in the Middle East or that the victim of some particularly heinous crime is in stable condition – 'mock "vérité" as Montgomery points out the actual spot in the dispassionate, upbeat manner of a TV street reporter, as if this happened to someone else. There are no screen tears of remembrance which only adds to the disturbance' (Nichols and Peary 1996: 36–37).

Like Montgomery's film, many of the documentaries and fiction works covered here attempt to lay bare the dark underside of middle-class American life. And like Montgomery's film, most of the works covered reject sentimentality. Grim episodes are recounted or, in the case of the fiction films, acted out, with irony, with a certain sense of matter-of-fact detachment and cool. Perhaps more disturbingly, violence is often exploited in the interest of provoking real sensation in the audience. Directly engaging the body of the spectator, the films frequently use the visuals and thematic tropes of 'low' genres such as horror and porn to make their point.[3] Even here they push the envelope of audience response. Vampire films show large, gaping, ragged-edged wounds where the victim has been bitten, rather than the neat pinpricks and clean incisions used in Hollywood movies. Graphic depictions of sexuality are often cinematically motivated and cued by violence. Addiction is depicted – as Burroughs depicted it in *Naked Lunch* – as the dominant organizing metaphor for life under late capitalism.

In the sense that they directly challenge the viewer, these films participate in the same kind of aesthetic practiced by Brecht and

Godard. They form a 'counter-cinema', one that, like real political encounters, can take you 'by the shoulders and shake you out.' (Kraus 1997: 156)[4] Unlike the works of Brecht and Godard, though, these films are rarely overtly polemical,[5] and they rarely try to disrupt the narrative or block traditional processes of spectator identification. Rather, as Todd Haynes has noted, they attempt to reveal the way narrative and traditional processes of cinematic identification work, 'without nullifying the process of identification' itself.[6]

Not all of the downtown filmmakers are young and not all of them live downtown. But they all share what Jennifer Montgomey has called a 'punk underground aesthetic' (Nichols and Peary 1996: 36), a sensibility that Todd Haynes labels 'East Village'.[7] The stories they tell – about hustling in the sex industry, about drug addiction, about alienation, racism, homophobia, environmental illness, cultural malaise, and AIDS – frequently are not the stories mainstream filmgoers want to see. There is a raw grittiness here, which often extends to the formal elements of filmmaking. Even when they have a budget, many downtown directors prefer their films to have a grainy, black-and-white look, which borrows equally from early Italian neo-realism and George Romero's *Night of the Living Dead*.[8] They shoot on location, and many of them make extensive use of real time. If there is a beauty here, it is, as Andrei Codrescu notes, a 'savage beauty' marked by the 'sophistication and brutality' of both the historic avant-garde and film noir (Rose and Texier 1998, cover).

Despite the frequent references to historic antecedents, downtown culture is not simply a reworking of previous avant-garde and popular styles.[9] Many of the works have strong links to postmodern theory, to a discursive strategy which Steven Shaviro has identified as no longer 'a theoretical option or a stylistic choice', but rather an endemic part of contemporary fin de siècle culture (Shaviro 1997: 1st page preface, no number). Many of the artists working downtown went to graduate school, and their works often explicitly reference the very theories which will be used to critique them. Writer-filmmaker Chris Kraus is one of the editors at *Semiotext(e)*, the leading US publisher of Jean Baudrillard and Félix Guattari. Furthermore, as the editor of the press's Native Agents Series – a series of American prose works (fiction and essays) – she has a certain economic stake in demonstrating the degree to which downtown *artistic* culture enacts a kind of radical postmodern theory. Todd Haynes studied feminist film theory at Brown and has talked about the conscious manipulations of the gaze in his films. Novelist-screenwriter Kathy Acker studied with Herbert Marcuse and frequently references philosophy in her work. Downtown cinematic culture positions itself, then, not only somewhere between 'high art' and 'low culture' ('between: because it draws equally from avant-garde and popular sources, and makes no cultural distinction between them), but also somewhere between official academic theory and a theory-savvy, streetwise 'lay' avant-garde style. If the surrealists opened a space for Marx's and Freud's ideas within avant-garde art, downtown film and literature have reconstituted theory as radical chic. In that sense they comprise what might be described as a postmodern or post-structuralist avant-garde, an avant-garde which is heavily indebted to and informed by academic culture.

What I'd like to do in the remaining space is talk a little about some of the downtown films that have crossed over into 'cult' status. Some – such as Lynch's *Eraserhead*, Tod Haynes's *Poison* and Abel Ferrara's *The Addiction* – are already well known.[10] So I'm going to concentrate on films that have remained fringe cult hits.

The 'transgressive films' made by directors such as Nick Zedd and Richard Kern have a cult following all their own. In fact, you could argue that the transgressive film movement is a kind of cult movement within underground or downtown film culture. The term was coined by *Village Voice* criticAmy Taubin in a review of Nick Zedd's feature-length, super-8 movie, *They Eat Scum* (1979). The film's narrative is 'a nihilistic combination of punk/juvenile delinquency/family melodrama/horror/Death Rock all shot through with satirical camp'.[11] The film follows Suzy Putrid and her Death Rock Band, The Mental Deficients. As the Death Rock movement grows, Suzy kills her dysfunctional family and causes a core meltdown at Indian Point nuclear power station. Years later the Death Rockers rule – they are the only people who have radiation-protective clothing, but a group of radiation mutants wants to take over. The film includes scenes of slice-and-dice cannibalism, oral bestiality and a fake punk being forced to eat a live rat. 'The scenes are uniformly revolting', Taubin wrote – adding that, with Zedd's film she felt a 'generation gap' she didn't feel with other punk filmmakers, such as Vivienne Dick (Sargeant 1999: 25). In 1982, three years after Taubin wrote her review, the film was broadcast on Manhattan Cable Television's Channel C (public access cable), a broadcast which prompted the *Wall Street Journal* to write a front-page article condemning public access (*Wall Street Journal*, 20 December 1982). The broadcast demonstrated two things – first that transgressive cinema (Zedd finally wrote a manifesto for *Underground Film Bulletin* – under the name Orion Jericho – in which he acknowledges and appropriates the label) had already achieved a certain punk cult status; and second that cult films were being increasingly disseminated outside the traditional midnight theatrical screening venue.

Another 'transgressive' film that has achieved an odd cult status is *Where Evil Dwells*, the 1985 film made by artist David Wojnarowicz and filmmaker Tommy Turner. The film is about the infamous 'Satan Teen' Ricky Kasso, who killed himself after he and a friend had been accused of murdering another kid in a satanic ritual. I say 'odd cult status' because the film was destroyed in an apartment fire, and all that remains of it is a 34-minute trailer – which you can buy on videocassette from Facets Multimedia or the Monday, Wednesday, Friday Video Club. The cult status of the movie is based entirely on this VHS trailer and the film script, which has been printed in Sargeant's *Deathtripping* (1999).

Within the more traditional arena of midnight screenings – director Stephen Sayadian deserves a mention. Sayadian made his career working in the adult industry – using names such as Rinse Dream, F. X. Pope, Ladi Von Jansky and Sidney Falco. He crossed over into more mainstream cult (as opposed to porn-cult) status when his hardcore film *Café Flesh* (1982) showed up on the midnight movie circuit. (The Kinsey Institute in Bloomington recently acquired a collection of 35mm films from an art house that used to do midnight screenings of the film, which included six 35mm prints of the movie; so it was a popular midnight show). *Café Flesh* (Stephen Sayadian working under the name of Rinse Dream) is a disturbing post-apocalyptic film which critics have alternately dubbed 'The Thinking Person's Porno Film' and the least erotic adult movie ever made (Lenzl and Lenzl 1996: 35). The film takes place in a viral future in which the only sexual relationships permitted are between so-called 'positives' who perform live sex acts onstage. As *Flesh and Blood* notes, 'since these performances are obligated by the government of the new world however – for the appeasement of the negatives . . . – the sexual motivation can be gauged as being well below the minimal requirements for erotic behavior. What remains is an absolutely mechanical, emotionless sex act' (Lenzl and Lenzl 1996: 35). As a film which, as *Flesh and Blood* warns, denies 'eroticising feelings' to the viewer, *Café Flesh* occupies an odd niche in porn history (1996: 35). It is a self-reflexive porn film, one that is not at all easy about the circumstances (mandated spectacularized sex) of its own production.

Sayadian followed this midnight success with *Dr Caligari* (1989), a film which appears to have been made specifically to appeal to the 'cult' market (its opening publicity dubbed it a 'cult' comedy classic). Inspired by the 1919 *Cabinet of Dr Caligari*, the film is set in the Caligari Insane Asylum (CIA) which is presided over by Dr Caligari, the granddaughter of Robert Wiene's mountebank. This new Dr Caligari treats sexual dysfunction with hormonal injections (which succeeds only in transferring one patient's dysfunction to another). The film was inspired by Wiene's 1919 film, but it also follows closely on the heels of another Caligari pastiche, which made the midnight circuit in the early 1980s. Chicago independent filmmaker Tom Palazzolo's 1983 *Caligari's Cure* uses Palazzolo's memories of Catholic school and adolescent sexual fantasies as part of his Caligari remake.

Sayadian's films initially played the midnight circuit. In the USA 'midnight movies' are cult films which are generally shown – in mainstream theatres – at midnight. They generally get very little by way of traditional publicity. The screening is announced on the theatre's marquee, and in special underground or downtown publications (such as New York's *Village Voice*), but usually receives no mention at all in mainstream newspaper ads. Audiences often hear about a screening, literally through word of mouth, from friends – or see a flyer posted in a coffee shop or club. Midnight screenings were most popular in the 1970s. They continue to be popular in urban areas, but the rise of video has attenuated the role they play in cementing a film's cult status.[12]

In addition to midnight screenings, clubs have played a major role in attracting audiences for downtown films. Most of the punk films (by filmmakers such as Beth B. and Vivienne Dick) were originally shown in clubs, both in special backroom screenings and as a visual backdrop to the bands. Transgressive films – by filmmakers such as Nick Zedd and Richard Kern – also were originally exhibited in clubs, at special film festivals (the New York Underground Film Festival, the Chicago Underground Film Festival, Mix – a New York-based festival of experimental gay and lesbian film) and at specialty cinema venues such as the San Francisco Cinématheque. Thanks to the work of people such as Alan Moore (the owner of the Monday, Wednesday, Friday Video Club) and groups such as Electronic Arts Intermix, these films too have increasingly turned up on video, so that audiences outside New York can finally see the films they've read about in the underground press.

As I mentioned above, video has played a key role in cementing the cult status of various films. Its easy availability means that people who don't live in major urban centres such as New York and Chicago have an opportunity to see films that originally played only in downtown clubs and at midnight screenings. Also, the rise of other direct-to-video films (usually low-budget, softcore thrillers which never get theatrical release in the USA) has created a wide market niche for 'movies that nobody's heard of'.[13] As a result, people who would ordinarily never watch avant-garde or experimental film pick up downtown titles. Attracted by the box and the plot synopsis, which usually stresses the film's depiction of transgressive sexuality or crime, patrons rent the films while they're still in the 'new release' or 'direct-to-video' part of the video store, before they're relegated to the 'cult and experimental' shelves. In addition, video release often ensures that films will turn up on local access cable channels (low-budget, independently owned, cable television channels which are always in need of material produced 'by the community').

Video has ensured the cult status of both Sayadian and Palazzolo's movies. Larry Fessenden's *Habit* is another example (like *Where Evil Dwells*) of a film which owes its cult status by and large to the video market. The script for this downtown vampire film was first read at the NuYo Rican Poets Fifth Night Series on 31 May 1994 (New York) and was finally released as a film in 1997. Fessenden, who had already made some downtown films, succeeded in taking the film to Sundance – but the film didn't get much theatrical distribution. Fessenden did get a video contract, though, and the first exposure most people got to the film was through the 'new arrivals' rack in the video store – and word of mouth. It's a great vampire film, which plays with the issues of substance addiction in the way that Ferrara's *The Addiction* does, but does so against a much more explicitly sexual backdrop. It has achieved that very curious status that many horror films have in the USA – it's a cult film (usually shelved in the horror or cult sections of video stores) but tthe U.S commercial videotape contains a preview of Jean-Luc Godard's *Passion*, an inclusion which seems to acknowledge the art film audience for downtown vampire films.

Finally, I'd like to mention Rik Little's *Church of Shooting Yourself*, a downtown NYC cable television programme that has attracted a cult audience both in and out of New York City (excerpts from the show are available on video and Little has won awards at the Media Alliance Hometown Video Festival (most innovative series) 1994, 1996 and 1997; and at the East Village International Film Festival (Jurors' Choice, 1996)). The 'show' is available outside New York via independently produced videotapes, which are advertised using the following quotation from Rik Little:

> Space aliens force me to think I am out of my apartment when I am in fact *in* my apartment. Probably sleeping or watching television. To combat this I have taken to shooting myself almost constantly with a camcorder to prove where I am and what I do. It is a tedious job to shoot my entire life and monitor it at night (when I used to watch the evening news), so I often act like a Newsman so that when I have to watch my 'daily tape' it seems more like a normal news show on television.
>
> The space aliens from outer space have devious ways of splitting my brain into parts to gentrify my soul, but they will not fool me because I have television with me all the time. I will survive by shooting myself.

The play on the word 'shooting', which can either refer to a camera or a gun, has special ironic resonance here. Part of the draw of *The Church of Shooting Yourself* is the troubled sensibility of Little himself, who one suspects *might* actually try to 'survive' by doing himself in. Like the abductees who populate the popular weekly television programme, *The X-Files*, Little seems to embody both an ironic sensibility and a paranoia which are perfectly suited to the times.

The first version of this article was written as a paper for the 'Defining Cult Movies' conference, held at Nottingham, England, 17–19 November 2000. At the time when I first wrote it, it seemed to me that the conditions – both material and socio-psychological – which I here attribute to the 1980s and 1990s still held sway. As is so often the case, the 1990s seemed to have extended their reach into the new decade, and so I conceived much of this article in the present tense. On 11 September 2001, while I was in the middle of preparing this piece for publication, everything changed. The World Trade Center in New York City was destroyed. And many of the people I've written about here were evacuated from their lofts and apartment buildings, told only to 'go north'. The geography of downtown Manhattan has changed. So has the mood in the USA. And it's not at all clear what new avant-gardes and cult films might rise up to address what seems at this point to be a new era (one in which irony, for example, may not be considered an appropriate response to anything). At such a time, it seems somehow more important than ever to remember what the fin-de-siècle avant-garde was – an attempt at what one graffiti writer called a 'last wake-up call', during a time when all the country's problems seemed internal.[14] It represents a moment of what – for want of a better term – I'm currently tempted to call nihilistic innocence, a time when direct intervention in the nation's spectacle seemed like the appropriate response to an American Dream turned terribly sour. A moment when we believed that direct intervention in the country's spectacle would do some good.

Notes

1 See, for example, individual entries in *TimeOut Film Guide*, seventh edition (London: Penguin Books, 1999).
2 The term 'downtown' was initially coined by writers, and adopted by 'zines such as *Between C & D* to describe a certain kind of work. Aesthetically the work is characterized by its heavy indebtedness to authors such as Céline and Burroughs. Revolving around graphic descriptions of drug addiction and life on the edge, it is written in language which ranges from lyrical to raw. As I mention later, however, the term 'downtown' derives from the urban areas where most of these artists lived. That is, it's a geographic epithet which serves as an aesthetic marker – as though where you live determines the kind of art you produce. And this is indeed the class point that many of the filmmakers and writers are trying to make. I should add that this is a profoundly radical stance to take in a society which prides itself (erroneously, as writers such as Kathy Acker continually point out) on being 'classless'.
3 I've used the quotation marks pointedly here. As my book *Cutting Edge* demonstrates, I believe that 'high art' and 'low culture' are closely related and intertwined terms.
4 Kraus 156. The term 'counter-cinema' here comes from Peter Wollen's essay on Godard, 'Godard and Counter-Cinema: *Vent d'Est*', in which Wollen identifies seven Godardian 'cardinal virtues' in terms which seem to be drawn directly from Brecht's Preface to *The Rise and Fall of the City of Mahagonny*. See Peter Wollen, 'Godard and Counter-

Cinema: *Vent d'Est'*, in Bill Nichols (ed.), *Movies and Methods Vol. II* (Berkeley and Los Angeles: University of California Press, 1985), pp. 500–509.

5 I'm thinking here of such Godard films as *La Chinoise* (1967), *Tout va bien* (1972), *Letter to Jane* (1972) and *Numéro Deux* (1975) in which characters quote Marx and directly discuss class oppression.

6 Todd Haynes, 'Risks of Identity' paper delivered at 'Knowing Mass Culture/Mediating Knowledge', The Center for Twentieth Century Studies Conference. University of Wisconsin. Milwaukee, Wisconsin. 1 May 1999 (conference was held 29 April to 1 May). The stress placed on 'identification' here is important. Even when works are frankly non-narrative and openly experimental – Michael Klier's *Der Riese* (1983), for example, which is composed entirely of surveillance footage – they are relentlessly curious about the way viewers identify (or don't) with the camera's gaze.

7 Haynes, 'Risks of Identity'.

8 This is not always the case, of course. Both Bette Gordon's *Variety* and Lawrence Fessenden's *Habit* use such lush, saturated color that my students find it distracting.

9 Downtown culture is careful to acknowledge and pay homage to those who went before, and it is very self-reflexive about its place in cultural history. Joel Rose's and Catherine Texier's *Between C & D*, for example, is dedicated to the French writer Céline.

10 These films are considered 'downtown' for a number of reasons. Filmed in grainy black-and-white and embodying a 'downtown punk aesthetic', they largely appealed to a young, hip, downtown audience. Also the subject matter – drug addiction, AIDS, dysfunctional family life – marked them as 'downtown' (as opposed to mainstream) films. For more on the downtown status of *The Addiction* see my '"No Worse Than You Were Before": Theory, Economy and Power in Abel Ferrara's *The Addiction'*, forthcoming in Steven Schneider and Xavier Mendik (eds.) *Underground U.S.A.* (London: Wallflower Press); and Xavier Mendik, 'Shooting up on Speech: The Female "Fix" of *The Addiction'*, in *Christopher Walken, Movie Top Ten* (ed.) Jack Hunter (London: Creation Books, 2000).

11 Jack Sargeant *Deathtripping: The Cinema of Transgression* (London: Creation Books, 1999), p. 25. Subsequent citations will be given in the text.

12 For more on midnight movies see J. Hoberman and Jonathan Rosenbaum, *Midnight Movies* (New York: Da Capo Press, 1983).

13 Not much has been written about the direct-to-video phenomenon. For more on the way video has impacted audience and viewing taste see Hawkins, *Cutting Edge*, ch. 2.

14 Graffiti from the woman's bathroom at the Whole Earth Restaurant, University of California at Santa Cruz, 1984.

References

Bordwell, David (1979) The Art Cinema as a Mode of Film Practice, *Film Criticism*, 4 (Autumn) pp. 56–64.

Hawkins, Joan (2000) *Cutting Edge: Art-horror and the Horrific Avant-garde*. Minneapolis: University of Minnesota Press.

Kraus, Chris (1997) *I Love Dick*. New York: Semiotext(e).

Lenzl, Augustus and Lenzl, Shamway (1996) 'I Know You Are Watching Me' . . . Night Dreamer, Stephen Sayadian', *Flesh and Blood*, 7.

Nichols, Bill, and Gerald Peary, (1996) Children, Art, Sex, Pornography: Jennifer Montgomery's *Art for Teachers of Children* (an interview), *Camera Obscura*, 39 (September).

Rose, Joel, and Texier, Catherine (eds.) (1988) *Between C & D: New Writing from the Lower East Side Fiction Magazine*. London: Penguin.

Sargeant, Jack (1999) *Deathtripping: The Cinema of Transgression*. London: Creation Books.

Shaviro, Steven (1997) *Doom Patrols: A Theoretical Fiction about Postmodernism*. New York: High Risk Books.

Siegle, Robert (1989) *Suburban Ambush: Downtown Writing and the Fiction of Insurgency*. Baltimore: Johns Hopkins Press.

Williams, Raymond (1982) *The Sociology of Culture*. New York: Schocken Books.

Index